The Art and Practice of
Leadership
Coaching

The Art and Practice of
LEADERSHIP
Coaching

50 TOP EXECUTIVE COACHES REVEAL THEIR SECRETS

Edited by Howard Morgan,
Phil Harkins, and Marshall Goldsmith

WILEY

JOHN WILEY & SONS, INC.

Published by John Wiley & Sons, Inc., Hoboken, New Jersey.
Published simultaneously in Canada.

An earlier version of this book was published in 2003 by Linkage Press under the title
Profiles in Coaching.

For general information on our other products and services please contact our Customer
Care Department within the United States at (800) 762-2974, outside the United States at
(317) 572-3993 or fax (317) 572-4002.

Wiley also publishes its books in a variety of electronic formats. Some content that appears
in print may not be available in electronic books. For more information about Wiley
products, visit our web site at www.wiley.com.

Library of Congress Cataloging-in-Publication Data:

The art and practice of leadership coaching : 50 top executive coaches
reveal their secrets / edited by Howard Morgan, Phil Harkins, Marshall
Goldsmith.
   p. cm.
Includes bibliographical references.
ISBN 0-471-70546-2 (cloth)
1. Leadership—Study and teaching. 2. Executives—Training of. 3.
Mentoring in business. 4. Business consultants. I. Title: 50 top
executive coaches reveal their secrets. II. Morgan, Howard J. III. Harkins,
Philip J. IV. Goldsmith, Marshall.
HD57.7.A77   2004
658.4′092—dc22

                                                 2004016225

Printed in the United States of America.

10 9 8 7 6 5 4 3 2 1

This book is dedicated to the memory of
P. Graham Hollihan,
a leader who coached to the strengths of many people,
encouraged confidence in their potential, and
put them in the best position to learn, grow, and succeed.

CONTENTS

ACKNOWLEDGMENTS

A project of this scope can only be realized through the outstanding contributions of a great team of people. Accordingly, the editors wish to acknowledge the spirit, creative talent, drive, and contributions of many. First, we'd like to thank our 50 coaches for so generously contributing their time and best thinking in an honest and open dialogue. In particular, Jim Kouzes was instrumental in the development of our ideas and our knowledge of top coaches, and generous with his perspectives and critique. We felt Warren Bennis's touch as well, with his early input. And we'd especially like to thank C. K. Prahalad, Beverly Kaye, Bill Bridges, and Richard Leider for their advice, counsel, and efforts. We'd also like to thank Steve Kerr, David Kepler, and Frank Morgan for their contributions on our behalf.

In the inner sanctum of the project team, the editors wish to acknowledge the efforts and contributions of a number of other key players. Translating great thoughts into a meaningful book is not an easy challenge—Keith Hollihan's project leadership, editorial skill, and writing talent helped us achieve our vision. It was his competence, perseverance, and commitment that allowed the editors to place their full confidence in his ability to deliver the highest quality product within a tight time frame. In addition, Todd Langton's initiative got us rolling, Erica Wright encouraged us to get connected, and Lyda Goldsmith helped us assemble a collection of contributors we are all proud to join.

Robert Tucker's foray into coaching literature was articulated wonderfully in his chapter on the ROI of coaching. David Schottland provided tremendous support wherever and whenever needed and assumed his own leadership over key areas of the book. Scott Young helped drive our survey research. Robin Craig kept us on schedule and facilitated the efforts of many key people in bringing the book to life. Jim Laughlin helped us make sure that we were saying what we wanted to say. Lori Hart turned the assembled pieces into a polished work under the usual deadline demands, applying her talents to the book's look and feel. And Jasmine Green and Rusty Sullivan made enormous contributions in helping take this book to the next level.

ABOUT THE EDITORS

Howard Morgan As an executive coach, Howard Morgan has led major organizational change initiatives in partnership with top leaders and executives at numerous international organizations. His clients include global businesses in the financial services, manufacturing, management consulting, communication, media, and high-tech industries.

Howard's profound understanding of the demands of executive leadership come from 17 years of experience as a line executive and executive vice president in industry and government. He has operated major businesses with full profit-and-loss responsibility; managed the people side of mergers and acquisitions; led international expansions and start-ups; and gained the respect of unions and corporations when negotiating agreements in volatile labor environments. He knows what it means to structure an organization, lead people, and manage a business to achieve quarterly objectives. This practical background, along with an understanding of the politics of leadership and the competitive pressures of today's global marketplace, is embodied in the roll-up-your-sleeves coaching work he does with executives.

The dramatic impact of Howard's approach is drawn from his ability to communicate the significance of people and performance issues in the context of business objectives. He has been a pioneer in the practical understanding of how motivation, productivity, and behavior are linked to organizational values, leadership approach, and employee satisfaction. He has done significant work on measuring the impact of leaders on long-term profitability and growth. He has helped leaders understand that the nuances of people management are a major influence on corporate success. He has shown managers how they can increase their effectiveness in that area in practical ways.

Howard is a managing director of Leadership Research Institute and is recognized globally as a top executive coach and leadership development expert. He specializes in executive coaching as a strategic change management tool leading to improved customer/employee satisfaction and overall corporate performance. He has led the development of an internal coaching model for a large international organization and has done significant work coaching executives on the art of managing managers. He has worked with many executive committees of the world's largest organizations on improving corporate and executive performance.

Howard holds an MBA from Simon Fraser University and has completed advanced studies at the University of Michigan. He currently serves on three boards of directors, in Europe and the United States. He is also committed to adding value back to the community through his volunteer efforts in the health care sector.

Phil Harkins   Phil Harkins has emerged as one of America's leading executive coaches and organizational development experts. His broad range of business experience and his knowledge of organizations, cultures, people, and psychology—combined with Linkage's proven process and tools—have made a significant difference for the hundreds of leaders, leadership teams, and organizations with whom he has worked and coached.

Phil prepared for his role as executive coach by first becoming a senior manager at Raytheon Company, and then studying with the foremost experts on human behavior at Harvard University. After completing a doctoral program under the advisement of Chris Argyris, the most widely respected authority on organizational behavior, Phil returned to industry, where he applied his expertise as part of the executive team at Keane, Inc. There, he helped this company become one of the fastest growing and most successful large software companies in the world. It was at this time that he formulated his process for helping executives and executive teams develop. This system, he believes, requires combining a clear perspective with building knowledge, skills, and tools to increase efficiency, effectiveness, productivity, and innovation in their work.

Over the past 15 years, Phil has had the opportunity to coach in long-term coaching relationships, as well as in short, specific assignments with internationally accomplished global leaders, leadership teams, and organizations. What's even more significant about Phil's experience is that he has worked in virtually every sector of business, as well as in nonprofits and government agencies.

Phil has also emerged as an authority on the subjects of communications and leadership. His landmark book, *Powerful Conversations: How High-Impact Leaders Communicate* is widely read and highly acclaimed as the textbook for honing leadership communications. His book, *Click!*, takes communications to the next level in helping leaders to combine communications with their ability to connect with others. His most recent book, *Everybody Wins*, provides the groundbreaking growth story and strategy of RE/MAX International, the real estate giant.

It is fortunate that in this very global world, Phil is comfortable with working and coaching in international settings. Phil has coached leaders, leadership teams, and organizations in more than 25 countries. His own experience of living, learning languages, and working abroad for seven years has made him comfortable in multinational settings. He is one of the few executive coaches who has the experience of working with and coaching leaders and leadership teams in Asia, North and South America, Europe, and the Middle East.

One of the reasons Phil connects so well with senior leaders is they respect the fact that he founded and leads a global company with offices throughout the United States, Europe, and Asia. Linkage, Inc., the company that Phil started (and the company that is the Research Sponsor for this book), has achieved noteworthy success, including appearing twice on the Inc. 500, a list of the fastest growing private companies in America. Phil knows what it's like to be responsible for revenue, profits, and people management. This has resulted in Phil's very practical and down-to-earth style. He believes in getting right at issues by creating blueprints for change and providing tools and techniques to get to the next level.

Phil is the president and CEO of Linkage. Along with leadership expert Warren Bennis, he also serves as cochair of the Global Institute for Leadership Development, which has trained and developed over 4,000 leaders from around the world. He has authored original research on emerging global leaders, leadership development, change management, and communications, and has written over 20 articles for magazines and journals.

Phil is a frequent speaker at public and in-house conferences, seminars, and programs around the globe. Since 1995, he has spoken at more than 400 such events. His business experience, strategic thinking, and teaching provide competitive advantage to meetings and real value to participants. He is also an expert on helping organizations work through difficult issues with teams during troubled times or in periods of rapid change, such as mergers and acquisitions.

Phil received three advanced degrees from Harvard University and a bachelor's degree from Merrimack College. He lives in Concord, Massachusetts, and has raised three sons (Matt, 32; Chris, 29; and John, 22).

Marshall Goldsmith   In the past few years, Marshall's work has been featured in a *New Yorker* profile, a *Harvard Business Review* interview, and a *Business Strategy Review* cover story (from the London Business School). Each of these publications described his distinctly creative approach to leadership development, a process that has helped thousands of leaders achieve positive change. He was featured in the *Wall Street Journal* as one of the "Top 10" executive educators, in *Forbes* as one of five top executive coaches, in the *Business Times* (of Asia) as one of 16 major thought leaders in his field, and in *Fast Company* as America's preeminent executive coach.

Marshall is consistently rated as one of the top executive educators and coaches in the world. He is one of the few consultants who has been asked to work with more than 60 major CEOs and their management teams. He teaches classes for executives, high-potential leaders, and HR professionals. He received a PhD from UCLA. He is on the faculty of executive education programs at Dartmouth College, University of Michigan, and Oxford (United Kingdom) University. His work has received national recognition from the Academy of Management, Institute for Management Studies, American Management Association, American Society for Training and Development, Center for Creative Leadership, the Conference Board, and Human Resource Planning Society.

Marshall currently heads Marshall Goldsmith Partners, a joint venture between Marshall and Katzenbach Partners LLC. He is a founder of the Russell Reynolds executive advisor's network. He is a partner with Hewitt Associates in providing global executive coaching. He served as a member of the board of the Peter Drucker Foundation for 10 years.

Aside from his corporate work, Marshall donates his time to nonprofit organizations. He has been selected as an American Red Cross "National Volunteer of the Year." He is currently a volunteer for the U.S. Army, where he is involved in leadership training for generals.

Marshall's 17 books include *The Leader of the Future* (a *BusinessWeek* "Top 15" bestseller), *Coaching for Leadership,* and *Partnering. The Organization of the Future* is a Library Journal "Best Business Book" award winner, and *The Leadership Investment* won a Choice award as an "Outstanding Academic Business Book." His newest books include *Global Leadership: The Next Generation, Leading Organizational Learning,* and *Human Resources in the 21st Century.*

RESEARCH SPONSOR

Linkage, Inc.

We are a global organizational development company that specializes in leadership development—and leadership coaching.

Along the way, we have developed a defined approach to coaching leaders. At Linkage, we believe that the best coaching occurs within context, working with individual leaders to drive personal behavioral change against the backdrop of the business strategy and the larger team. We believe that the coaching must be grounded in the practical—and geared toward action. And we believe in:

- Employing proven assessment tools for insight and perspective
- Using clear measurements to track behavioral change and its impact on performance
- Providing tools and techniques so that coaching happens "on the playing field"
- Respecting confidentiality while also connecting back to the key people around the coachee
- Imparting wisdom but insisting upon action

This is the approach that our cadre of experienced coaches employ when coaching individuals and teams. And this is the approach at the center of our programs and events revolving around coaching, including the industry-leading *Coaching Leaders Certification Program.*

We also recognize that the Linkage approach to coaching leaders isn't the only one. That's why we have such a passion for leadership coaching. And that's why we decided to sponsor the development of this book.

We have other books that we are sponsoring on mission-critical leadership topics that are in the process of being published. We offer a range of integrated leadership development and strategic change solutions that include strategic consulting services, customized on-site training experiences, tailored assessment services, and benchmark research. And we offer a full range of conferences, institutes, public workshops, and distance learning programs on leading-edge topics in leadership and OD.

If you are interested in finding out more about our company and our array of programs, products, and services, please call 781-402-5555 or visit www.linkageinc.com.

Please let us know what you think about this book. We already know that the topic of leadership coaching is critical. We know that this book captures the latest and best thinking on the subject. While we have no way of knowing for certain what all of this will mean to you, our expectations are high. Here's hoping that they will also prove to be correct.

RESEARCH PARTNER

Hewitt Associates

Executive Assessment and Coaching: A Critical Building Block for Leaders at Top Companies

The facts are compelling. A company filled with great leaders has improved business performance. Hewitt Associates' 2003 *Top Companies for Leaders* study found that companies with stronger leadership practices outperformed their industry peers in long-term measures of both financial growth and return.

One practice specifically separating the Top Companies from the others was the use of executive coaching. Our study found that 47 percent of our Top 20 Companies for Leaders regularly assign coaches to their high potential employees. Meanwhile, just 10 percent of the other 300 firms surveyed made a similar claim. We conclude that the Top 20 know that executive coaching provides a powerful tool to accelerate the performance of successful executives.

The Art and Practice of Leadership Coaching is a landmark resource that shares many of the perspectives we have gained through our survey and in the field. Tapping into the experiences of top coaches, it describes exactly what kind of coaching is going on with today's top executives. Coaches everywhere should take notice of its findings and strive to adhere to the high standards of those leading the way.

Trained to Provide the Best Services

Our organization is proud to work closely with Marshall Goldsmith in this regard. All Hewitt coaches are personally trained by Marshall, one of the world's leading executive coaches, in his behavioral coaching process. This ensures a consistent coaching process for company executives worldwide.

We also believe that experienced coaches need to be familiar with local cultures and customs. As such, we have 81 offices in 37 countries, allowing us to provide a trained executive coach who is well-versed in the business and cultural context of each client. Through our partnership with Marshall Goldsmith Partners, we extend this global reach even further.

Measuring Impact

In addition, as many of the coaches in this book have also stated, we believe that coaching effectiveness can, and should, be measured. Like Marshall Goldsmith, Hewitt Associates will accept payment for coaching services only when positive behavioral change occurs.

A proven return on investment makes executive assessment and coaching one of the best tools for building a top company for leaders. *The Art and Practice of Leadership Coaching* provides much valuable guidance in exactly what top companies and their leaders should be looking for to meet their own business and leadership development needs. We encourage readers to dig deep into its findings. It is our firm belief that those companies not investing in their best leaders will find it increasingly difficult to compete against those that do.

To learn more about our survey of *Top Companies for Leaders,* please contact us. We hope that you enjoy this valuable book.

MARC EFFRON
Hewitt Associates
(203) 523-8291
marc.effron@hewitt.com
www.hewitt.com

CHAPTER 1

❧

The Coaching Landscape

by Linkage, Inc.

Coaching is exploding as an industry. Today, more and more coaches, from an ever-widening circle of backgrounds and schools of thought, offer their services to organizations and individuals. The need within organizations, particularly at senior levels, for this form of development work has grown at an equally rapid rate.

As coaches ourselves, we care deeply about the work that we do and the profession we represent. We are aware that there is a great deal of debate in the field today. What is best practice? What is the optimal length of a coaching engagement? Who is the client—the coachee or the organization paying the bill? How should impact and return on investment be measured? What is the line between personal and business issues? How can confidentiality be preserved when supervisors and colleagues are part of the mix? Should coaching be limited to top executives or extended to deeper levels of the organization? What are the benefits of using external coaches rather than internal coaches and vice versa?

As with any new discipline, much remains to be settled. In this book, we define coaching, describe some categories it falls into, outline the skills and attributes that we think make for best practice, and guide clients and coachees to maximize the impact of their coaching engagements. In short, we hope to provide some of the structure that a relatively new and rapidly expanding field needs.

Our perspectives derive from personal experience, extensive research, and much discussion. Nevertheless, we recognize that, like coaching itself, our views are evolving. Although we hope to mark out territory that will come to be adopted as an industry standard, we also want to engage in an open dialogue. In fact, this book has been designed not as a final declaration, but as one volume in a series of observations and analyses of trends, best practices, and leading-edge thinking. As such, we invite coaches and clients alike to join the debate. We want to encourage an inflow of other viewpoints, experiences, and perspectives. Perhaps, in the best of all outcomes, this book will serve as a forum to maximize the impact of coaching, by being rigorous, critical, and forward-thinking about how coaching can meet the needs of those we aim to serve.

Our Methodology

Working in conjunction with the editors, we designed this book with three constituents in mind: the coach, the coachee, and the client organization. We developed our conclusions by triangulating a number of data streams.

First, we held extensive conversations with more than 50 top coaches and recognized thought leaders working today. Each coach provided us with a profile of his or her own personal philosophy and area of expertise by describing his or her approach, methodology, and attributes. From those interviews and profiles, we developed our ideas of coaching by category and best practice. We also learned a great deal about the trends and issues shaping the field.

Second, we surveyed coaches and organizations, primarily in North America but with some representation all over the world, to determine how coaching services are being bought and sold in the marketplace. This research gave us an indication of what consumers are looking for, what coaches are providing, how much is being spent, what areas are considered to be priorities for the future, and how all of this has changed in recent years.

Finally, by doing a wide literature search and analyzing the emerging trends and findings, we looked at what others are saying about coaching. In one chapter, we present our conclusions about the most critical of all current issues: How the impact of coaching should be measured in terms of return on investment.

Although we have drawn our conclusions from this three-pronged approach, the observations are there for anyone to interpret on his or her own. This book represents a collection of views rather than a statement of fact. There are many valuable opinions, perspectives, and approaches that can be lifted from the pages that follow.

We divided the content into four sections:

Part I: Working with Coaches. Includes an overview and summation of what we considered to be the latest thinking on how to select the right coach as well as best practices in partnering with a coach for maximum impact. Both were written for the client/coachee/consumer perspective.

Part II: 50 Top Executive Coaches. Fifty profiles of top coaches are divided into five coaching categories.

Part III: Internal Coaching. A look at trends in building internal coaching systems as well as an essay on the very topical issue of developing the "leader as coach" capability.

Part IV: The Coaching Almanac. Includes an analysis of trends, an overview of the coaching marketplace, and a discussion of the latest thinking on the issue of return on investment.

Linkage's 50 Top Executive Coaches

How They Were Selected and Who They Are

In trying to find 50 of the top coaches in North America, we began the search by examining our own large customer base of over 100,000 representatives in business, government services, and nonprofits. We regularly seek such advice on who should be featured in our national conferences, institutes, workshops, summits, and other internal and external programs. As a result, we are frequently a referral source for external and internal coaches. With this in mind, we asked who our customers consider to be the top executive coaches. We developed our primary list from this survey. We then went to the experts and asked the world's top thought leaders who they considered to be the top coaches. After much interviewing, using a rigorous process of de-selection, we made our choices and determined our coaching classifications (for more detail, see below).

Our customers' first choice as a speaker on executive coaching was Marshall Goldsmith. Marshall's keynotes on behavioral coaching at Linkage events have always received the highest ratings. In the past two years, his work in coaching has been featured in a *New Yorker* profile, a *Harvard Business Review* interview, and a *Business Strategy Review* (London Business School) cover story. Marshall has also been listed in the *Wall Street Journal* as a "top 10" executive educator, in *Forbes* as one of five leading executive coaches, in the *Business Times* (of Asia) as one of 16 top thought leaders of his field, and in *Fast Company* as America's preeminent executive coach. He was, without question, an easy decision and a logical place to begin our search.

Marshall agreed to sign on and become a coeditor of the book. We strongly agree with one of Marshall's basic beliefs about coaching. There is no one "best coach" who fits all situations. The best coach is the coach who has unique skills that fit the specific needs of the coaching client. For example, Marshall only does coaching that is related to leadership behavior. He does not do strategic coaching, organizational development, or life planning.

We next decided to focus on the various *types* of coaching and tried to find great representatives from these categories. As you review our list of 50 leading coaches, you will see frequent references to our Linkage customer base. For example, three of our most requested speakers are Beverly Kaye (career development and retention), Roosevelt Thomas (diversity), and Warner Burke (organizational development). All of these thought leaders have coaching practices in their various fields and are on our list of 50 coaches. We have also tried to build on research that has been done in related studies by publications like the *Wall Street Journal, Forbes, BusinessWeek,* and *Fortune.*

Rather than focus on business school professors or independent consultants, we decided to include both. Many professors, like C. K. Prahalad, have very active practices in coaching and advising top executives. Many consultants, like Jim Kouzes, sometimes work in university executive education. To the person being coached, it probably doesn't matter. Top executives want the best advice from the best people.

Every "50 top" list has to have limits. We decided not to include coaches or consultants in technical or functional fields. There are great coaches and advisors in marketing, sales, finance, accounting, operations, and information technology who are not in this book. We decided to focus only on coaching that related to the various aspects of *leadership*—from strategic leadership (at the macro level) to changing individual behavior (at the micro level). We also decided not to include internal coaches who are currently employed by major corporations. Although these internal coaches may be doing a great job, they will not be available to help the readers of this volume. Our book is also limited to coaches who are currently in North America. Although there are fantastic coaches around the world, we realized that we do not have enough information at the present time to do a high-quality assessment of global talent.

Selecting Categories for Types of Coaching

To say, "I am an executive coach," may seem meaningless. An important question is "Coach who to what?" There are many types of coaching and advising. Even narrowing the field to coaching that is related to leadership left a wide range of options. Some executive coaches are helping people plan their lives; others are helping clients become more effective leaders of people; some are changing organizations and others are discussing global strategy. Although there are some overlaps in coaching categories, there are also some vast differences. For example, Vijay Govindarajan focuses on business issues, not behavioral issues, while Marshall Goldsmith focuses on behavioral issues, not business issues. Neither is "better" or "worse." Both are experts in their own fields and are readily willing to state what they *don't* do.

In determining the categories for types of coaching, again in close conjunction with the editors, we began with the micro level (changing individual leadership behavior) and moved on to the macro level (determining global strategy). In settling on five categories for coaching, we realize that we do not have a perfect classification. There are many other ways in which we could have "sliced the pie" of coaching. On the other hand, these five categories are a start. We hope that they help you better understand the different types of coaching and how to select a coach that more closely fits the needs of the coaching client. We reserve the right to change and modify these categories over the years as our knowledge of the field of coaching grows.

Coaching Leaders/Behavioral Coaching

Behavioral coaches focus on helping leaders achieve a positive long-term change in interpersonal behavior. They give advice on how leaders can build better relationships and become more effective in motivating people. Although the coaches represented in this book tend to work with executives, this type of coaching can be useful for all leaders, including first-line supervisors. Most people who call themselves executive coaches specialize in behavioral coaching. Most requests for coaching involve behavioral issues.

Career/Life Coaching

Career or life coaching frequently crosses the line between personal coaching and business coaching. Nevertheless, the coaches in this category saw their work on personal growth, career development, and life issues as having demonstrable value to the organization. The degree to which this tension was an issue is related to the natural difficulty that businesses that are oriented to the bottom line have in connecting the more holistic needs of today's knowledge workers with the challenge of making the numbers. In one way, this group of coaches may do work that is broader than that of behavioral coaches; they spend more time on personal values, personal mission statements, and the broader aspects of life. In another way, these coaches may do work that is narrower than that of behavioral coaches; they focus on the intrapersonal world of one person more than the interpersonal connections with a group.

Coaching for Leadership Development

In selecting categories, it seemed important to distinguish between coaches who help leaders become more effective individual leaders, and coaches who help leaders and organizations develop leaders. Coaches in this category ran the gamut of activities from helping an organization develop a cadre of leaders who are great coaches to helping install leadership development programs and systems that ensure an ongoing pipeline of great leaders. Some of these coaches play the role of coach as teacher while others played the role of coach as architect. As opposed to the first two categories, most coaches in this category were striving to help large numbers of leaders or the entire organization, not just the individual or team.

Coaching for Organizational Change

This group of coaches focused largely on the execution of organizational change. They engage in a wide variety of challenges, including the organization's capacity for innovation, its view on strategic diversity, its implementation of a merger, and its ability to execute a new strategy. The coaches themselves were defined primarily by the fact that they worked closely with a number of senior leaders (and their teams) to make the change initiative a success.

Strategy Coaching

Our strategic coaches worked at the most senior levels, helping top executives set the tone for the long-term direction of the organization. Some coaches worked primarily with the CEO, others with the senior team, still others with "converts" or champions throughout the organization. All mentioned a commitment to guiding the organization's quest for its *own* future path, rather than imposing a belief or vision of their own.

As mentioned, the way that coaches fit in categories is far from perfect. Some coaches fell distinctly into their set areas, while others straddled different categories in different parts of their practice. Furthermore, there was a continuum of skills, approaches, and perspectives within each category. Coaches, like all humans, have great variation in their degree of specialization.

What about General Practitioners?

What about the general practitioner (GP) coach? Is there a coach who does everything well in all of the categories? We did not find this at the top of the coaching hierarchy.

Coaches who work at lower levels in the organization may be seen as doing a good job of providing life coaching, strategic coaching, behavioral coaching, and organization coaching at the same time. An experienced coach (with a broad background) may be able to help a first-line manager better solve a wide range of problems and do a good job as a generalist.

Top executives want to deal with serious experts. This is true from the micro level to the macro level. If top executives are dealing with a micro-level behavioral issue that is alienating top talent, and potentially costing the company millions of dollars, they want the best. If they are dealing with a long-term strategic decision that will impact the company's future, they want the best. Every coach listed in this book is a true expert at something. Some are legitimate experts at two or three things. None claims to be an expert at everything.

Who Is a Coach and Who Is a Consultant?

For the purposes of this book, our *coaches* are world-class advisors who help individuals, teams, and/or corporations increase their leadership effectiveness. We make no claim that we have the ideal definition of *coach*. This is merely the operational definition we have chosen. Almost all of these advisors could be called both coaches and consultants. We (the editors) have chosen to focus on the portion of their work that they describe as coaching.

Selecting Both Thought Leaders and Practitioners

One of the great challenges that we face in Linkage conferences and summits is simultaneously providing speakers who are seen as the world's greatest thought leaders, yet consistently introducing our customers to new and different people. We faced the same challenge in this book. How could we share the thoughts of the best-known people in each of the five categories of coaching, yet still publish the thoughts of professionals who may not be as well known, but are doing excellent work. To solve this problem, we decided to list two different types of coaches in each of the five categories: *thought leaders* and *practitioners.* Thought leaders tend to be the coaches that you may have heard of before. They are mostly noted authors and speakers whose work is reasonably well known. They have a proven track record of success, and their message has appeared in different forums. In each of our five categories, we began with six thought leaders. We then let the thought leaders nominate four practitioners—professionals who do great work, but may not be quite as well known.

Just as the categories of coaching sometimes overlap, the thought leaders and practitioners overlap as well. Some of the practitioners were reasonably well published and could arguably be called thought leaders. Many of the coaches we describe as thought leaders were more doers than academics and could be called practitioners. In any case, we think we have selected a terrific group of 50 coaches. We hope that you will be able to learn from the comments of the coaches you may know, as well as the coaches that you may have never encountered before.

Why "50 Top Executive Coaches" and Not "The Top 50 Executive Coaches"?

Executive coaching is an emerging field. We reserve the right to be wrong in selecting our list of top coaches. Although we feel the coaches we have included (after consulting with the editors) are excellent choices, we are sure that there are other great coaches that we did not learn about and inadvertently left out. Five of the thought leaders we asked to join chose not to participate (Warren Bennis, Richard Bolles, Michael Useem, Jon Katzenbach, and Ram Charan). The most common reason for not participating was that they felt they were now more largely focused on writing and speaking as opposed to coaching and advising.

Selecting 10 Top Coaches in Each Category

Coaching Leaders/Behavioral Coaching

Marshall Goldsmith was the first coach selected in this category. His unique "pay only for results" process has been widely publicized and is being used by hundreds of coaches around the world. Marshall has coedited or coauthored 17 books. His article, *Try Feedforward Instead of Feedback*, has been reproduced in seven different publications and is changing leaders' entire orientation toward behavioral coaching. It was easy to choose Marshall for this category, since he does nothing but help "successful leaders achieve a positive, long-term change in behavior: for themselves, their people, and their teams."

Marshall's first two choices for behavioral coaches were Warren Bennis and Jim Kouzes. Warren is an obvious choice for any listing of top experts in leadership. Both Marshall and Jim consider Warren to be a role model for professionals in the field. Ultimately, Warren decided to decline because most of his work is now in writing and teaching, not coaching. Jim accepted, and Jim and Marshall began screening nominees in this category.

Jim Kouzes is clearly a world authority in helping leaders understand the behavior that will lead to increased effectiveness. Linkage customers have also rated him as Linkage's top teleconference speaker. This is no small honor, since many of the other speakers are among the world's top thought leaders. He has been listed as a *Wall Street Journal* "top 10" executive educator. Jim's coauthor, *Barry Posner,* is also one of the key thought leaders in our behavioral coaching section. Barry is the Dean of the Leavey School of Business at Santa Clara University. Jim and Barry's classic book, *The Leadership Challenge,* has sold over one million copies and is a standard in the field. They are pioneers in doing research that involves real leaders, at multiple levels, who are doing great things. Aside from helping individual leaders, both Jim and Barry are great teachers.

Dave Ulrich is an obvious choice for the book, but in what category? Dave could be included in behavioral coaching, coaching for leadership development, or coaching for organizational change. His work on *results-based leadership* gives a clear road map for how individual leaders can make a difference. His work on leadership development design and action learning give him high credibility in two other categories. Dave is Linkage's most requested speaker on human resource (HR) issues. He was also listed in *Forbes* as one of five leading executive coaches and in *BusinessWeek* as one of the outstanding educators in his field.

No one is better known as a coach and advisor for leaders in the nonprofit world than *Frances Hesselbein.* Her book, *Hesselbein on Leadership,* helps leaders understand "how to be" not just "how to do." Frances is one of the few top coaches who also has a track record of success as an executive. She was the National Executive Director of the Girl Scouts of America for 13 years. She is now the chair of the Leader-to-Leader Institute. Peter Drucker declared that she was the greatest executive that he had ever met. Frances's diversity of clients is illustrated by the fact that she is currently advising generals in the U.S. Army. Her many publications include *The Leader of the Future,* which may well be the best-selling edited book on leadership ever written. Frances is a winner of the Presidential Medal of Freedom, the highest award that can be given to a U.S. civilian.

Jay Conger was another of our choices for the thought leader category. Jay is a widely publicized author in the field. His participant-observation approach to coaching is different, yet complementary to approaches suggested by the other thought leaders. Having joint appointments at the University of Southern California and the London Business School gives Jay a multinational perspective that is somewhat unique in the field. His book *Building Leaders: How Successful Leaders Develop the Next Generation,* could also place him in the "coaching for leadership development" category.

Although Warren Bennis decided he did not want to be included in this list, he did nominate *Ken Siegel* to be in the top practitioner group. Ken's coaching practice is unique and very intensive. He usually works with clients over a three-to-five-year period. He helps leaders challenge the status quo and, like Marshall, measures the success of his work based upon impact on others, not just self-assessment.

Bobbie Little is a Regional Director, Executive Coaching at Personnel Decisions International (PDI). She has multinational leadership experience. Bobbie works with C-level executives and sets clear metrics to document change. Rather than view coaching as a "popularity contest," she strives to achieve a "return on the individual" that is measured by other people besides her and her coaching client.

Kim Barnes has over 30 years of experience in the field. She is a performance coach who helps high-potential leaders develop their skills and helps HR managers and key staff members become great internal coaches.

Marshall Goldsmith's nominee for the practitioner list was *Howard Morgan.* Howard is one of the few coaches who has extensive experience with Fortune 500 CEOs and their management teams. He not only works with key executives, he has also managed leadership development processes that have been shown to have a positive impact on thousands of leaders. Luckily for us, Howard also agreed to sign on to edit this book along with Marshall and Linkage CEO Phil Harkins.

Career/Life Coaching

In the area of career/life coaching, the first four professionals who were nominated were Richard Leider, William Bridges, Beverly Kaye, and Richard Bolles. Richard Bolles declined our invitation for reasons that were very similar to Warren Bennis'. He was focused primarily on writing and teaching, not coaching. The others, however, accepted our invitation.

Richard Leider is an expert on life planning and helping people live "on purpose." Richard has a unique distinction. Not only do other coaches recommend him, he has actually been a life coach for five of the coaches on our list of 50. Richard is the author of several books, including the international bestseller, *Repacking Your Bags.* His work as a speaker on life planning with Linkage has been very well received.

In the areas of career development and employee retention, *Beverly Kaye* is one of Linkage's most requested and highest-rated speakers. Her book, *Love'em or Lose'em,* is the best-selling book ever written on the topic of retention. Beverly is also one of the world authorities on career systems and she could also qualify in the "leadership development" category. She is an expert on helping managers develop their people and helping employees take responsibility for their own careers.

In the field of coaching through the transitions of life and work, *William Bridges* is in a class by himself. He has published multiple books in the field and is a role model for sharing how his teaching relates to his own personal transitions. Bill's newest book, *Creating You & Co.,* is a handbook for creating and managing a twenty-first century career. Bill has been ranked as a *Wall Street Journal* "Top 10" executive educator.

The next nominee is one of the most popular authors and speakers in the field, *Barbara Moses.* Over one million people have used Barbara's *Career Planning Workbook. Fast Company* called her a "career guru." When publisher Dorling Kindersley decided to produce a "career bible," they conducted an international search of experts and selected Barbara to be the author. She has a very practical approach that focuses on the complexities of the new workscape and the needs of the new worker. Along with speaking and writing, Barbara is also a coach for coaches.

One major segment of the life-coaching category is coaching for personal productivity. This type of coaching helps leaders (and people in general) understand the "nuts and bolts" of what they need to do to achieve success and get things done. Two thought leaders who stand out in this field are Brian Tracy and David Allen.

Brian Tracy may be the most prolific author in all of our thought leader groups. As we go to press, he has authored 35 books and is the author/narrator of more than 300 audio and video learning programs. His writings, recordings, and speeches have impacted millions of people. Brian is known for providing practical advice that people can understand and use.

David Allen is the leading authority on organization and time management for the new work force. His best-selling book, *Getting Things Done: The Art of Stress-Free Productivity,* has become a classic in the field. David's work is based on years of practical experience. He helps leaders make the hard decisions required to get organized and "move on with life."

Leadership thought leader and best-selling author Ken Blanchard nominated *Shirley Anderson* for the practitioner group. Shirley is a pioneer in the coaching profession and has worked with a wide variety of influential leaders. She helps very successful people who become "stuck" or find that they are struggling with something that they have never struggled with before. Shirley is also Ken's coach.

Although Richard Bolles declined to be on our list of 50 leading coaches, he did make a nomination. *Joel Garfinkle* is the founder of Dream Job Coaching, the top online resource for creating fulfillment at work. He is also a widely published author and speaker who could be considered for the thought leader category.

Richard Leider's nomination was *Richard Strozzi-Heckler*. Richard has more of a focus on the body than the other coaches in this field. He has a sixth-degree black belt in aikido that has greatly influenced his coaching practice. He helps leaders determine their authentic self.

Beverly Kaye nominated *Marian Baker*. Marian's coaching technique revolves around the use of questions. She helps clients come up with their own answers. Marian sees herself as a catalyst who helps her clients achieve true fulfillment. She is also an author whose work has been featured in newspapers and magazines.

Coaching for Leadership Development

Ken Blanchard may well be the best-known author and speaker on leadership in the world. His books have sold millions of copies, and he has spoken in front of hundreds of thousands of managers. Ken's work goes beyond his books and talks. His company and his materials are used to develop millions of leaders. Although he could be considered in the behavioral coaching category, we saw his biggest contribution as large-scale leadership development. Ken is also one of Linkage's most requested and highest-rated speakers.

One of Ken's former teachers and a mentor to many people in the field of leadership development is *Paul Hersey*. Ken worked with Paul in developing the Situational Leadership model. Hersey and Blanchard's *Management of Organizational Behavior* is in its eighth edition and is one of the most widely used texts in the world. Paul's focus is on teaching leaders to coach and develop their people. He is a pioneer in the field of leadership development whose work has made a difference to millions of people over the past 40 years. Along with Ken, Paul has served as a mentor to Marshall Goldsmith.

Noel Tichy is probably the world's best-known authority in helping organizations develop their entire leadership team. He is a frequent Linkage speaker who receives consistently great feedback. He is also a *Wall Street Journal* "top 10" executive educator. Noel headed up the famous leadership development effort at General Electric and helps leaders develop a "teachable point of view" that they can share with people throughout their organizations. Noel directs the University of Michigan's Global Leadership Partnership and is the author of several top books in the field, including *The Leadership Engine* and *The Cycle of Leadership: How Great Leaders Teach in their Organizations.*

Nancy Adler is a foremost authority on cross-cultural management and women's global leadership. She is a noted author and speaker who has published over 100 articles and has spoken to leaders around the world. She is a professor at McGill University. Nancy is also a pioneer in integrating the arts into the leadership development process. Her books include *International Dimensions of Organizational Behavior* and *Competitive Frontiers: Women Managers in a Global Economy.*

Al Vicere is engaged in coaching clients on how to develop leaders in several of the world's premier organizations. He works closely with human resource development professionals to help them design systems, programs, and processes that are being used to develop the leaders of the future. He is a professor of executive education at Penn State. Al has published over 80 articles on leadership development. His books include *Leadership by Design* and *The Many Facets of Leadership.*

One of Al's coauthors on *Leadership by Design* is *Robert Fulmer.* Bob is the academic director of Duke Corporate Education and a professor at Pepperdine. He has been involved in the design of leadership development efforts that have impacted thousands of leaders in major corporations. Like Noel Tichy, Bob moved from the corporate world, where he formerly headed up worldwide management development for Allied Signal. His many publications include *Executive Development and Organizational Learning for Global Business* and *The Leadership Investment.*

BusinessWeek has ranked the Center for Creative Leadership (CCL) as the number one organization for leadership development for the past two years. CCL has trained countless thousands of leaders from around the world and has made a huge impact on the entire field. *John Alexander* is the president and CEO of CCL, and the first nominee in the practitioner group. His organization provides coaching and feedback to leaders and has developed a wide range of assessment tools. John is a gifted practitioner as a teacher, coach, and leader in the field.

Jim Bolt was nominated as a top practitioner in this category by almost everyone who was asked. He coaches CEOs and their senior management teams on how to build great processes for developing the leadership capabilities they need to successfully execute their strategy. Jim's clients have included 50 of the Fortune 100 companies. He also manages a series of networks that enable top HR professionals to connect with other leaders in their field.

Phil Harkins selected *David Giber* to be the lead consultant for leadership development at Linkage. David has served as a coach and advisor in leadership development for over 20 years. He has designed and implemented leadership development programs around the world. David is coeditor of the *Best Practices in Leadership Development Handbook* as well as *Best Practices in Organizational Development and Change.*

Very few people have more experience in managing large-scale leadership development processes than *Jim Moore.* Jim led the leadership development efforts at BellSouth, Nortel, and Sun Microsystems. His work is well known by several of the coaches on our list. Today, he coaches either the head of human resources or the head of executive development in building strategies to grow future leaders. Jim has taken what he learned as an internal coach and is applying this with his new clients as their external coach.

Coaching for Organizational Change

Given the broad nature of organizational change, this category may have the greatest amount of differentiation between coaches. Each one of the coaches listed is an expert in helping organizations change. However, they have very different areas of emphasis on *what* to change and *how* the change process occurs.

Phil Harkins is not only the CEO of Linkage but is also one of the most-requested and popular speakers on Linkage programs. Phil's publications include *Powerful Communications: How High-Impact Leaders Communicate* and *Everybody Wins,* a book focusing on RE/MAX's growth story and strategy. He has had the opportunity to speak to thousands of leaders, and, through the organization he founded, has impacted hundreds of thousands of people. Phil could easily be put in the "coaching for leadership development" category. His work involves facilitating teams across the organization. Phil's goals as a coach include creating positive long-term change, increased organizational learning, and sustainability.

Warner Burke is Linkage's most requested speaker in the field of organizational development. Warner is a professor at Columbia and faculty member in their creative, multidiscipline organizational psychology program. Two of his

14 books include *Organizational Development: A Process of Learning* and *Organizational Change: Theory and Practice.* As opposed to the coaches who focus on changing individuals or teams, Warner is best known for helping change entire organizations.

Roosevelt Thomas is Linkage's most requested speaker in the field of diversity. He is also a *Wall Street Journal* "top 10" executive educator. Roosevelt is a widely published author. His many publications include *Building a House for Diversity* and *Beyond Race and Gender.* Roosevelt generally coaches executive teams (as opposed to single individuals), and his work may impact the entire organization. He is the founder of the American Institute for Managing Diversity.

Sally Helgesen uses a unique anthropological approach to coaching. She engages in a deep narrative study of how leaders in the organization do their jobs, in the context of the organization's culture. Sally builds upon her background in journalism to ask the right questions and try to uncover the deeper answers. She is the author of *The Female Advantage* and *The Web of Inclusion,* two of the most successful books ever written about women in leadership.

Gifford Pinchot is predominately focused on helping organizations achieve greater levels of innovation. His best-selling book, *Intrapreneuring: Why You Don't Have to Leave the Corporation to Become an Entrepreneur,* set the ground rules for an emerging field: the courageous pursuit of new ideas in established organizations. Gifford helps individuals and teams turn innovative ideas into successful business propositions.

Strat Sherman is on the board of the Leader-to-Leader Institute and was recommended by Frances Hesselbein. Along with being a master practitioner, Strat is the coauthor of the bestselling *Control Your Destiny or Someone Else Will,* the first serious study of Jack Welch's transformation of GE. His coaching practice is devoted to helping successful senior executives and high-potential leaders expand their capabilities in the context of change.

Like Marshall Goldsmith and David Ulrich, *Gary Ranker* was listed in *Forbes* as one of five leading executive coaches. Steve Kerr, the dean of corporate CLOs, also recommended Gary. Gary has a great track record of coaching in GE and in the financial services industry.

David Dotlich works with organizations, teams, and individual executives to help create positive change. He is a world authority on action learning, and one of his many books is *Action Learning: How the World's Best Companies Develop Their Top Leaders and Themselves.* David is one of the few top coaches with extensive experience in the business, academic, and consulting worlds.

Leigh Fountain has been one of the highest rated coaches and facilitators at Linkage's *Global Institute for Leadership Development* (GILD). Leigh combines both coaching and consulting in a process he calls *Embedded*

Coaching. His work has impacted tens of thousands of people. Before becoming a coach, Leigh was a senior executive on Wall Street.

Bruce Pfau is the Vice Chair—Human Resources at KPMG LLP. Bruce has worked with groups of executives at some of the world's largest corporations to undertake significant organizational improvement and culture change. He has made numerous contributions to professional journals and is a regular speaker at professional societies.

Strategy Coaching

C. K. Prahalad is one of Linkage's most requested speakers. His keynotes on strategy receive outstanding positive feedback. C. K. has been listed in *BusinessWeek* as one of the "top 10" teachers and in the *Wall Street Journal* as one of the "top 10" executive educators. C. K. is a professor at University of Michigan and one of the most successful CEO-level advisors in the world. C. K. was our first nominee in the category of strategic coaching. His several books include *Competing for the Future*. Three of his articles have won the McKinsey Prize.

C. K. nominated *Christopher Bartlett* as one of the top strategic coaches. Chris is a professor at the Harvard Business School and has published eight books in the field, including *The Individualized Corporation*. He is a specialist at coaching CEOs and their senior management teams. His approach involves a long-term commitment with each client. He is focused on developing the capabilities of the entire top management team.

Vijay Govindarajan is clearly one of the top teachers, coaches, and advisors in the strategy field. He is a professor at Dartmouth's Tuck School and the founding director of their Center for Global Leadership. V.G. has been listed as one of the "top 10" professors in executive education in *BusinessWeek*. One of his articles is one of the most cited in the history of the *Academy of Management Journal*. Like C. K. and Chris, V.G. works with the CEOs and top management teams of major corporations. He helps organizations generate fresh ideas, explore different frameworks, and benchmark best practices. He engages with CEOs in a frank, challenging dialogue about the company's future direction.

Our first three strategic coaches seem to fit clearly in the strategy area. Our next two could be considered in both strategy and organizational change. While both Fariborz Ghadar and Michael Hammer provide strategic advice, both focus heavily on operational excellence and execution.

Fariborz Ghadar specializes in global corporate strategy and implementation. He is the author of 11 books and numerous articles. Fariborz is a gifted teacher and a chaired professor at Penn State. His focus is not just on providing strategic advice, but advice that can be realistically implemented. His goal is to make strategic implementation a fun and dynamic process that engages the management team.

Michael Hammer defines himself as focusing on the "operational nuts and bolts of business." He strives to provide coaching that is nontraditional, relentlessly pragmatic, and immediately relevant. Michael was formerly a professor at MIT. His books include *Reengineering the Corporation*, which has been called the most important business book of the 1990s. He was named on *Time* magazine's first list of America's "25 most influential individuals."

Strategic coaches, like coaches in all of the other categories, vary in a number of different ways. While Michael Hammer prides himself on being relentlessly pragmatic and immediately relevant, *Joel Barker* prides himself on being a visionary and a futurist. Joel is know as the "paradigm man" because of his pioneering work in helping leaders understand the power of our paradigms and how they can shift. He is a widely published author and has produced some of the most popular training and development tapes that have ever been made. He popularized the term "vision" before it became part of regular leadership vocabulary. Joel helps leaders look to the future, explore new options, and create visions for tomorrow.

Like Warren Bennis, Jon Katzenbach was nominated for this list, but chose not to be included. Jon, like Warren, said that much of his practice today involves writing, leading a business, and doing other things besides coaching executives. Also like Warren, Jon nominated someone for our list. *Niko Canner* is a partner with Jon in Katzenbach Partners LLC. Niko is unique to this list in that he is especially interested in service firms, whereas most of the other strategy experts work primarily with large public corporations. A former McKinsey consultant, he is working with his firm to develop a new kind of advisory work around strategy. He wants to help clients overcome the sometimes-artificial distinction between "strategy" and "implementation." Niko has published articles on a wide range of topics.

Dave Ulrich nominated *Judy Rosenblum.* As chief operating officer for Duke Corporate Education, Judy could also qualify for the "coaching for leadership development" list. She helps develop organizational capability by integrating organizational learning and corporate strategy. Like Noel Tichy, Jim Moore, and Bob Fulmer, she has made the transition from an "internal" coach to an "external" coach. Aside from providing personal advice to leaders, Judy helps organizations analyze the effectiveness of their entire coaching process.

Fariborz Ghadar nominated *Bill Davidson*. Bill could easily qualify as a thought leader. His book *2020 Vision* was selected as a "Best Business Book of the Year" by *Fortune* magazine. He was also the most widely cited authority in international management between 1985 and 1995. Bill and his group specialize in the area of enterprise strategies—"integrated master plans that require focused and coordinated implementation across the entire organization over an extended period of time."

Sally Helgesen nominated *Julie Anixter*. Julie is the head of R&D for the tompeterscompany! Her area of specialization is a little different from that of anyone else on our strategy list. Julie focuses on the areas of communication, brand, and innovation—and how these three disciplines can help an organization create competitive advantage.

The Profile of Our Coaches

The thought leader coaches were largely a mix of academics and consultants. While 70 percent have a PhD, 40 percent still held academic positions and another 20 percent were former academics. All have published books, and most have published more than four. Fifteen of the 30 have received national recognition in at least one major magazine (e.g., the *Wall Street Journal, Forbes, BusinessWeek*). Almost 60 percent are instructors in university executive education programs, and almost all are asked to speak for large corporations. Although all of the thought leaders were coaches, most were actually better known for their work in publishing and speaking.

In general, each person:

- Had more than 10 years experience coaching at the top three senior levels in organizations
- Was experienced in more than one industry in a number of Fortune 500 level companies
- Had strong subject expertise, interpersonal skill, and ethical practice
- Was the author of one or more seminal works in their field
- Held what could be considered to be a unique and possibly trend-setting point of view

The practitioner coaches were more likely to work as independent coaches or be part of a larger consulting firm. Most of their time was spent in coaching, consulting, or managing other consultants. They were less focused on writing, speaking, and working in universities. All had thousands of hours of experience in their unique fields.

A Message on Ethics and Responsibilities

Before we turn matters over to our editors, our 50 coaches, and our other special contributors, we'd like to end our introduction with a brief discussion of the significance and responsibility of coaching. We think that coaching plays a critical role in driving performance improvement in leaders and organizations today. But we also think that coaching is an awesome responsibility. Coaches enter engagements as experts and sometimes saviors. The organizations they work with have opened not only their doors and their budgets, but also their vulnerabilities and secrets. The coach gains privileged access to critical information relating to financial situations, career concerns, strategies, challenges, fears, hopes, and, most of all, dreams. Organizations, careers, and lives are at stake. As Frances Hesselbein has said, the primary rule of the coach must be: "First, do no harm." Or, as Phil Harkins advises for those who enter organizations, above all, "Don't make it worse."

We advocate for coaching that is done in the spirit of the moral responsibility—responsibility that the people and organizations affected by our work deserve. Coaching, unlike management science, academic theory, or consulting, is an exciting interpersonal journey. Coaches and clients form strong bonds built on trust, openness, confidence, and achievement. We hope that we enhance the coaching experience for all who read this book, whether they are coaches by profession, or using coaching as a tool. For inspiration, career enhancement, and thrill, the ride is incomparable. We believe that it should be the time of your life.

Part

WORKING
WITH COACHES

CHAPTER 2

※◆※

Selecting the Right Coach

Executive coaching is a precision tool for optimizing the abilities of leaders. Most often, coaching focuses on the leader's individual effectiveness. In other cases, the coaching aims more at the leader's effectiveness within a team environment or at his or her capacity to drive organizational change. Regardless of where coaching aims on the leadership spectrum, the executive coach works in close, trusted partnership with the leader. The coach applies experience, know-how, and insight to key areas, and judiciously pushes the client beyond his or her comfort zone to reach levels of performance greater than the client would have achieved alone—all within an accelerated time frame.

If that sounds like a tall order, it should. Top executive coaches are well paid. The organization that hires a coach makes a significant financial investment, not to mention an investment of resources, energy, and focus. Coachees are almost always key individuals whose performance levels greatly affect the performance of others. The coach who works with that leader must be able to help him or her achieve superior results within the organization's business goals. Otherwise, the organization has wasted its money.

Despite this imperative, the coach selection process does not always receive the attention it deserves. In part, this results from lack of clarity about what coaching should accomplish and how it should accomplish it. Although a powerful idea, as its definition broadens to accommodate new approaches and demands, *coaching* is threatening to become a watered-down term. Is coaching limited to achieving business objectives and higher levels of performance, or does it also extend to personal satisfaction and achievement? Is coaching just for individual performance, or can it drive team and organizational performance as well? Is coaching dedicated to specific objectives from the beginning, or does it take on new challenges as they arise? Does the engagement take place within a set period of time, or does it go on indefinitely, with no clear end, as an extended partnership or "coach-for-life"?

A spectrum definitely exists and over the course of this book we will define our perspective on the optimal boundaries of that spectrum. Nevertheless, as the number of practitioners joining the coaching industry increases, the inherent looseness within the coaching discipline can create confusion and dissatisfaction among consumers. How can the consumer know what his or her organization's needs are and whether a particular coach can fill those needs efficiently? Despite the rise of accreditation and certification programs, it can be difficult to ascertain whether a coach's expertise and skill are sufficient for meeting the challenges the organization or leader is facing. The best coaches come from a wide variety of backgrounds, experiences, and points of view, although they also share a narrow range of talents and approaches. Many of these talents and approaches (perception, empathy, the ability to put oneself in another's shoes, etc.) seem more inherent than trainable. Without knowing who the best coaches are, how does an organization make a choice? Organizations today have a greatly reduced capacity to put up with the distraction and expense of outside interventions that don't accomplish the job.

The number of effective and dedicated coaches working today, however, is greater than ever before. As leaders face increasingly complex interpersonal, strategic, and organizational issues, more and better coaches are becoming available to help their cause. The current success of coaching as an industry demonstrates the need at top management levels for outside expertise, free from any personal agenda. The continuing success of coaching depends on how well coaches define, structure, and deliver their services in the future.

This book aims to create more clarity about how coaching meets the demands of today's leaders, not from a theoretical vantage point, but from an analysis of how top coaches actually *practice* their art. We hope to educate clients and coaches to recognize when coaching is necessary; what goals it can achieve; and what skills, attitudes, and backgrounds the coach needs to produce successful results.

This chapter describes the considerations, steps, and questions a client should keep in mind when choosing a coach. To cover these issues, Part I looks at what a coach does and what common attributes, skills, and orientations are common to successful coaches. Part II looks at the causes behind the decision to hire a coach and the criteria that need to be in place to ensure a superior return on investment. Finally, Part III looks at how to ensure fit between the coach and the organization's needs.

Part I: What Is Coaching?

Coaching is not just for problems anymore. Ten years ago, coaching primarily concentrated on people with performance issues. A coach came on board because a leader's personal style had a negative impact on peers and reports, or because his or her skill set was inadequate—conditions that were leading to career derailment. Sometimes, the coach was simply a bulletproof way to communicate bad news about performance before dismissal. Coaching was often viewed pejoratively as something applied to failing leaders or as a last-ditch effort to salvage a career in which the organization had made a long-term investment it didn't want to throw away.

Today, that impression has turned 180 degrees. As the marketplace has become increasingly competitive and fast-moving, organizations now recognize they must work with speed and precision to enable key people to achieve critical business objectives. In response, coaching has embraced a whole new focus: how to take good people and make them the best they can be, positioning them to work more effectively and cohesively in their environments, and making the most of their capabilities. In other words, coaching is now most often applied to top performers whose leadership and growth potential are highly valued by the organization.

Performance issues will always arise in any development plan or in any dynamic that a leader must work through when trying to execute strategy or change. However, coaching is not intended to focus on those issues any more than absolutely necessary. The orientation is always forward, with a focus on efficiency, effectiveness, and impact. The personal and interpersonal challenges a coach encounters are no less complex than they were years ago, but the coach and coachee now work together, with a different kind of urgency and creative energy, to discover the best solutions to meet the organization's objectives.

Selecting the right coach is a challenge. Coaching is an approach, a viewpoint, and a technique as much as it is a profession. There are no defined backgrounds or sets of skills for coaches, just as there are no defined sets of problems or challenges. The coach is a highly specific resource of knowledge, expertise, intuition, and experience. He or she brings to the table the ability to deal with dynamic challenges. Although this dynamic character makes coaching difficult to codify, it also ensures that a good coach, with the right expertise, can work with a coachee to find a path to success. That path may differ from coach to coach, but the impact will still be positive.

What Coaching Isn't

To define what coaching is, let's examine what it isn't. Coaching often differs, for example, from consulting. Although a consultant and a coach both have a body of research or a theory from which to draw, the coach may very well not bring a model or framework into the engagement. As outsiders, neither coach nor consultant is likely to understand the client's business environment as well as the client does, but although the consultant provides ready-made answers, the coach's advice is extremely customized. Both consultant and coach rely on data gathering to interpret the organization's or individual's challenges. However, although the consultant uses that data to prepare a path for others to follow, the coach uses it to build the critical capabilities of key people so that they themselves can forge their own paths. Unlike the consultant, the coach works in partnership with the client to discover solutions together, finding them through careful listening, provocative questioning, enlightened guidance, and the right level of prompting at the right time. To a great degree, the coach's goal is to enable the client to find the right answers by him or herself.

It is not surprising, therefore, that a successful relationship between coach and client depends on the highest levels of trust and openness. Nevertheless, boundaries do exist. Although coaching may sometimes feel like something halfway between the couch and the confessional, coaching is not therapy. The orientation is very different. Depending on personal background and skill, a coach may use some of the listening and analytical tools of therapy to build connection, trust, and openness. But although personal issues or deeper problems are likely to arise in the course of working together, the coach is not meant, and is usually not qualified, to provide more than supportive, confidential advice in those matters. Should serious personal issues emerge, a coach may be well positioned to provide a referral to a psychologist, counselor, or medical doctor. But, inasmuch as it is healthy to do so, a coach will maintain the focus of the engagement on moving the client forward, in line with business objectives. Although the client may control the pace and direction of a therapy session, the coach is being paid to facilitate the pace and direction of the coaching engagement—in the service of specific business-related goals.

Despite the coach's close working relationship with the client, the coach is not a substitute colleague or fellow executive. Many coaches have been successful in business in earlier incarnations, usually at the most senior levels.

This provides a sense of comfort and familiarity in the client's world, allowing him or her to communicate in the same language. It also provides key insights into the complex and competing pressures of the client's work environment. This enables the coach to recognize a business opportunity or roadblock when it appears. However, the skills and interests that make the coach successful in coaching would probably not lead to success as a full-fledged member of the organization. If the coach were on board permanently, the orientation toward questioning, pushing the envelope, prompting alternative answers, and closely managing the personal dynamic might very well wear out the welcome. The coach's stay in the organization is meant to be short, usually less than two years, and longer only if intermittent challenges are pursued in a way that builds on the foundations that have already been established. A best practice coach, by design and ethic, is not in the business of creating a dependant relationship. Although this may be a sensible business model, akin to logging billable hours at a law firm, it violates one of the principle ethics of coaching: do everything in the service of the client, not in the service of oneself.

Skills and Attributes of Best Practice Coaches

Coaching takes place across a broad spectrum of areas, challenges, and situations. By its very nature, coaching is a flexible, adaptable, and fluid way of achieving measurable results. What are the skills and attributes that make for successful coaching? Chemistry, expertise, and experience are all very important—and we will define those in more detail shortly. But, the following sections help distinguish what it truly means to be a *best practice coach*.

Technical Skills

A best practice coach is able to:

- Set the stage for the coaching engagement by establishing ground rules, reporting lines, confidentiality, and trust.
- Assess the current situation fully and accurately.
- Achieve alignment and agreement (with the coachee, client, and key stakeholders) around critical needs and achievable objectives.
- Develop and execute an approach that will lead to a successful outcome.
- Recognize emerging problems and opportunities in advance and adjust the plan accordingly.
- Provide follow-up, to whatever degree necessary, to ensure sustainability.

Experience and Background

A best practice coach has:

- A good working knowledge of the industry and the kind of organization for which the client is working.
- A deep understanding of the coachee's level within the organization and the associated pressures, responsibilities and relationships.
- A keen knowledge of where his or her expertise starts and stops, and how that will match the client's needs.
- The insight to judge whether the client is serious about working toward the kind of change, development, or direction the coach is able to drive.
- The ability and resolve to assess personal fit and to go forward, or part ways accordingly.
- The structure and discipline to manage the coaching relationship for the needs of the individual, whether the individual fully recognizes those needs or not.
- The ability to distill a great deal of information while recognizing important patterns and uncovering key nuggets.
- The ability to distinguish between matters of short-term urgency and long-term significance.
- The ethics to maintain strict personal and business confidentiality.

Coaching Attributes

A best practice coach is able to:

- Put the coachee's needs ahead of his or her own ego.
- Listen with nuance and sensitivity.
- Establish the highest levels of trust, openness, and personal connection.
- Ask probing questions that draw forth information the coachee could never have arrived at independently, despite superior knowledge and experience.
- Understand the coachee's relationships with the insight of a participant-observer.
- Make intuitive leaps that will lead the coachee to new levels of performance.
- Judge actions or words to determine whether development is occurring at the appropriate rate and in the correct direction.
- Manage the coaching dynamic to the ever-shifting mood, attitude, and will of the coachee.

- Back away from an area or direction that is not in the coachee's best interest to pursue or one that he or she is highly resistant to working on.
- Change the coachee's behavior gradually, but steadily, even in the coach's absence.
- Push the coachee to new levels without putting him or her in a position that would lead to compromise or embarrassment, or that would otherwise decrease the desire and willingness to change.
- Create an independent capability in the coachee by building her strengths, instead of building reliance on the coach.

Given this complex matrix of skills, attributes, and capabilities, it might seem that a best practice coach is born, not made. The hard truth, however, is that every coach learns through doing. The coach often begins his or her calling because of a passionate desire to take a leadership roll in a particular area of expertise or interest. This passion carries the coach through a sometimes painful growth of skills and abilities in the service of his or her calling. A coach is always learning, growing, and developing key behaviors as they are required. Each of the best practice coaches we interviewed spoke of a two-way dynamic in coaching relationships, which is frequently described as teaching that flows in both directions, the coach providing insight to the client, while the client does the same for the coach.

A coach, like a leader, can be developed if she possesses the original passion. But this is a personal journey more than an educational attainment. Coaching accreditation programs probably can't teach the art of coaching any more than golf instruction can teach the art of golf. Skills can be learned and techniques replicated, but true understanding only comes from carefully honed practice in real-world situations.

We recognize that there are different levels of capabilities in the coaching profession, just as there are different categories of coaching. Higher levels can be attained over time, given limitations of experience, innovative capability, and personal growth. The thought leaders profiled in this book are widely recognized as among the top coaches working today. Each of them has been practicing for many years. Other coaches can learn from them, not to attain a higher level of mastery tomorrow, but to become better each day.

Areas of Coaching Expertise

Another problem with the term *coaching* is that it describes the mode of the working relationship without differentiating the variety of aims and objectives.

In this book, we are generally talking about business or executive coaching. The distinction is most clear when compared to coaching that helps an individual achieve a personal aim such as happiness, work-life balance, wealth, or better relationships. There are several important exceptions to this distinction, and many coaches speak of the continuum between business and personal life encountered during any engagement; but, for the most part, executive or leadership coaching is meant to meet organizational needs.

Within that domain, we have made further differentiations. The following five categories seemed to provide adequate "boxes" for all of the coaches that were interviewed. A qualification is necessary, however. Some coaches were very firmly members of their particular box. Others recognized that although they belonged mainly in one category, there were aspects of their coaching that occasionally crossed over.

Coaching Leaders/Behavioral Coaching

This is the largest and most inclusive category. Typically, the focus of such coaching is on a leader's behaviors, style, vision, or practice. The coach works with the coachee to understand and optimize his or her effectiveness in key relationships.

Career/Life Coaching

All coaching involves change, but coaching for transition focuses on change that is a part of distinct shifts in level or circumstance. Some coaches work on guiding a leader or leadership team through a major organizational shift such as occurs during a merger or acquisition. Others work at optimizing a leader's capabilities as required by a new level of responsibility. Still others define the career options for an individual who is seeking a new position, level of responsibility, environment, or role.

Coaching for Leadership Development

Leadership development coaches work to instill a capability in the leader or leadership team to bring the organization to another level of effectiveness. In some cases, this means helping the leader become a coach himself or herself.

Coaching for Organizational Change

To some degree, coaching for organizational change is another catchall category, defined more by its variety than by any unifying approach. However, each of the coaches interviewed focused on the leader's ability to steer the organization through a period of change or to a distinctly different level of capability. Some coaches, for example, focused on developing the organization's capacity to innovate, others on the capacity of the leadership team to guide the organization through crisis and uncertainty. In any case, coaching for leadership behaviors, competitive strategy, team building, and change were common ideas acknowledged by each coach.

Strategy Coaching

Coaching for strategy, because it is more organizationally focused, can cover a broad range of challenges. Primarily, it is focused on coaching a leader or leadership team to understand its emerging competitive landscape, in order to dominate that future space, five to seven years down the road. Hardcore analysis, development and deployment of strategy, and implementation of organizational change are all aspects of strategy coaching. As a result, the coach must be able to guide the leader through the important stages of the journey. This means that coaching for personal effectiveness, leadership behaviors, team building, and organizational change can all be important to the engagement.

When deciding whether to select a coach, it can be helpful to think in terms of these five categories. It is common sense that one should understand the imperative for coaching before determining how to fill that need. Nevertheless, a framework for considering available options can create greater clarity and define expectations for all involved.

Part II: The Mechanics of Selection

Who Should Make the Coach Selection Decision?

To establish the foundation for a successful coaching engagement, the ground rules and objectives must be clear. When it comes to who should make the coach selection decision, the issues can be broken down into three areas of concern.

Who Is Paying for the Coach and Why?

Nearly 100 percent of the time, the organization is paying for the coach. If so, the organization must own the coach selection process. In other words, the organization is hiring a coach because it needs the coachee to improve his or her performance. That organizational need must be front and center throughout the engagement. Allowing the coach selection process to be ceded to someone who doesn't have the organization's clear objectives in mind is a mistake.

Choices of coaches can be presented to all who are concerned. The coachee must feel reasonably comfortable with those choices, but the client should be the ultimate decision maker.

Who Is the Client?

When defining who the client is, a gray area may exist between who is being coached and who is paying for the coach's services. To some degree, this ambiguity is inherent to the confidentiality and trust necessary to the coaching relationship. A vocal minority of coaches is very clear that the coachee is their client. Although the organization is paying for their services, and the achievement of organizational goals is the ultimate objective, the relationship between coach and coachee is akin to a doctor-patient, or lawyer-client one.

The main concern in this approach seems to be confidentiality and trust. Other coaches, perhaps the majority, are equally clear that although trust and confidence between coach and coachee are inviolable, the coach is being hired in service of the organization. Clarity in that relationship moves the ball along. The coachee knows that his or her agenda must be aligned with the organizational agenda, and that success or failure will be measured on those terms. During times of disagreement, the organization's wishes are paramount. If the coachee is to believe that he or she is the client and in control, a very different dynamic might result.

The actual client is almost always the coachee's superior. In those frequent cases when the CEO is the coachee, the client and the coachee may be one. Regardless of who the client is, the coach is always working to the best of his or her abilities for the betterment of the coachee.

What Is the Role of Human Resources?

Frequently, Human Resources is given the opportunity to provide a list of appropriate coaches. Although this can become tantamount to actually selecting the coach, it should not. Human Resources, with its insight into organizational and behavioral change, may be well informed about an individual leader's needs—especially when it is involved in executive development, succession planning, and organizational strategy. But the selection decision should remain with the client, because the client is most affected by the pay-off or lack thereof from hiring the coach.

Nor should HR allow the coachee the opportunity to select a preferred coach among three or four choices. In such cases, coachees will typically make the choice based on personal criteria, likes and dislikes, connection or chemistry, or sometimes even based on seeing particular coaches as stronger advocates for their careers. Rarely will this help the coachee push into un-comfortable areas or make desired performance improvements.

When it comes to reporting relationships, a discussion covered in the next chapter, HR needs to step aside from this dynamic as well. If HR is closely involved in the selection process and is also involved in checking up or re-viewing the progress of the engagement, there are a number of risks. First, HR may be viewed as the de facto client. Second, the department's personal views about the coachee's and client's needs and objectives may overly influ-ence the belief structure of the coach.

The coach should feel empowered to set the ground rules regarding client and coachee, to clarify reporting relationships, and to work to align the coachee's challenges with the client's or manager's objectives. All of these is-sues will be discussed in greater detail in the next chapter.

Why Is a Coach Being Hired?

As the paying client, the organization needs to be clear about why a coach is being hired to work with the coachee. What is the root cause of the decision to hire a coach? Is it positive or negative? Is it obvious on the surface (i.e., is there a clear goal in mind), or are there unstated reasons related to politics, performance issues, or interpersonal dynamics? The reasons for hiring can usually be broken down into two distinct areas: performance correction and performance development. Both influence the cost, time, and energy the or-ganization should be willing to invest.

Performance Correction

How valuable is the coachee to the organization? What is the cost of replace-ment as opposed to fixing the problem? Would the organization be able to move faster and more efficiently without that person, or do their other con-tributions make the effort, expense, and time of coaching worthwhile? Will performance levels of colleagues and reports improve if that person's perfor-mance improves, or will they improve at even greater rates if that person is no longer in the organization? When performance correction is the reason for coaching, there is nothing wrong with the organization thinking in such blunt terms. In fact, clarity in those matters can ease or guide the decisions that occur along the way—for everyone involved.

It is human nature to avoid dealing with unpleasant or uncomfortable issues, particularly at senior levels, where collegiality, territorial politics, and personal history can create a great deal of willful ambiguity. Organizations have clear mandates for dealing with the most egregious performance correction issues, such as sexual harassment, anger management, and so on. But in gray areas, it's not uncommon for an external coach to be engaged as a substitute for the manager's own leadership duties. Sometimes, a coach is actually being hired as a kinder, gentler way of moving the coachee to a life outside of the organization—a very expensive mode of outplacement.

The client needs to consider some critical issues. Is coaching going to help the problem? What's the probability of success, and what's the payoff for success? When these variables are measured against the cost of the coach and the cost to the organization's resources and capabilities, the answer should be clear.

Performance Development

Because of the cost and investment required to hire a coach, organizations today more often focus their external coaching budget on valued leaders whose contributions are considered critical. The question whether to hire a coach or not, however, is still one of cost benefit. The organization must answer some key questions. Who is worth coaching? What areas of skill or capability development are important enough to warrant coaching? In what direction does the organization want to move, and can its current leadership develop the requisite capabilities? What is the final result that is desired?

Despite the economic downturn since 2001, the competition for talented performers continues to skyrocket. Such people have unlimited options. What is the cost to the organization in providing or in not providing growth opportunities? If that star performer's capabilities are improved by 25 percent through coaching, will there be a place within the organization for her to perform at higher levels? If not, the investment will likely have been wasted—painfully so, if the individual moves to a competitor.

Coaching for performance development is almost always applied in advance of or slightly after a change in circumstance. The coach's role is to provide objective, continuous advice to the coachee on how to position himself most effectively within his or her environment. The following list provides concrete examples of when coaching can help with performance development. Specifically, coaching applies when the individual leader is:

- Taking on a new role or rising in level within the organization.
- Slated for development because he or she has been identified as high potential or as someone who fits in the succession management process.
- Expanding the scope of his or her responsibilities to include new challenges, for example, an increase in geographic, multinational, or cross-cultural territory or the rolling in of other divisions or departments.
- Charged with driving some kind of organizational change or strategy critical to organizational success.
- Working with senior team members in a new way that requires external counsel, advice, and support.
- In need of optimizing his or her own capabilities to improve the performance of others.
- In need of developing critical, interpersonal skills in order to work better in a nontechnical, leadership role.
- In need of help presenting, developing, and articulating a message, vision, plan, or strategy.
- In need of counsel, advice, or critical thinking from an outside perspective to reconfigure the organization's direction, structure, or capabilities.

What Are the Desired Results of the Coaching Engagement?

Just as the organization's objectives should be clear, so should the desired results. In the case of performance correction, the cost of coaching should be no more than the cost of replacement. In the case of performance development, the cost should be considered an investment that sees a greater return through the coachee's new level of contribution.

As much as possible, return on investment should be measured in dollars and impact. This is one of the most challenging aspects of coaching for almost all of the coaches we surveyed. When goals are clear from the outset, success can be judged by whether those goals are met. But goals often evolve throughout the course of the engagement, or the impact of coaching may be intangible, or the foundation that is being laid for impact will have its effect at some time in the future. Satisfaction of coachee and client is one measure of success, but does it gauge the sustainability or long-term success of the impact, or merely the success of the relationship?

Part III: Ensuring Fit

Once the decision to hire a coach has been made, how does the client judge whether a particular coach will be a good fit for the coachee and the organization's needs? It is necessary to consider the appropriateness of the coach in terms of background, ability, organizational fit, and human chemistry. This will increase the likelihood of success.

Alignment of Values

Although alignment of values is rarely considered, a mismatch in values set lead to failure. The coach's values, demonstrated in his or her approach, methods, and personal philosophy must be a good match for the organization. A hard-driving organization that values internal competition over team harmony, for instance, would not be well served by a coach who works to increase effectiveness by improving interpersonal relations. An organization oriented toward short-term profits might be out of line with a coach whose work is most effective at instilling long-range capabilities. Stark contrasts in these points of view will lead to conflict between coach and client, and result in a poor return on investment. It might even place the coachee in some degree of career jeopardy.

Wisdom, Insight, and Intuitive Leaps

Has the coach walked a mile in the coachee's shoes? The coach must be able to understand the challenges of the person being coached. Ideally, the coach has had direct, personal experience that relates to the coachee's current concerns and needs. Quite often, coaches who advise senior leaders have been senior leaders themselves, or have worked so closely with such people that familiarity is very high. It shouldn't be assumed, however, that because a coach works well with senior leaders, his or her ability transfers automatically to more junior levels. Pressures, responsibilities, challenges, and opportunities can be very different.

Experience provides the coach with credibility. The coach should know how to present him or herself in a way to make his or her messages heard and understood. It doesn't matter how wonderful the advice or counsel is. If the coach does not project credibility, the message will go unheeded.

Technical knowledge or expertise can also matter, but is not nearly as important as one might think. The coach, to a certain extent, can actually be well served by a lack of direct technical knowledge. This forces the coachee to articulate issues in greater detail, and opens the door for the fresh perspective of a newcomer. Regardless of the level of technical experience and understanding, the coach's questioning and insight must add value to the situation. If suggestions and questions are inappropriate or unhelpful, frustration will build.

But the expectations for the value that coaches provide should be even higher. Best practice coaches absorb information about the organization, the individual, the technical concerns, and the objectives—not just to steer the coachee appropriately, but also to bring him or her to entirely new levels of performance. The coach does so by making intuitive leaps. He or she has an ability to see patterns and connect the dots in ways that the individual could never manage alone.

Evaluating the coach's experience, wisdom, and intuitive capabilities is no easy feat. One method of doing so is to ask concrete, behavior-based questions about past coaching engagements.

What Are the Coach's Other Dealings in the Industry?

Just as the network of senior leaders and board members is a tangled web, so the network of best practice coaches may extend beyond the client's organization to competitors. The client can be excused for asking the question, "Can the coach serve two masters?"

Confidentiality is not the issue. Coaches have strong personal ethics when it comes to confidentiality and would damage their reputations if they ever violated their obligations. Nevertheless, clients should consider how the coach's other dealings in the industry may affect the guidance being given. Can the coach be a committed partner in success? That's a judgment that can only be made based on the individuals involved.

On the other hand, many coaches that we surveyed frequently found themselves in exactly this scenario—and declared it to be a benefit rather than a detriment to their ability to provide service. A knowledge of the industry, the competitive landscape, the innovations taking place and overall best practices are resources to the client in terms of crafting solutions unique to his or her circumstances. The essence of coaching is customized help. Whereas a consulting organization might provide the same plug-and-play advice, even to direct competitors, the coach is working in partnership with the client to discover unique solutions together.

Can the Coach Operate Effectively with More Than One Coachee in the Same Organization?

Quite often, the success of a coaching engagement with one leader will lead to the coach being retained by another leader in the same organization. The quality of results and impact can lead the coach to be passed around like an exciting new book that simply has to be read. In particular, if the coach has worked with a senior leader or CEO, it might be considered important for others to become schooled as well.

Each individual coach knows whether he or she can operate effectively with multiple leaders, or when tasked at different levels within the organization. Some coaches see that as a desired state because they are able to work most effectively at driving change, strategy, effectiveness, or team work when they become roving coaches. Some clients and coachees may view this with alarm when they consider possible breaches of trust and confidentiality. Certainly, trust and confidentiality are at issue, but problems can be avoided if the ground rules are clear and followed openly. In some organizations, the mandate for development is so insistent and clear that coaches will be working openly with superiors, colleagues, and reports to drive performance improvements. The organization needs to determine what is acceptable for its culture and direction.

Human Chemistry

Coaching is a partnership that thrives on trust, confidence, and forward progress. Coaches and coachees often develop a very strong relationship, even a strong friendship, during the course of working together. Best practice coaches are able to inspire that foundation from the very first stages of the engagement.

Nevertheless, a coachee will not obtain a great deal of benefit from someone he or she dislikes or, conversely, someone he or she likes a great deal but who is unwilling or unable to push him or her in the right direction. Personal likes and dislikes shouldn't be prime factors, but coaching will not be successful if the coachee is highly resistant to the coach. Where's the balance?

The client must make that decision by weighing all factors. For example, if the coachee is uncomfortable with assertive people but needs to develop more assertive behavior, a coach with a dominant and hard-driving personality may be the ticket. If a coachee is from the old school and does not respect the contributions of female reports, then a determined female coach may rearrange their worldview. There are times when likes and dislikes, personal preferences, comfort levels and biases should be ignored.

Best practice coaches develop the human chemistry needed for success. By the end of any successful coaching relationship, the bond between coach and coachee will be present. See Figure 2.1 on page 39 for a tool to use when selecting the right coach.

❑ Are you looking for a long-term or short-term coach?

❑ What are the characteristics of the coach that will have the greatest impact on success?

❑ What style of coach will be most effective?

❑ Has the coach had enough "real" experience at this level?

❑ Has the coach the appropriate experience in the type of coaching required?

❑ What is the level of knowledge that the coach has in your industry?

❑ Does the coach have the skills that you think are important for success?

❑ Are you looking for a coach to enhance or adjust the performance of an individual of a team?

❑ Are you using coaching appropriately—or using it as an alternative for dealing with the problem?

❑ Can the coach command the respect of the coachee?

❑ Can the coach relate to the coachee?

❑ Can the coach manage the relationship effectively?

❑ Is the coach building capacity in the coachee(s) or building dependence on them?

❑ Is there a benefit or risk in the coach working with more than one person in the organization?

FIGURE 2.1 Coaching Checklist: Selecting the Right Coach

CHAPTER 3

---—◆◆◆◆—---

Creating a Powerful
Coach-Coachee Partnership

Organizations are demanding a high return for their coaching investment dollar. Accordingly, best practice coaches must deliver levels of productivity, effectiveness, innovation, and impact that could not otherwise have been obtained. Selecting the right coach for the organization's specific needs is the basis for producing those superior results. But the power of that coaching engagement flows from:

- The structure of the relationship
- The coach's skill in moving the coachee toward high impact goals
- The coachee's commitment and willingness to change

The coach-coachee relationship is best described as a partnership, one in which both sides work to reach an agreed-upon destination. Obviously, neither coach nor coachee could get to the goal alone. From such mutual reliance, confidence, trust, and even friendship develop along the way.

The relationship is not one of equals, however. The coach, not the coachee, controls the pace and direction of the journey. It is within the coach's realm of responsibility to set the ground rules; collect the necessary information; assess, analyze, and judge the situation; define the right action plan; push or prod accordingly; monitor progress; adjust approach as required; and deliver the goods. All of this needs to be done openly and with the full cooperation of the coachee—but the coach's skill, experience, and adaptability are driving the process.

The coachee has his or her own responsibilities. As in any form of counseling that is oriented around change, the coachee must commit to the hard work, risk, and awkwardness that are part of real, sustained impact. In other words, the coachee must take ownership over his or her own progress, working at it consistently and with commitment, while trusting the coach to be there with all necessary support and expertise. Further, it is important for everyone to understand the risk of a person's taking on change and the subsequent fear of failure that can result. If the coachee is not willing to make that level of commitment, or, as sometimes happens, if the organization is not truly willing to be supportive, then it's up to the coach to identify that problem, clarify expectations, and continue or abandon the project as appropriate.

The coaching journey, especially for a top leader or executive, does not take place in a vacuum or during a time-out from other responsibilities, pressures, and interpersonal demands. It is not surprising that the regimen of change can sometimes become lost amidst so many day-to-day concerns. The coach is there to watch over the small steps in what can be described as the microplan. It is, after all, only through small steps that we achieve larger aims. As Hesiod, one of the earliest Greek philosopher-poets, stated 2,600 years ago: "If you add little to little, and do it often, soon the little will grow, and become big."

The coach must also link the microplan to the larger vision; otherwise, the coachee will not be reinforced by his or her steady accomplishments. As anyone who has ever driven a change process will recognize, the steps leading toward that change are lost to many people in the details of the daily grind. By deliberately and frequently linking the coachee's efforts to the overall objective, the coach creates the sense of forward momentum and purpose valued by action and goal-oriented organizations.

This chapter describes the coach-coachee partnership from two vantage points. Part I looks at how the coach designs the engagement's system in order to create the conditions for a true partnership. Without this structure, both sides are liable to seek paths of least resistance whenever they encounter pressures or roadblocks. Easy solutions reduce the power potential of the change. Part II looks at the human dynamic of the relationship and the means by which the coach leads the coachee to the depth of understanding necessary for creating sustainable results. Separating the process of coaching into two distinct aspects is a purer approach than would ever arise in the messy dynamics of real life. Nevertheless, that division will help coach, coachee, and organization communicate expectations with more clarity and purpose.

Part I: Structuring the Coaching Engagement

The results-driven nature of the coach-coachee relationship requires clear ground rules to operate effectively. One purpose of the first meeting is to establish exactly what those ground rules are.

Establishing the Ground Rules

Setting the ground rules is not a process of negotiation but one of clarification. The coach is in charge and up-front. Ground rules cover most of the following key areas:

- Confidentiality, expectations, and commitments
- Reporting relationships
- Methods of information gathering
- Making judgments, setting objectives, and monitoring progress
- How, why, and when the coaching will end

The coachee will have concerns and anxieties, some which are bound to be self-serving or protective, and with the danger of limiting the coach's effectiveness. An experienced coach has encountered these before and knows how to provide assurances or sound reasons to overcome reluctance. One of the key issues raised in the last chapter comes to the forefront at this very stage—who exactly is the client? If the coach and coachee understand that the client is the organization footing the bill, the ground rules become much easier to accept. Acceptance won't automatically generate the trust and openness required for success, but establishing ground rules that are clear, and clearly followed, is one of the steps necessary for trust to grow.

Once ground rules have been set, they cannot be bent along the way. The relationship needs the discipline and boundaries of that structure for the coachee to experience the creativity and energy of real change.

Confidentiality, Expectations, and Commitments

Although trust is a feeling and a bond, confidentiality is more of a contractual agreement. Over time, it can serve as one of the pillars of trust. But in the beginning of the relationship, confidentiality is about establishing expectations and the lines or boundaries of communication.

Confidentiality between coach and coachee is inviolable, no matter who is paying the bill. For the relationship to be effective, the coachee must be able to honestly discuss personal feelings, concerns, and attitudes that can encompass a broad range of subjects, including the coachee's superiors, peers, reports, and even family, as well as the organization and its strategy.

As much as possible, the coach should keep such discussion within the realm of the predetermined objectives, but essentially the floor is open. Without confidentiality, the relationship cannot progress to trust, nor can the coach understand the coachee's challenges with sufficient complexity.

The protocol of confidentiality runs both ways. The coachee does not betray the coach's confidences any more than the coach would. Commitment to the process must also be mutual. The coach is willing to do everything for the coachee as long as the coachee demonstrates commitment with consistent effort. The coachee should expect the same from the coach. A coach's rules are simple: "You can fire me. I can fire you. The organization can fire both of us."

Reporting Relationships

Strict confidentiality does not mean that the coachee's progress is never discussed outside of that relationship, but it does mean that what gets discussed, when, and with whom is clearly determined and consistently followed.

The goal of the engagement is not to make the coachee happy but to provide value to the organization. Whoever is paying the coach is the client. Although confidentiality needs to be respected, the line of command and the flow of communication must be clear. There should be one point of contact in that information flow, ideally the coachee's boss or someone even higher in the same line of command. Once this contact is decided, the coachee's progress should not be discussed or broadcast beyond that person.

The initial Human Resources point of contact, for example, may not be the best choice for the reporting relationship. That person set up the engagement and the conditions, and can help keep things on track, but should not be an active participant in the process. The client's interest in the business objectives can adequately serve as the compass that points the coach and coachee in the right direction.

Coaching can fail, especially if coach and coachee have little regard for time frame, expense, and meeting objectives. Often, this is a symptom that arises from a poor understanding of reporting protocol.

Methods of Information Gathering

Another aspect of coaching that may be unsettling to the coachee is how much information the coach will be gathering and how he or she will be gathering it. Unfortunately, the coach cannot learn everything he or she needs to know by talking to the coachee alone. Such data provide only part of the picture, since the coachee's knowledge may be limited and his or her point of view is personally biased. In strategy coaching, for example, the CEO or division head may not be aware of everything that is going on with the organization's operations. In leadership coaching, the coachee's perception of his or her leadership style may be completely out of line with how that style affects peers or reports. What's intended as a joke or a motivational dressing down by a CEO may be interpreted very differently by a new vice president.

To gather critical information, a coach must understand the coachee's environment and interpersonal relationships to whatever extent the objectives dictate. There are a number of approaches or techniques that coaches use, each with its own limitations and advantages. The following is a representative list:

- *Survey:* To gauge the climate of the organization or assess the impact of a strategy or change initiative
- *360-degree feedback survey:* To assess the coachee, from the perspective of superiors, reports, peers, and even customers.
- *Interviewing:* Similar to 360-feedback, except that the coach will spend time personally with superiors, reports, colleagues, and so on, discussing the coachee and his or her challenges confidentially.
- *Internal source:* With permission, the coach works closely with one or two key stakeholders who know the coachee very well.
- *Shadowing:* The coach follows the coachee through daily assignments, in team settings, during key meetings, and so on, observing how the coachee works, how that impacts others, the dynamics involved, the information exchanged, the power relationships, and so on. Shadowing is similar to the participant-observation techniques of anthropology.
- *Monitoring output:* This is used when tasks and deliverables are good gauges of the coachee's current performance and progress.
- *Past performance:* To understand a coachee's current situation, a coach sometimes needs look no further than the past. Behaviors, attitudes, values, and approaches are difficult to change. What may have been a benefit at one level can be a liability in another context. With access to information about past performance, the coach can intuit a good deal of quality information about current challenges.
- *Outside influences:* In some cases, what is going on in the coachee's personal or family life may have a drastic impact on performance. If the coach has no knowledge of such personal issues, coaching can be directed at entirely wrong areas.

It's understandable that the coachee will need to define a comfort zone when it comes to information gathering. In establishing the ground rules, the coach informs the coachee about preferred approaches, but permission needs to be secured and boundaries agreed upon. If those boundaries threaten to get in the way of a successful engagement, another solution needs to be found.

Making Judgments, Setting Objectives, and Monitoring Progress

Following the information-gathering stage, a best practice coach will end up with too much data. This data needs to be filtered, narrowed down, and focused, a process that requires a significant amount of judgment.

The coach must be careful not to apply all of the data to the coachee unreservedly. Some of it may not be true; some may not be relevant; some may be relevant but not significant in meeting key objectives as they shape up. The coach overlays his or her own expertise on the data by looking for clues, echoes, and patterns. As the coach begins to grasp what the issues are, he or she reframes them for others to respond or push back, adjusts them as required, and secures alignment. The coach does not bring biases to this process. Instead, the coach brings structure, thought, experience, instinct, and knowledge to shape the information and focus it on a reduced number of significant objectives that are worth accomplishing.

The coach and coachee must come to agreement on these objectives and then on a plan of action. It is important that the objectives be in alignment with the client's or organization's needs or concerns, and that the action plan be part of the flow of information in the reporting protocol.

Objectives must be concrete, outcome-based, accomplishable in a defined time period, and limited in number. Most coaches focus on only two or three objectives. Many coachees want to be more ambitious, but experience has shown that increasing the number only blurs focus and reduces impact. Instead of doing two or three things well and benefiting in a lasting way, the coachee or the organization partially accomplishes five or six objectives with less impact. On the other hand, once the initial critical objectives have been accomplished, others can be tackled in turn.

Objectives need checkpoints at progressive stages. With any end goal, there are always steps that must be accomplished along the way. Those steps should be flagged and serve as markers, both for monitoring progress and celebrating small wins.

The coach needs structure and skill to monitor progress effectively. Systems must be in place to measure how well the coachee is delivering on the identified actions. Frequency of follow-up is based not only on the coachee's need for counsel but also on how frequently the coach needs to check in to ensure progress. The spectrum of approaches is quite variable. Some coaches work intensely with a coachee for a few months, then sporadically monitor progress and make adjustments along the way. Others do a few initial sessions, monitor from afar, and revisit when needed.

During follow-up, the coach is disciplined about having a specific objective in mind for each contact. Although the coachee may not always be aware of the underlying agenda, the coach is probing to monitor progress and adjust the plan as necessary. Without that discipline, coaching follow-up would lack structure. This might lead to unfocused sessions, filled up by friendly chatter and confession; or the sessions might swing chaotically from one challenge to another, preventing steady progress on preset goals.

How, Why, and When the Coaching Will End

When the objectives are accomplished, the coaching engagement is over. Depending on their relationship, the coach may occasionally check in with the coachee, but only off the clock. Alternatively, if the objectives aren't accomplished and the time frame is exceeded, the coaching engagement may have failed. That's up to client and coach to evaluate. A useful exercise is to assess levels of blame. Rarely is it one person's fault that a coaching engagement doesn't work. The percentage of blame allotted to the coach, coachee, and others can be insightful.

How a coach ends the engagement can be as important as how it begins. An exit strategy must be in place. Some coaches will hang on for as long as the client will pay, but a best practice coach lets go at the optimal time. The goal of coaching is not to create dependency but to give the coachee the tools and capabilities to excel and grow on his or her own.

Part II: Creating Lasting Impact

Best practice coaching is a combination of empathy and structure. Coaches develop the structure by setting the stage, assessing the current situation, creating alignment around needs, focusing on objectives, laying out a future plan and executing it with sufficient follow-up. The art of coaching lies in the human dynamic, however. It encompasses the means by which the coach builds trust, adjusts the coaching process to meet the coachee's personal strengths and pace, and fosters the conditions necessary for success.

Personal style has a lot to do with how best practice coaches create lasting impact Describing that dynamic helps coachees and clients know what to expect.

Building Trust

Trust is both a foundation and an outcome of the coaching partnership. Best practice coaches are able to create the foundation of trust from the outset, by the end of the first meeting. How do they do it?

- *Self-awareness:* Coaches are people with a high degree of self-knowledge, gained over time. They are not without ego, but they are humble and open, and can project these qualities clearly. They have a strong personal ethic and set of values, which they demonstrate in their behaviors.
- *Empathy:* Coaches are skilled at listening, questioning, and empathizing. They develop an understanding of the coachee's position and personality very quickly. The focus keenly on that person's needs. They adjust their own style to fit the coachee.
- *Credibility:* Coaches have a level of experience that provides them with instant credibility. They can communicate in a language and style with which coachees are familiar. They have a knowledge base, which is now at the disposal of the coachee.
- *Real relationship:* Coaches do not just give, they receive. Coaching is a journey of learning and growth for both coach and coachee. If the relationship were one way, it wouldn't foster the highest levels of trust.

The coaching partnership achieves its impact because of the foundation of trust. The more trust the coach can generate, the more the coachee can achieve.

Managing the Dynamic

Whether the coaching objectives are directed toward strategy, personal leadership, transitions, or organizational change, at least 75 percent of that coaching focuses on the human dynamic over the more technical aspects of the challenge. In order to meet the coaching objectives in the desired time frame, the coach must be able to skillfully manage that dynamic, allowing the coachee to learn, grow, and succeed at an optimal rate. This growth takes place at the very edge of the coachee's comfort zone, where creative possibility is just within reach.

How does the coach produce such magic? First, the coach has a clear understanding of what needs to be worked on, in large part because he or she is able to think in terms of behaviors. For example, most people are quick to hold a person's personality at fault if they are not accomplishing some objective. Manager X is ineffective because he is not assertive or does not take enough risks, while manager Y is overbearing and closed off to new ideas. As personality traits, these can be intimidating challenges, but when viewed as behaviors, they are eminently changeable.

As an example, a manager who is not assertive enough or who is too risk averse needs to:

- Understand the context in which that behavior occurs
- Have the behavior pointed out when they demonstrates it
- Be trained to have an alternative behavior available for future occasions
- Be encouraged to continue practicing that alternate behavior even when it feels awkward or meets with less than spectacular success
- Become a natural and skilled user of that learned behavior over time

Although this is a basic example in the domain of leadership coaching, there are parallels with other kinds of coaching as well. There is a behavioral change aspect to the manager who is unable to accept the new responsibilities of a merger, or the COO who needs to work with a senior team in a different way to manage an organizational shift, or the CEO who must think in radical terms to create the organization's new competitive strategy. By focusing on behaviors and measurable outputs instead of on personality traits and characteristics, the coach is able to deftly manipulate the levers of growth and change.

Overall progress is not judged by the person making the change but by those who view the change. In other words, the coach doesn't measure success by measuring the coachee's level of satisfaction, but by measuring the impact on the surrounding environment.

For example, the manager who needs to be more proactive about providing feedback is not the best judge of whether he or she is doing a better job. Even though that manager may be much more deliberate than in the past, the important question is whether direct reports feel the same way. If they don't, is it because the manager is truly failing to change or because reports have not noticed the change that has taken place? The coach must judge and adjust tactics as needed, suggesting perhaps that the manager tag a feedback moment more openly in the future so that reports are made consciously aware of it.

As another example, in the case of an organizational change initiative, the coachee's success at developing and implementing that change can't be measured by how well the coachee feels but rather by how clearly the organization has been impacted. Again, the coach takes the pulse of that impact and adjusts the coachee's approach accordingly, keeping in mind that not everyone's perception of macrochange is always clear.

A behavioral change or a strategy implementation will not succeed if the coach is only there to provide the initial push, no matter how solid and insightful the advice. Progress must be monitored at appropriately frequent intervals to ensure the change. The coach understands the coachee, the environment, and the challenge well enough to know when to apply more gas, when to touch on the brake, and when to change direction. The coach is always trying to create the most powerful and sustainable results in the shortest time frame. How fast can the coachee be moved along? How is the coachee doing emotionally and mentally with the changes taking place? Is there a danger zone approaching in which the coachee will be placed in a situation that might jeopardize chances of success or reduce his or her willingness to take further risks? Is the organization providing sufficient support for the change?

The coach modifies the approach as required, recalibrating it to optimize the pace of the coachee's development in a way that allows the coach to meet his or her commitments and agreed-upon objectives. The coachee's best interests are kept in mind throughout this recalibration. Even though the organization may be the paying client, the coach is nevertheless not going to be part of any measures that harm or undermine the coachee. The ethic of coaching requires the coach to manage the client's expectations just as skillfully as he or she manages the coach's progress.

Sustainable Success

Success isn't measured by how well the coachee performs with the coach's direct help; it must be judged by how well the coachee performs after the coach has left the scene. If the coach has truly done the job, the coachee will have the capabilities and tools to succeed independently.

How does the coach create sustainable success? First, the coach must ensure that the coachee is actually anchored to the change they've experienced. It's easy to change in the short term. It's more difficult to change permanently. In some ways, this is the difference between technique and understanding. In other words, just because the coachee is making a conscious effort to think or behave differently, that doesn't mean he or she won't go back to old habits when that conscious approach falls off the daily to-do list.

That's the internal battle. There will also be a great deal of external pressure on the coachee to leave their new performance zone for the familiarity and comfort of the old zone. To manage the external pressure, the coach tries to create the conditions for success in the coachee's environment. That might involve preparing the people around the coachee for the changes that are taking place, by enlisting their support and understanding. Not all of the coachee's reports and colleagues will be actively rooting for his or her success, especially if behavioral problems have been part of the mix. But if 80 percent of those people can be brought on board, the chances of that success being sustained are much greater.

Creating sustainable success is part of the coach's exit strategy. The process of weaning the coachee from the coach's guidance involves checking in to ensure the change is still effective. It's the coach's duty to help the

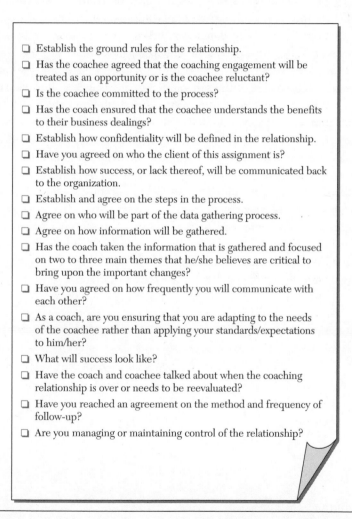

❏ Establish the ground rules for the relationship.
❏ Has the coachee agreed that the coaching engagement will be treated as an opportunity or is the coachee reluctant?
❏ Is the coachee committed to the process?
❏ Has the coach ensured that the coachee understands the benefits to their business dealings?
❏ Establish how confidentiality will be defined in the relationship.
❏ Have you agreed on who the client of this assignment is?
❏ Establish how success, or lack thereof, will be communicated back to the organization.
❏ Establish and agree on the steps in the process.
❏ Agree on who will be part of the data gathering process.
❏ Agree on how information will be gathered.
❏ Has the coach taken the information that is gathered and focused on two to three main themes that he/she believes are critical to bring upon the important changes?
❏ Have you agreed on how frequently you will communicate with each other?
❏ As a coach, are you ensuring that you are adapting to the needs of the coachee rather than applying your standards/expectations to him/her?
❏ What will success look like?
❏ Have the coach and coachee talked about when the coaching relationship is over or needs to be reevaluated?
❏ Have you reached an agreement on the method and frequency of follow-up?
❏ Are you managing or maintaining control of the relationship?

FIGURE 3.1   Coaching Checklist: Creating a Powerful Coach-Coachee Relationship

coachee prepare for the change, accomplish the change, and sustain the change. The occasional phone call to the coachee or the coachee's key stakeholders can evaluate how well the coaching impact has lasted. The impact of monitoring after the engagement is formally over cannot be underestimated.

As coaching comes under more and more pressure to demonstrate its return on investment, demonstrating sustainability of success is becoming critical. Revenue for even the blue-chip consulting firms has fallen recently, in large part because clients were never actively weaned from consultant-dependency and capabilities were not sufficiently transferred. The business model of best practice coaching is clearly aligned with these new demands, but coaches must be able to demonstrate that their results are living up to those demands.

Ultimately, the success of the coaching partnership is not measured by coach-coachee chemistry or the satisfaction of the coachee; it is measured by business results. Nevertheless, the partnership is one of mutual benefit and the satisfaction in that should be felt by both parties. The coachee has taken a journey from vulnerability to competence with a new base level of high performance. Along the way, he or she has received side benefits of greater satisfaction in their work, more authenticity in their personal calling, and increased creativity in their role. The coach has also taken a journey, although it is perhaps one more leg on an even longer adventure. By working closely with another human being and seeing that work come to success, he or she has gained a valuable experience while developing in approach, insight and self-awareness. See Figure 3.1 on page 51 for a Coaching Checklist to use when creating a powerful coach-coachee relationship.

Part II

50 TOP EXECUTIVE COACHES

———◆———

Nancy J. Adler	Leigh Fountain	Howard Morgan
John Alexander	Robert M. Fulmer	Barbara Moses
David Allen	Joel Garfinkle	Bruce Pfau
Shirley Anderson	Fariborz Ghadar	Gifford Pinchot
Julie Anixter	David Giber	Barry Posner
Marian Baker	Marshall Goldsmith	C. K. Prahalad
Joel Barker	Vijay Govindarajan	Gary Ranker
Kim Barnes	Michael Hammer	Judy Rosenblum
Christopher A. Bartlett	Phil Harkins	Stratford Sherman
Ken Blanchard	Sally Helgesen	Ken Siegel
Jim Bolt	Paul Hersey	Richard Strozzi-Heckler
William Bridges	Frances Hesselbein	R. Roosevelt Thomas Jr.
W. Warner Burke	Beverly Kaye	Noel M. Tichy
Niko Canner	Jim Kouzes	Brian Tracy
Jay Conger	Richard J. Leider	Dave Ulrich
Bill Davidson	Bobbie Little	Albert A. Vicere
David Dotlich	Jim Moore	

CHAPTER 4

Coaching Leaders/ Behavioral Coaching

Thought Leaders

MARSHALL GOLDSMITH
JIM KOUZES
FRANCES HESSELBEIN

JAY CONGER
DAVE ULRICH
BARRY POSNER

Practitioners

HOWARD MORGAN
KEN SIEGEL

BOBBIE LITTLE
KIM BARNES

THOUGHT LEADERS

Marshall Goldsmith

CHANGING LEADERSHIP BEHAVIOR

 Marshall Goldsmith currently heads Marshall Goldsmith Partners, a joint venture between Marshall and Katzenbach Partners, LLC. He frequently teaches high-potential leaders and is on the executive education faculty at Michigan and Dartmouth. His newest books are *Global Leadership: The Next Generation* and *Human Resources in the 21st Century*. Amazon.com has ranked six of his books as the "most popular" in their field. In the past two years, Marshall's work has been featured in a *New Yorker* profile, a *Harvard Business Review* interview, and a *Business Strategy Review* cover story (from the London Business School). He was featured in the *Wall Street Journal* as one of the "top 10" executive educators, in *Forbes* as one of five top executive coaches, in *Business Times* (of Asia) as one of 16 major thought leaders in his field, and in *Fast Company* as America's preeminent executive coach. Marshall's books include *The Leader of the Future* (a *BusinessWeek* "top 15" bestseller), The *Organization of the Future* (a *Library Journal* "Best Business Book" award winner) and *The Leadership Investment* (which won a Choice award as an "Outstanding Academic Business Book"). He can be reached via the Internet at www.MarshallGoldsmith.com or by phone at (858) 759-0950.

My mission is to help successful leaders achieve a positive change in behavior: for themselves, their people and their teams.

While I am best known as an executive coach, coaching represents only 25 percent of what I do. The remaining three-quarters of my time is spent in teaching others (executives, high-potential leaders, human resource professionals, or university executive education participants) what I know, writing or editing books and articles, or working in consulting networks that can provide a wide range of coaches to leaders around the world. Almost everything that I do as a professional is related to my mission.

Our "Pay for Results" Behavioral Coaching Approach

All of the behavioral coaches that I work with use the same general approach. We first get an agreement with our coaching clients and their managers on two key variables: (1) what are the key behaviors that will make the biggest positive change in increased leadership effectiveness and (2) who are the key stakeholders that should determine (one year later) if this change has occurred.

We then get paid only after our coaching clients have achieved a positive change in key leadership behaviors as determined by key stakeholders.

I believe that many behavioral coaches are paid for the wrong outcomes. Their income is a largely a function of "How much do my clients *like me*?" and "How much *time* did I spend in coaching?" Neither of these is a good metric for achieving a positive, long-term change in behavior. In terms of liking the coach—I have never seen a study that showed that clients' love of a coach was highly correlated with their change in behavior. In terms of spending clients' time—my clients are all executives whose decisions often impact billions of dollars. Their time is more valuable than mine. I try to spend *as little of their time as necessary* to achieve the desired results. The last thing they need is for me to waste their time!

Qualifying the Coaching Client: Knowing When Behavioral Coaching Won't Help

Since we use a "pay only for results" process in behavioral coaching, we have had to learn to *qualify* our coaching clients. This means that we only work with clients that we believe will benefit from our coaching process.

As this book so clearly points out, there are several different types of coaching. I only do behavioral coaching for successful executives—not strategic, life planning, or organizational change coaching. I have the highest respect for the coaches in the categories that are represented in this book.[1] That is just not what I do. Therefore, I only focus on changing leadership behavior for individuals and teams. If my clients have other needs, I refer them to other coaches.

Have you ever tried to change the behavior of a successful adult who had no interest in changing? How much luck did you have? Probably none. I only work with executives who are willing to make a sincere effort to change and who believe that this change will help them become better leaders.

Some large corporations write people off; but rather than just fire those people, the organization engages in a pseudobehavioral coaching process that is more seek and destroy than help people get better. We only work with leaders who are seen as potentially having a great future in the corporation. We only work with people who will be given a fair chance by their management.

Finally, I would never choose to work with a client that has an integrity violation. I believe that people with integrity violations should be *fired,* not coached.

When will our approach work? If the issue is behavioral, the person is given a fair chance and is motivated to try to get better, the process that I am going to describe will almost always succeed.

Involving Key Stakeholders

In my own development as a behavioral coach, I have gone through three distinct phases.

In phase one, I believed that my clients would become better because of *me*. I thought the coach was the key variable in behavioral change. I was wrong. Since then, we have done research with over 86,000 participants on changing leadership behavior. We have learned that the key variable for change is *not* the coach, teacher or advisor—it is the people being coached and their coworkers.

In phase two, I spent most of my time focusing on my coaching clients. This was much better. I slowly learned that hardworking clients were more important than a brilliant coach! I learned that their ongoing efforts meant more than my clever ideas.

In phase three (where I am now), I spend most of my time not with my coaching client but with the key stakeholders around my client. My results are dramatically better.

How do I involve key stakeholders? I ask *them* to help the person that I am coaching in four critically important ways:

1. *Let go of the past.* When we continually bring up the past, we demoralize people who are trying to change. Whatever happened in the past happened. It cannot be changed. By focusing on a future that can get better (as opposed to a past that cannot), the key stakeholders can help my clients improve. (We call this process feedforward, instead of feedback.)[2]
2. *Be helpful and supportive, not cynical, sarcastic, or judgmental.* If my clients reach out to key stakeholders and feel punished for trying to improve, they will generally quit trying. I don't blame them! Why should any of us work hard to build relationships with people who won't give us a chance?
3. *Tell the truth.* I do not want to work with a client, have her get a glowing report from key stakeholders and later hear that one of the stakeholders said, "She didn't really get better, we just said that." This is not fair to my client, to the company, or to me.
4. *Pick something to improve yourself.* My clients are very open with key stakeholders about what they are going to change. As part of the process,

our clients ask for ongoing suggestions. I also ask the stakeholders to pick something to improve and to ask for suggestions. This makes the entire process "two-way" instead of "one way." It helps the stakeholders act as "fellow travelers" who are trying to improve, not "judges" who are pointing their fingers at my client. It also greatly expands the value gained by the corporation in the entire process (see the following case study).

Steps in the Behavioral Coaching Process[3]

The following steps outline our behavioral coaching process. Every leader that I coach has to agree to implement the following steps. If they don't want to do this, I make no negative judgments. There are many valuable things that leaders can do with their time other than work with me! Our research indicates that if leaders won't do these basic steps, they probably won't get better. If they will do these basic steps, they almost always get better!

1. *Involve the leaders being coached in determining the desired behavior in their leadership roles.* Leaders cannot be expected to change behavior if they don't have a clear understanding of what desired behavior looks like. The people that we coach (in agreement with their managers) work with us to determine desired leadership behavior.
2. *Involve the leaders being coached in determining key stakeholders.* Not only do clients need to be clear on desired behaviors, they need to be clear (again in agreement with their managers) on key stakeholders. There are two major reasons that people deny the validity of feedback: wrong items or wrong raters. By having our clients and their managers agree on the desired behaviors and key stakeholders in advance, we help ensure their "buy in" to the process.
3. *Collect feedback.* In my coaching practice, I personally interview all key stakeholders. The people that I am coaching are all potential CEOs, and the company is making a real investment in their development. However, at lower levels in the organization (that are more price sensitive) traditional 360-degree feedback can work very well.
4. *Determine key behaviors for change.* As I have become more experienced, I have become simpler and more focused. I generally recommend picking only one to two key areas for behavioral change with each client. This helps ensure maximum attention to the most important behavior. My clients and their managers (unless my client is the CEO) agree upon the desired behavior for change. This ensures that I won't spend a year working with my clients and have their managers determine that we have worked on the wrong thing!

5. *Have the coaching clients respond to key stakeholders.* The person being reviewed should talk with each key stakeholder and collect additional "feedforward" suggestions on how to improve on the key areas targeted for improvement. In responding, the person being coached should keep the conversation positive, simple, and focused. When mistakes have been made in the past, it is generally a good idea to apologize and ask for help in changing the future. I suggest that my clients *listen* to stakeholder suggestions and not *judge* the suggestions.

6. *Review what has been learned with clients and help them develop an action plan.* As was stated earlier, my clients have to agree to the basic steps in our process. On the other hand, outside of the basic steps, everything that I give my clients is a *suggestion.* I just ask them to listen to my ideas in the same way they are listening to the ideas from their key stakeholders. I then ask them to come back with a plan of what *they* want to do. These plans need to come from them, not me. After reviewing their plans, I almost always encourage them to live up to their own commitments. I am much more of a facilitator than a judge. I usually just help my clients do what they know is the right thing to do.

7. *Develop an ongoing follow-up process.* Ongoing follow-up should be very efficient and focused. Questions like "Based upon my behavior last month, what ideas do you have for me next month?" can keep a focus on the future. Within six months, conduct a two-to-six item minisurvey with key stakeholders. They should be asked whether the person has become more or less effective in the areas targeted for improvement.

8. *Review results and start again.* If the person being coached has taken the process seriously, stakeholders almost invariably report improvement. Build on that success by repeating the process for the next 12 to 18 months. This type of follow-up will assure continued progress on initial goals and uncover additional areas for improvement. Stakeholders will appreciate the follow-up. People do not mind filling out a focused, two-to-six-item questionnaire if they see positive results. The person being coached will benefit from ongoing, targeted steps to improve performance.

The Value of Behavioral Coaching for Executives

Although behavioral coaching is only one branch in the coaching field, it is the most widely used type of coaching. Most requests for coaching involve behavioral change. While this process can be very meaningful and valuable for top executives, it can be even more useful for high-potential future leaders. These are the people who have great careers in front of them. Increasing effectiveness in leading people can have an even greater impact if it is a 20-year process, instead of a one-year program.

People often ask, "Can executives *really* change their behavior?" The answer is definitely yes. If they didn't change, I would never get paid (and I almost always get paid). At the top of major organizations, even a small positive change in behavior can have a big impact. From an organizational perspective, the fact that the executive is trying to change anything (and is being a role model for personal development) may be even more important than what the executive is trying to change. With top executives, behavior may be the *only* leadership attribute that can be changed in a cost-effective manner. At that level, it is usually "too late" for technical or functional education.

<hr />

Jim Kouzes

COACHING FOR CREDIBILITY

Jim Kouzes is the coauthor with Barry Posner of the award-winning book, *The Leadership Challenge,* with over one million copies sold. The third edition of *The Leadership Challenge,* released in the fall of 2002, debuted as number 4 on the *BusinessWeek* best-seller list. Jim and Barry have also coauthored *Credibility: How Leaders Gain and Lose It, Why People Demand It, Encouraging the Heart,* and four other books on leadership. They are also creators of *The Leadership Practices Inventory,* a 360-degree assessment tool that has been completed by over one million individuals. Jim is not only a highly regarded leadership scholar and experienced executive, but the *Wall Street Journal* has also cited Jim as one of the 12 most requested "nonuniversity executive-education providers" to U.S. companies. Jim is also the Chairman Emeritus of the Tom Peters Company, a professional services firm that specializes in leadership development, and an executive fellow in the Center for Innovation and Entrepreneurship, Leavey School of Business, Santa Clara University. He can be reached at jim@kouzesposner.com.

Leadership is a relationship. It's a relationship between those who aspire to lead and those who choose to follow. Sometimes, the relationship is one to one. Sometimes, it's one to many. Regardless of the number, leaders must master the dynamics of this relationship. The mastery of the leader-constituent relationship has been the focus of my leadership development work for over twenty years. Whether I'm speaking, teaching, coaching, or researching I am a fanatic about improving the quality of the relationship between those who aspire to lead and those who choose to follow.

So, what's the foundation of this relationship? For over two decades and across six continents, my coauthor, Barry Posner, and I have asked people what they look for and admire in a leader, someone whose direction they would willingly follow. In all those years, the response has been the same. The most important quality people look for and admire in a leader is personal credibility. *Credibility is the foundation of leadership.* If we don't believe *in* the messenger, we won't believe the message.

And what is credibility behaviorally? The most frequent response we get is "Do what you say you will do," or "DWYSYWD" for short. You hear this message reinforced daily in expressions such as:

- Practice what you preach.
- Put your money where your mouth is.
- Walk the talk.
- Actions speak louder than words.
- You have to have the courage of your convictions.

Embedded in these everyday expressions are the two essential ingredients to earning and sustaining personal credibility. First, leaders must be clear about their beliefs. They must know what they stand for. That's the *say* part. Then, they must put what they say into practice; they must act on their beliefs. That's the *do* part.

But leaders don't just speak or act in their own personal interests. Leaders represent groups of people, and when leaders speak and act they're doing so on behalf of others. Personal credibility is maintained when *you* do what *you* say, but *leadership* credibility means that you have to "Do what *we* say *we* will do," or DWWSWWD.

This simple and intuitive framework, but one based in solid research, forms the foundation of all the coaching work that I do. We call it the Say-We-Do model. It involves three challenges in the developmental effort:

- The Clarity Challenge
- The Unity Challenge
- The Intensity Challenge

A successful coaching engagement is one in which the leader embraces these challenges and arrives at a place of effortless performance and leadership authenticity—a place where the person does not just *do* the message, but *is* the message.

The Clarity Challenge

Commitment to credibility begins with clarifying one's personal values, visions, and aspirations. It's impossible to do what you say until you have clarity about what you want to say. The first coaching challenge is to guide leaders in finding their voice and in making sure they really *care* about what they espouse. The Clarity Challenge involves engaging leaders in an exploration of questions such as:

- What are the values and principles that guide you?
- What do you care about?
- What keeps you up at night?
- What legacy do you want to leave?
- What's your framework for living?

Once a leader can clearly articulate values and beliefs, we've taken the first step on the road to sustainable credibility. But only the first step. No matter how noble the principles, constituents want to have leaders that can execute. Clear values are necessary, but insufficient. You cannot do what you say if you don't know how to do it. That means that leaders must be aware of their strengths and weaknesses. The Clarity Challenge also involves engaging the leader in gathering and processing valid and useful information about leadership skills and abilities.

In my coaching and development work, I base the development of leadership competencies on the research in our book, *The Leadership Challenge.*[4] In our extensive exploration of personal best leadership experiences, we found that individuals engaged in The Five Practices of Exemplary Leadership™. When leaders are operating at their best they:

Model the Way

Leaders *find their voice* by clarifying their personal values and then expressing those values in their own style. Then they *set the example* by aligning their personal actions with shared values.

Inspire a Shared Vision

Leaders *envision the future* by imagining exciting and ennobling possibilities, and they *enlist others* in their dreams by appealing to shared aspirations.

Challenge the Process

Leaders *search for opportunities* by seeking innovative ways to change, grow, and improve. Leaders also *experiment and take risks* by constantly generating small wins and learning from mistakes.

Enable Others to Act

Leaders *foster collaboration* by promoting cooperative goals and building trust. They *strengthen others* by sharing power and discretion.

Encourage the Heart

To keep hope and determination alive, leaders *recognize contributions* by showing appreciation for individual excellence. They also *celebrate the values and the victories* by creating a spirit of community.

When providing individuals with feedback on their leadership competencies, I use The Leadership Practices Inventory (LPI),[5] which Barry and I developed during our research. The LPI is a highly valid and reliable measure of leadership behavior, and we've used it since 1986 in a wide variety of organizational settings and in numerous countries.

Contrary to some in the field of leadership development who advocate only building on strengths, we believe it's essential to work on weaknesses as well. We liken it to a pentathlon. There are five events in a pentathlon, and if you're going to compete in it, you have to compete in all five. You can't say, "Well, I'm really not a very fast runner, so I think I'll skip that event." If you do, you're disqualified.

It's the same with leadership. There are five practices (in our model), and if you're going to lead, you have to engage in all of them. Sure, you may be better at some than others, but you still have to improve in all of them. If you chose not to participate in all of them, you're disqualified. You're saying with your behavior, "I really don't want to be a better leader."

The Unity Challenge

To build strong and viable organizations, people must be united in a common cause—united on where they're going, united on why they're going there, and united on the principles that will guide them on their journey. Although members may comply with what the leader says, they will not be fully committed until they own those words themselves. None of us perform at our best when we are doing something because we have to. We only perform well when we want to. Unity cannot be forced. It must be forged.

Credible leaders are able to build a community of shared vision and values. To become fully committed, constituents must understand the aims and aspirations, and they must agree that these aims and aspirations are important to the success of the organization. The second coaching challenge is to guide leaders in gaining consensus on shared values and in building trust among members of the group.

The process of gaining consensus is a highly collaborative process. It involves listening, patience, and the capacity to resolve conflicts. Sometimes, these are not easy things for leaders to do. They just want to get on with it. But we've learned over the years that this phase of the process cannot be cut short. At some level, people will resist when values and visions are imposed or do not fit with personal beliefs.

The Intensity Challenge

People who feel strongly about the worth of the vision and values will have energy to act on them. They'll have passion and intensity for them. They'll set the example by their own behavior. The third coaching challenge is to make absolutely certain that leaders are passionate role models for the organization.

When coaching leaders on how they set the example, I look at how they spend their time and how they handle critical incidents. I listen to their language and to the stories that they tell. I examine the measures they use and how people are rewarded and which individuals get recognized. All these things send signals to the organization about what the real values are. Credibility is built only when there is alignment between words and deeds.

Passion is the dividing line. Intensity demands enthusiasm, hope, self-sacrifice, and a never-say-die attitude. The real test of credibility comes when the times are tough and when leaders have to show the *courage of their convictions.* As one leader told us, "Adversity does not build character, it reveals it."

Coaching for intensity is the most demanding phase of the process. It requires a high degree of confidence in one's skills, a willingness to stand up to some very strong individuals, and a willingness to walk away from an engagement if the person is not willing to convert words into deeds. It also requires a unique relationship between coach and leader. The late John Gardner—leadership scholar and experienced executive in his own right—once commented, "Pity the leader caught between unloving critics and uncritical lovers." Sycophants are of no use to leaders. Always hearing that everything you do is wonderful and right, is a sure route to derailment. Always hearing that everything you do is wrong only causes you to stop listening. What leaders need are "loving critics." I've often thought about putting that on my business card!

Coaching for Character

At a recent character education conference at Santa Clara University's Markkula Center for Applied Ethics, Thomas Likona, author of *Educating for Character,* began his talk with this anonymous poem:

> Be careful of your thoughts, for your thoughts become your words;
> Be careful of your words, for your words become your deeds;
> Be careful of your deeds, for your deeds become your habits;
> Be careful of your habits; for your habits become your character;
> Be careful of your character, for your character becomes your destiny.

This poem summarizes in five lines the rationale behind my approach to coaching for credibility. The way I see it, strategy is not a biological imperative. It begins in our minds, gets expressed in words, and then gets translated into action. Over time, those actions become who we are. What we do repeatedly will determine the legacy we leave.

Coaching people to use the tools of commerce is necessary but insufficient to creating a healthy and prosperous society. The right tools in the wrong hands invite evil ends. The more we study leadership, the more we're persuaded that leadership development is not about the tools. It's about the person. Leadership development is character development.

⟫◆⟪

Frances Hesselbein

FIRST DO NO HARM

 Frances Hesselbein is the Chairman of the Board of Governors of the Leader to Leader Institute, formerly the Peter Drucker Foundation. She was CEO of the Girl Scouts of the USA from 1976 to 1990. Mrs. Hesselbein is Editor-in-Chief of the quarterly journal *Leader to Leader,* and a coeditor of a book of the same name. She also is the author of *Hesselbein on Leadership,* published in August of 2002. She is reachable by e-mail at frances@leadertoleader.org or by visiting her corporate web site www.leadertoleader.org.

I listen very carefully when people talk about coaching. It must be said that not everyone is talking about the same thing. Before we develop a practice that has the potential to influence someone's life, I think we should clarify our own aims and beliefs. The ethical and moral responsibilities of the coach cannot be taken lightly.

First, we need to have a very clear, compelling definition of coaching. Without that definition, we are like organizations without a mission. We also need to be sure that we are defining what we are doing in such a way that the person being coached shares that understanding. The expectations must be clear. There must be a beginning and an ending. The parameters must be set. Overarching those criteria should be one unbreakable creed: first, do no harm. As in the medical profession, everything must be done in service of the person whose life we are affecting.

If we begin our coaching by saying that we know what is good for a person, then we will fail. We cannot have preconceptions, a Case A and Form B, which we will use to fit that person into an established solution. We need to truly know and take into account our clients' needs. What do they value? What do they expect? What are they looking for? The depth of understanding that is needed to do this well says something about how many people we can coach at any given time.

To coach someone takes everything we have ever done and everything we have ever been. If we are faithful to our mission, then it will also take a great deal of our emotional reserve. Our obligation to the person we are coaching requires us to be at our very best—intellectually, emotionally and responsively. If, in the end, the person we are coaching has been diminished by the experience, then shame on us.

What I do, I don't call coaching. I talk with people. I advise and discuss. It's circular. My "coaching" is based on what each person needs. That need is always different and must be discovered through the course of our working together. It's a partnership. Together, we draw closer to answers that are meaningful.

When we define coaching in such human and respectful terms, then that definition will carry us with its sense of moral and ethical obligations. We have an enormous responsibility to the people whose lives we are influencing. The job cannot be done lightly. We need to answer for ourselves, can we do this? If we lack that clear imperative, then we should refrain. Out of such introspection and deep self-assessment comes our answer, our definition, and our mission.

━━◆━━

Jay Conger

COACHING LEADERS

 Jay Conger received his bachelor's degree from Dartmouth College, his masters from the University of Virginia, and his doctorate of business administration from the Harvard Business School. Currently, Dr. Conger is a Professor of Organizational Behavior at the London Business School and a senior research scientist at the Center for Effective Organizations at the University of Southern California in Los Angeles. Jay is the author of 11 books including *Building Leaders: How Successful Companies Develop the Next Generation* and *Winning 'Em Over: A New Model for Managing in the Age of Persuasion.* He can be reached by e-mail at jconger@london.edu.

In my view, executive coaching meets a very basic need. All managers eventually finds that certain strengths that were extremely valuable early in their careers can become powerful liabilities with a rise in level and responsibility. At the same time, there are always one or two weaknesses that become increasingly exposed and exaggerated. As a coach, my role is to help leaders address these strengths that transform themselves into weaknesses and the weaknesses that now loom larger.

The talented executive, for example, who is seen as too controlling and hands-on to effectively lead at the enterprise level, may have excelled at more supervisory levels where demands are more tactical and immediate. Their poor ability at managing upwards was compensated by superior results. With a promotion to senior levels, this weakness becomes problematic as bosses may be geographically removed and political networking becomes a require-ment of the executive suite. Coaching is often critical to help individuals manage these transitions. It is about changing behaviors in line with the lead-ership demands of a role and the needs of the organization.

The people I coach usually come to me because they are not as effective as they feel they should be in their leadership roles. Since my expertise relates to leadership style, interpersonal behavior, and communications, my coaching falls into a fairly broad range. Nevertheless, it focuses on behaviors and style rather than on strategic thinking, functional expertise, or technical skill.

The First Meeting

At the initial meeting with the client, I begin with a set of open-ended ques-tions about the executive's perceptions of her own strengths and gaps; then I get her to rank order her development needs by priority. I ask her to gauge which will be the more difficult to change and why. I also lay out an informal contract of what the coaching process will entail and how it will likely unfold.

I see the first meeting as an opportunity for both coach and client to make a set of personal assessments. Am I the right coach for the person, and is this the right client for me? I don't use the word "chemistry" to describe this de-termination, but there is an evaluation of fit going on. For my part, I'm gaug-ing the person's motivation level, whether she really understands the areas around which she needs development help and how perceptive she is about herself. I test how receptive she is by sharing some initial impressions I have of her. I provide her with a few scenarios and ask how she would respond in those situations. From these, I can gauge her versatility and thoughtfulness. I'm looking, ideally, for someone who is open, reflective, curious, and moti-vated. If we don't engage in that kind of discussion I won't get a full picture. We may end up working on issues that don't really hit the mark.

I pay a lot of attention to the voice tone and the body language in this interview. Obviously, I need to be physically present to do that sort of assessment. I may be in a minority today, but I don't believe that coaching by phone can be effective, particularly before rapport has been established. In any event, I am trying to make a decision about the probability of her sincerity and her capacity for change.

Participant-Observation

If we decide to proceed, I come back and observe her for two to three normal days. I watch what she does and how she interacts, using what anthropologists might call the "participant-observer" technique. The value of that approach is simple. Most people can't fully describe what they do on a daily basis. It's very important to see them in their environment under normal circumstances to get an accurate picture. I watch how they work with different individuals. I look to see if those patterns are consistent across all individuals or if they are specific to particular subordinates and issues. I look to see how my client spends her time and how she communicates. I also make note of what she doesn't talk about or doesn't spend time on. What people don't do is often just as telling as what they do.

At checkpoints, during those first few days, we will take time out so that I can ask questions. I want to get clarity about what I have seen. I'm not only interested in observing; I need to learn her personal perceptions about the things she did and why. In doing so, I am also trying to instill a discipline for self-reflection. That's an underdeveloped capacity in many executives since they are typically, by nature, action-oriented people focused on making things happen.

Next, I'll interview the people around that manager. If she's a senior executive, there are usually only one or two levels above her; so I will interview those individuals, as well as a number of peers and direct reports. If I have time, I like to go one or more levels below the direct reports as well. Most coaches assume that close perceptions and distant perceptions are identical; but research holds that those perceptions can vary greatly. A leader's style must be effective at close range and far away.

If 360-degree surveys have been previously done, I ask for access. I research the coachee's past performance to see how she has behaved in other circumstances. I'm trying to confirm or raise questions about the coachee's personal perceptions and where she has had persistent problems. All of that data helps me get a fully informed sense of her two or three most important developmental needs.

I'm looking for patterns, not one-off situations. If specific relationships are problematic, I put those into a separate pile. I am also looking at patterns of behavior by level. Some people are terrific at managing upwards, for example, and you hear wonderful things about them from their superiors, even as you uncover difficulties in their downward capabilities. Other managers don't spend enough time thinking consciously about managing upwards, because they mistakenly believe that results are their best insurance policy.

Setting and Meeting Objectives

Following this observation and information gathering period, I meet with the executive to decide which development areas we should focus on over the near term—say six or nine months. Personally, I'm of the school that we should limit that number to one or two. We make that decision jointly by synthesizing a number of factors. Where does the client have the highest motivation to focus? What do others see as that person's greatest development needs? And finally, knowing the person and her motivation level, as well as what others view as the areas that need work, what's the likelihood of successful change in that behavior over a period of several months?

In the intersection of those three questions, we choose one or two areas to focus on. The alignment is never perfect. Sometimes, the client wants to focus on an area that overlooks what others have been saying loud and clear. I'm also hesitant to focus on areas that are personality-dependent because I don't see myself as a psychotherapist. As much as possible, we're looking for behavior-specific areas that will help the person succeed in her role.

After we choose one or two areas for development, we have a conversation about what the final outcome will look like. We talk about how others will recognize when the manager is working on that behavior. What realms of the job will be affected on a typical day? How can we measure that? How will we and others know whether the manager is succeeding? We also discuss what factors or circumstances will make that change difficult to accomplish, and strategize ways around those problems.

Usually, we uncover new stuff in the process. What might initially have been perceived as the biggest need turns out to be symptomatic of something else. Often, it's like peeling layers on an onion. The initial interview and the observation help to peel back a few layers; as we go deeper into the work, we pass through more and more layers together.

It's also important at this stage to know the organization's direction and demands. What's going on in this person's business? Who does the coachee report to and what do they reward and encourage? Understanding the context of the person's circumstances helps peel back more layers. Maybe the manager has been placed in a new assignment or has a new boss. Maybe the organization's strategy has changed or new demands are being made. Perhaps those changes or circumstances are exaggerating certain behaviors and magnifying the absence of others.

When the coaching outcomes have been set and the manager has a strategy for action, her work is clear. I come back to visit her occasionally, to observe her in action and to provide additional guidance. I get feedback from her colleagues to see how she's progressing. We have contracted around a specific time frame that we both think is reasonable for successful change. To measure that success, sometimes we'll administer a 360-degree survey around those specific behaviors or I'll interview key individuals about their perceptions on those behaviors. If we've been successful, we may or may not go onto another behavior afterwards.

The Coach and the Client

Every coach brings different experience. My strength comes from my varied but integrated background. I was educated as an anthropologist but have a PhD in organizational behavior. I've spent time training to be a psychotherapist and I have an MBA. I understand business, personal, and organizational issues. As an anthropologist, I'm able to read situations across multiple levels and environments.

The ability to gather different perspectives and synthesize them, especially across levels of analysis, is what distinguishes the very good coaches from the average. The drawbacks are obvious for those with limited areas of expertise. A therapist-coach, for example, focuses on the interpersonal issues but has no appreciation for the organizational. A coach overly versed in business matters may not have sufficient appreciation or empathy for the manager's life, personality, and dilemmas.

It's critical that a coach be able to put the executive at ease early on. Much of that, in my case, relates to interpersonal style and even nuances like my tone of voice. I think a tone works best when it shows it is open to information, joint exploration, somewhat soft and paternalistic, but conveying the offer of help. Even so, there is as much variety in approaches as there are coaches in the field. While I use a mix of probing questions, concise observations and humor, other coaches have more confrontational or intense listening styles. In some analogous research, studies done on the effectiveness of a variety of psychotherapists have shown that more important than a particular method is the quality of the relationship between the helper and the helped. Likewise, I don't think there is one correct coaching method. It's possible that two coaches with very different methods could get the same results with the same person if chemistry and a trusting relationship are established. At the same time, I do think it is important to have a methodology. It helps create the discipline and focus that coaching needs to drive change and results.

The executives who are most receptive to coaching are usually in some type of transition. Perhaps they've been promoted to an enterprise role or have a new boss or have been assigned to a high-visibility task force. Research shows that transitions are the most likely windows where people are open to learning. If people are in a certain degree of pain, that can be quite helpful because it makes them more open to relief, learning, and reflection. The greater the stakes and the pain, the higher the motivation for achieving successful change.

It's also important for an executive to have a fairly healthy reflective side. It is a great sign when people are curious. Are they good observers of themselves? Have they been in trouble or hit a plateau before? If so, how did they respond and learn? I'm looking for that kind of mix of qualities and background.

Not everyone is open to coaching. It has its limitations. Sometimes, the change requires a fundamental change in personality, which can be difficult to manage in a timely way under real business circumstances. Sometimes, the person has no desire to change and perceives himself to be highly successful, which is usually a precursor to failure. Sometimes, perceptions about what needs to be changed are inaccurate. On top of all these limitations rests the most critical restriction of all: Coaching is expensive. It's an intervention that only a few in a company can afford. Naturally, those few are most often at the very top of the organization. We are already moving to new models of coaching to address this challenge. Increasingly, I am teaching executives how to be better coaches!

Dave Ulrich

VISION, STYLE, AND STRATEGY

 Dave Ulrich is on leave as Professor of Business, University of Michigan, and currently serving as Mission President Canada, Montreal Mission, Church of Jesus Christ of Latter-day Saints. He is the author of over 100 articles and book chapters, including *Why the Bottom Line Isn't: How to Build Value Through People and Organization* (with Norm Smallwood); *Results Based Leadership: How Leaders Build the Business and Improve the Bottom Line* (with Norm Smallwood and Jack Zenger); *Tomorrow's (HR) Management* (with Gerry Lake and Mike Losey); and *Human Resource Champions: The Next Agenda for Adding Value and Delivering Results.* He can be reached by phone at (514) 342-2243, by e-mail at dou@umich.edu, or via the Internet at www.daveulrich.com or www.rbl.net.

Leaders envision a future and invest in the present. They need to have a sense of where they are headed through their strategy, mission, purpose, vision, goals, or whatever word works. Then, they need to see how their decisions today move toward that endgame. Connecting present decisions with tomorrow's visions is a key part of coaching. Often, we articulate a glorious future but cannot translate it into the routines of today.

Professionally, I work with senior line and HR leaders who want to articulate a vision for the future and make it happen today. I begin coaching by asking leaders to define their personal style and organization strategy. Personal style deals with how they make decisions, interact with others, accomplish work, and determine what matters most to them. Organization strategy deals with envisioning a future state and investing in the present to get there.

I then help them review the key stakeholders they have to serve (e.g., investors, customers, employees, community) and articulate specific goals for each stakeholder. Then, I help them think about what decisions they can and should make to meet these stakeholder goals. With the decisions in place, we then prepare a time map where leaders figure out how and where to allocate time to meet stakeholder goals. This time map deals with who they meet with, how much time to spend on each decision, what issues they should deal with versus someone else, and so on.

I try to instill a spirit of learning into the coaching experience. Learning often comes from failure and the cycle of making choices, having consequences, and taking corrective action with the consequences. Mistakes are okay if they are sources for learning in the future. Letting go of the past comes from learning how to respond in the future. Sometimes, that means starting small. Out of small things come great and wonderful outcomes. Leaders who try lots of small things build an infrastructure of success. In the short term, many of the small things may not work, but in the long term the cumulative effects of small things are great outcomes.

For coaching to go well, there are some key tenets I try to keep in mind. First, it's important to focus on what we do, not what we don't do. It is easy to go after the negative. This is often done with assessments when we do a 360-degree survey and find someone weak in two or three areas and say, "You are weak, let's fix it." I would rather find the two or three areas where the person can and should excel, and try to drive that. I like to help people feel that they each have strengths that they can build on to deliver value and that they should identify and use those strengths. This also means overcoming the weaknesses by bringing them at least up to par.

The coach needs to care about the person more than the program. I find that until the person I coach knows that I care about him or her at a personal level, the professional suggestions are distant. This means talking about "what matters most" to the person and listening to find out. Most people I coach are already professionally successful or on the path to be so, and yet they have paid a price in their personal lives to get there that they sometimes want to recover. I have found coaching lets me talk about personal issues and what matters. This might get into family, personal life, values, and how to find a way to deal with the pressures of business leadership while maintaining personal balance. It's the most important thing I do.

Leaders give back. Most successful people have earned their right to prominence, but they also have an obligation to share with others. Until we give something away, we don't really feel ownership of it. This means giving back to people who have helped, by being grateful or giving back through family, religious, or community groups to gain a sense of the responsibility leaders have to share with others.

It's important to enjoy the journey. Things go wrong. This is inevitably the case. If nothing is going wrong, you are not trying hard enough to do something new. Learning to laugh when things go wrong, sharing credit when they go right, and being consistent gives one a sense of personal joy along the journey. Leaders should frequently be asking, "Is this what I really want to be doing right now?" Generally the answer should be, "Yes, even if it is hard."

Barry Posner

THE LEADER'S PASSION

Barry Posner is Dean of the Leavey School of Business at Santa Clara University, also serving as a Professor of Leadership at that university. He has also served as Associate Dean with responsibility for leading the School's MBA programs and as Managing Partner of the Executive Development Center. He has received the Dean's Award for Exemplary Service, the President's Distinguished Faculty Award, the School's Extraordinary Faculty Award, and several outstanding teaching and leadership honors. In 2001, he was one of the recipients of the McFeely Award, given to the nation's top management and leadership educators. Barry is the coauthor (with Jim Kouzes) of the award-winning and best-selling leadership book, *The Leadership Challenge.* Barry can be reached or by e-mail at bposner@scu.edu or via the Internet at www.leadershipchallenge.com.

How can I be a leader? How can I be a better leader than I am today? These are the sorts of questions I'm typically asked by students, alumni, and executives from both nonprofit and corporate enterprises. Neither the questions, nor often the answers, vary much depending upon the background of the questioner (i.e., age, education, organizational level, years of experience, gender, and so on) nor the characteristics of their organizational setting (i.e., large or small, public or private, marginal or exceptional performance). Not that these matters are insignificant, because they form an important context in which leadership emerges and is exercised, but essentially because these aren't the bases from which leadership begins.

Leadership begins with determining what you care about, and what you care deeply about. Some refer to this as passion, and others call it vocation or calling. Regardless of terminology, the important point is that leadership development is an inside-out process of development, a bringing forth of talents, energies, motives, determination, and the perseverance necessary to make something happen. Indeed, another critical point is working out how we'll determine "success." Another way of saying this is "Who and for what purpose are you trying to serve?" Clarifying this issue goes a long ways toward determining both passion and ego, for in the end leadership is selflessness, and caring more about another person (or cause) than one cares about oneself.

It's in this same vein that Jim Kouzes and I have written about how leaders are in love: "Of all the things that sustain a leader over time, love is the most lasting." It's hard to imagine leaders getting up day after day, putting in the long hours and hard work it takes to get extraordinary things done, without having their hearts in it. The best-kept secret of successful leaders is love: staying in love with leading, with the people who do the work, with what their organizations produce, and with those who honor the organization by using its work. Leadership is not an affair of the head. Leadership is an affair of the heart.

Another essential characteristic of would-be leaders is their willingness to experiment with new behaviors. Increasingly, I've been more effective when we've determined not what the individual wants "to change" but rather what they want "to improve." Even at the university, we recently revised our language from "strategic planning" to "strategic improvement" and found a world of difference in people's energies and excitement for the challenges and opportunities. Leaders are great learners, and, in fact, we found this to be empirically true in a recent study. We found all five of the leadership practices of exemplary leaders to be positively correlated with the individual's active learning inclinations and strategies. What's the motive for change? Consider, do you think you could be even more effective than you are today? If so, what do you think it would take? Are you willing to try some new behaviors (perhaps even some neglected or unappreciated behaviors) in order to become even more effective?

Leadership, at any level, is fundamentally about the relationship between people. Without a relationship, there is no trust, and without trust, leadership doesn't seed itself and grow. Mutual respect is essential in the leadership development process, and just like the leader, leader-coaches must care about their developing leader more than they care about themselves. Listening, patience, encouragement, imagination, energy, and spirit are additional personal characteristics that help both parties, both inside and outside of the developmental process.

PRACTITIONERS

Howard Morgan

 As an executive coach, Howard Morgan has led major organizational change initiatives in partnership with top leaders and executives at numerous international organizations. Howard's insights into the demands of executive leadership come from 17 years of experience as a line executive and executive vice president in industry and government. He is a Managing Director of Leadership Research Institute and is recognized globally as a top executive coach and leadership development expert. He specializes in executive coaching as a strategic change management tool leading to improved customer-employee satisfaction and overall corporate performance. Howard can be reached by e-mail at howardmo@att.net, via the Internet at www.howardjmorgan.com, or by phone at (858) 756-6912.

I work with senior leaders and/or executive teams on maximizing their effectiveness on both an individual and team level. The majority of my practice is building the depth of executive talent in organizations and ensuring that practices are in place to retain the top talent.

While the approach that I use varies depending on the need, the majority of my engagements begin with gathering the views and opinions of the persons that are significant players in the day-to-day success of the coachee. It is their perceptions that become critical in the coaching relationship. In most cases, they are the reason that the coach is being hired in the first place. In today's companies, most of the really problematic performers have been removed. We are now dealing with individuals whose financial and technical performance is noteworthy, but the impact of their behavior on others in the organization cannot be ignored. They can fall into one of two categories: either they have such strong technical skills that the organization believes that they would not benefit from their departure, or they are the strong choice for future roles in the organization, but there are several areas that need attention for the coachee to be successful at the next level.

To be a good coach, you need to understand that effectiveness is based on the ability to provide another level of understanding on how the coachee and the organization can be more effective together. To be successful today, organizations need to harness the unique skills and characteristics that each successful individual has and find a way for them to succeed within the team or organization. Most coaching finds ways for individuals to lose some of their unique characteristics in the interest of organizational harmony. True success comes from the ability of a coach to build on those strengths, while helping the coachee manage the offsetting "irritations" that can hamper their effectiveness in a team or company setting.

What are the qualities that coachees must have for my coaching to be successful? They need to believe that coaching will help them become more effective both personally and professionally. Many times when I first meet coaching candidates, they ask why they should consider a coach when they have gotten to their level without any assistance. Typically, they also state that they are highly marketable and wonder why they should change. Both are valid points! But coaching is about optimizing performance, not about doing okay. I generally tell coaching candidates that they should not engage a coach just because the company thinks that they would benefit from having one. Instead, the engagement should take place because they think that a coach will help them navigate the "white-water" of today's business climate and enable them to use their skills more effectively. In fact, any coaching that is focused on changing behavior makes a much more persuasive case for the coachee. Bringing about the desired behavior change helps the coachee not only inside the organization, but also with their families and any other work settings they may find themselves in.

The coachee's ability to focus on the benefits of change in the future rather than analyzing the past is key. Can they leave the past behind? Equally important, can others around them leave the past behind? The coachees' desire to be the best they can be and commit fully to that effort defines the value for them. They must be able to trust the coach and themselves before any movement can happen. Furthermore, they have to be able to experiment and find the right solution. After all, if the solution were easy to find, why would they need a coach?

For coaching to be successful, a coach also needs to have a number of critical traits. The first is the ability to leave his or her ego at the door. It is important to remember that the coaching relationship is not about the coach—it is about the coachee. To truly add value, the coach also needs to be able to listen not only to what the coachee is saying, but also to the meaning of their words. There are times when the last thing that a coachee needs is more feedback. Some days, they just need solutions. The coaching relationship hinges on the coach's ability to help them grow and evolve. Thirdly, it is about the ability of the coach to build trust quickly. In today's business world, speed is everything. It does not help for the coach and coachee to take several months to get to know each other. The time span of several months is an eternity in a business setting. Finally, it is the coach's ability to judge the pace and frequency of interaction that could be one of the most important traits. Over the years, I have learned that some coachees require contact every week while others require little communication, once they are clear on the action required and are comfortable about the next steps. This does not mean that the relationship should be totally guided by the coachee's wishes, but rather, on their needs.

The coach knows their efforts have been successful when the coachee and the key players around the coachee agree that the coachee's actions are providing more positive impact and effectiveness in their day-to-day business conduct. The sustainability of the change goes unquestioned when the coachee feels comfortable that he or she is more effective and has adopted the steps necessary to perform at their highest level. Put another way, sustainability feels secured when the return on investment for the company and the coachee has become clear.

━━◆◆◆━━

Ken Siegel

 Kenneth N. Siegel, PhD, ABPP, is President of The Impact Group, Inc., a Los Angeles-based group of psychologists who consult to management. Over the past 20 years, Dr. Siegel has provided management-consulting services to a broad array of multinational companies. He has lectured around the world in his specialty areas of leadership development, cultural clarity, strategic alignment, team enhancement, management development, conflict, and executive coaching. Ken is also the author of the recent book, *So . . . You Call Yourself a Leader: 4 Steps to Becoming One Worth Following.* He can be reached by e-mail at KSiegel105@sbcglobal.net.

In my view, executive coaching is somewhat symbolic in nature and ultimately hollow because it rarely acknowledges (let alone treats) the self-absorbed arrogance and interpersonal ineptitude extant in positions of power. Even the use of the word "coach" taken from the socially competitive, high-flying world of sports, is a euphemism—a corporately acceptable dimension of what is really (and should be) going on . . . psychotherapeutic intervention. When it comes to subordinates, most managers are blissfully comfortable with themselves, blindly indifferent to the needs of others, and relatively disinclined to do anything that does not provide immediate self-benefit. Should we be surprised? Anyone who works for a company today knows how self-interest gets rewarded, understands the pressure to self-aggrandize, and recognizes that corruption has been made interpersonally legal. It's the rare and special leader who sheds those self-imposed limitations on the way up the ladder to become someone truly worth following.

Typically, we are called in to "coach" when high-flying executives have hit an abrupt interpersonal wall. Either they have suddenly—and for no apparent reason—lost the support, commitment and admiration of "their people"; or they have so alienated colleagues, customers, or staff that their careers are in immediate jeopardy. This is not a rare occurrence. In fact, it happens all the time. Managers, by nature, rarely figure out what it takes to be a real leader without the healthy shock of imminent derailment. They are simply not hard-wired to let go of the technical skills, capabilities, and intelligence that got them where they are today, in order to embrace a new, softer skill set that will serve themselves and others better from now on.

The work that we do is (and must be) developmentally based. Generally, we engage with a client over a two-to-five-year time frame. Anything less is nothing more than assuaging upper management that something is being done. We are not interested in what might be considered palliative; what we really want to accomplish is something meaningful.

To be effective, our approach must be developmentally integrated for the individual and done in a group context. In other words, we rely on the expertise and help offered by those surrounding the manager who have the true experience of interacting with him or her. This differs from the typical 360-degree feedback love fest. In our view, traditional 360s are a waste of time because they never enjoin the people who provided the data as part of the solution. Instead, they get everyone to fill out the right paperwork, throw it into some vat, and provide it to managers in sanitized form for later retaliation. In the approach we take, we gather the perceptions and experiences of a variety of stakeholders as data input; but we also recruit those people as part of the therapeutic intervention.

In our model, we teach managers to develop three behavioral constructs, which are probably different from the methods of most coaches. First, we guide managers in learning how to be irreverent. Leaders need to look at themselves from the point of view that who they are and what they are doing is worth examining, doubting, and changing. Second, we try to invoke in managers a sense of courage. Leaders need courage to confront the dark corners where so much of their dysfunction resides, and they need courage to become someone fundamentally different in overcoming those handicaps. Third, we help managers develop a sense of passion. Leaders must have a sense of passion about creating a better "them" because that is the only thing that creates a better "us." Without the irreverence to question assumptions, the courage to act and grow in ways that are fundamentally awkward and risky, and the passion to really care about what happens to themselves, their people, and the world—a leader is not worth following.

Irreverence, courage, and passion are equally important for the coach. A good coach has to have real problems with authority and the ability to look at people who are in those positions as no better (and quite often worse) than others. A coach also needs the courage (if not the narcissism) to want to create an impact on others that will completely transform them. And the coach must believe that in doing so he is helping to make that person and the world a little better.

We measure the success of our coaching in two ways. First, is the manager now producing the interpersonal results that they intend to produce, as opposed to having those effects occur haphazardly and caustically? Second, do the people that the manager affects feel better toward them, have greater respect for them, and view them as more credible, responsible, and trustworthy? In other words, the criteria for success lie outside the manager we are coaching. We evaluate the impact of the leader by the impact on the followers.

"What kind of manager am I?" "How do I affect the people around me?" "Who do I need to become to bring out the best in others?" Real leaders ask those sorts of questions of themselves all the time. They know that introspection, critical self-examination, painful honesty, and a willingness to change and grow are essential leadership tools. To accomplish that sort of deep, behavioral shift, many coaches claim that the manager's own desire to change is the critical ingredient. I respectfully (if not irreverently) disagree. In my narcissistic opinion, what managers really need is a solid dose of panic. Anything less will fail to provide them with sufficient motivation to try something different, let alone become someone different—a person who is **R**esponsible, **E**mpowering, **A**ccountable, and **L**oving to themselves and others.

⫸◆⫷

Bobbie Little

Bobbie Little is a Regional Director, Executive Coaching at Personnel Decisions International (PDI). She is based in Washington, DC, and specializes in coaching senior executives and CEOs. Before joining PDI, she was a founding member of DBM Inc.'s executive coaching practice from 1999 to 2003, responsible for global strategy and ensuring coaching quality and consistency worldwide. A pioneer in the corporate coaching and leadership development field, Ms. Little, a British-born American citizen, has held senior management positions in the United Kingdom and Australia. She has also worked in Italy and France. Ms. Little has also been Chairperson of the Board of the Research Triangle Area Chapter of the American Society for Training and Development (ASTD) and President of the Raleigh Professional Women's Forum. She is a member of The International Coaching Federation (ICF) and a certified Leadership and Master Coach. She can be reached via e-mail at bobbie.little@personneldecisions.com.

I am a master business coach for senior executives in a wide variety of industries. I work with highly talented men and women who want to optimize their performance and stay at the leading edge of their business. Such people are bright, committed, and curious, and set very high standards for themselves. They want to be exemplary leaders. They may already be C suite executives or are aspiring to be in a senior position.

I am currently in a global leadership role with PDI and can readily identify with the challenges my clients face. My international experience gives me an instant connection with many different nationalities and some of the cultural issues they face. I have extensive coaching and assessment experience from both private practice and from working with senior executives during a number of international mergers. It has been a privilege to work with some outstanding corporate leaders and others who have had the courage to try to change long-standing behaviors.

At PDI, we have designed a comprehensive development pipeline for corporate use. This coaching pipeline starts where our clients currently are and takes them to the next level. We do not mandate a slew of assessments for our time-starved executives. We look at the most appropriate form of information gathering, including 360-degree surveys, standardized interviews, performance reviews, and other assessment tools, and use what is most relevant to the coaching engagement. A key difference is that after analyzing the data, we create written action plans that align the individual to the organization's imperatives. These plans are firmly grounded in real-life events on the client's calendar. A critical by-product of my coaching is to create focus on what's really important. I often assign a not-to-do list for my most overscheduled clients.

It is easy to write action plans, but I hold my clients accountable for results. They know I am going to check the metrics with their boss, peers, and direct reports, and I am not going to cut them any slack if they do not take coaching seriously or can't find the time. I look for a return on the company's investment and a "return on the individual." They have to desire change and sustain the change in order for me to report that they have moved the needle on their action items. I interview key stakeholders after an agreed period of time to check how they are doing. I ask for the quantitative as well as the qualitative impact of any changes made. It is very powerful to document their progress and give them feedback. This is when I know I have made a difference.

I think I have been successful because I have honed my skills over a long period of time with very diverse clients. My leadership role with PDI keeps me current on business issues and gives me peer status with many senior executives. I have run my own business, and I can talk their language. I can empathize with some of the tough situations they face, and I can also be tough myself. I don't let them get away with much. They have to make a commitment to making a change that will benefit not only them but also their organization, and we have firm deadlines. I do not want to create codependent relationships.

My creative and flexible personality allows me to enable my clients to see themselves differently. I ask a lot of open-ended questions to help them gain critical insights about themselves. I challenge them to see things differently, using my sense of humor to lighten up some of my more serious executives. Most of all, I provide a confidential safe place where we can discuss their progress against the backdrop of what's going on in their company at that time. It is not unusual for me to read about the people I coach in the *WSJ* or *New York Times*. They are often stressed, high achievers who, despite their many talents, can be very vulnerable in today's economic churn. I like to believe that I can increase not only their leadership effectiveness, but also their confidence to deal with whatever comes next.

Kim Barnes

Kim Barnes is the President and CEO of Barnes & Conti Associates, Inc., of Berkeley, California, an independent learning and organization development firm. She holds a Master's degree in Human Development and has over 30 years of experience in the fields of management, leadership, and organization development. Kim has been a frequent speaker at national and international professional conferences and meetings, and has published many articles in professional journals in the United States and abroad. Her book, *Exercising Influence: A Guide for Making Things Happen at Work, at Home, and in Your Community,* was published in 2000. She can be reached via the Internet at www.barnesconti.com or by phone at (800) 835-0911 or (510) 644-0911.

My coaching practice in the past few years has focused on two areas: Coaching high-potential leaders with a need to develop more effective interpersonal skills and developing HR managers and key staff as coaches for their clients. The first usually involves a person who has been very successful as an individual contributor and is seen as a technical expert, but with some blind areas in his or her relationships with others. The second kind of coaching may be either formal or informal and is focused on supporting internal HR or OD staff who are in a position to coach senior leaders.

I would describe my approach as performance coaching. Literally, this means that I work with the client toward achieving excellent results in a series of performance opportunities. This is similar to the way a coach might work with a top athlete, singer, or actor. I was moved to develop this approach several years ago by a colleague, Edd Conboy, and find it particularly useful for working on interpersonal skills. If you define a performance as something that happens in public, in real time, with the purpose of achieving a specific result, then focusing coaching on important performance opportunities is an efficient and effective method.

Once a coaching contract has been established, I begin my work with individual leaders by using a 360-degree instrument and interviewing individuals identified by the leader as critical to his or her success. The results enable the two of us (or three, if we include the person to whom the leader reports) to establish clear performance goals for the coaching process. We also at this time identify or create upcoming performance opportunities that will require the leader to use the skills he or she has decided to focus on with precision and effectiveness. Philosophically, this approach assumes that people best learn the skills they need to use in order to be successful. Urgency trumps importance most of the time in real life, so I believe in creating urgency as part of a coaching strategy.

If the leader is working on interpersonal skills, I often recommend that he or she attend an intensive class so that he or she has a good basic understanding of the skills involved and has experienced some practice and feedback. This provides us with a common language to use. We then meet a week or two before the first performance opportunity we have agreed on and practice using the skill in that situation. At times, we have what amounts to a rehearsal, stopping for feedback and rethinking the approach. We work on a strategy for success in the situation; we also troubleshoot the performance, identifying ways to recover and succeed if problems occur.

After the actual performance, we debrief either in person or on the phone, discussing what worked well, what did not, what was learned from the experience, and the next steps to take. This process continues until the goals we established at the beginning are met or until we mutually agree that it is time to identify new goals or bring the process to a close.

The most successful coaching experiences are always ones where the client is personally eager to learn and develop, seeing it as in his or her own interest rather than going through the motions to fulfill a requirement or please a boss. Sometimes, this is because he or she sees an important opportunity; sometimes, it is because the person feels an urgent sense of dissatisfaction with his or her own performance; occasionally it is both.

A successful coach is one who is willing to partner with the client and is not afraid to confront the client with difficult feedback or challenge him or her with possible difficulties and complexities. I personally judge a coaching engagement as successful when the client surprises him or herself with the successful results of performances we have worked on and applies the learnings to other opportunities. I am always happy when we end a coaching engagement with the sense that the person has developed an "internal coach" to take him or her to the next level.

CHAPTER 5

---◆---

Career/Life Coaching

Thought Leaders

RICHARD J. LEIDER   DAVID ALLEN
WILLIAM BRIDGES   BARBARA MOSES
BEVERLY KAYE   BRIAN TRACY

Practitioners

SHIRLEY ANDERSON   RICHARD STROZZI-HECKLER
JOEL GARFINKLE   MARIAN BAKER

THOUGHT LEADERS

Richard J. Leider

THE INHERENT DILEMMAS OF CAREER/LIFE COACHING

 Richard J. Leider is the Founder and Partner of The Inventure Group, a training firm in Minneapolis, Minnesota. He is the author of the international best-sellers *Repacking Your Bags, Whistle While You Work* and *The Power of Purpose*. Richard is a speaker, writer, and coach, and is a nationally recognized leader in the career development field. He can be reached by e-mail at RJLPurpose@aol.com.

Gertrude Stein once wrote that "a rose is a rose is a rose." For most executives, the poem might read, "a coach is a coach is a coach." Many assume that coaching is a generic activity for which any good coach will do. Executives who think that w ay fail to ask the question "Why do I need a coach?" and tend to focus on "How do I get a good one?" Although both questions are important, answering the first is a prerequisite to getting the right answer for the second.

Executive coaching runs a continuum of approaches ranging from working with individual leaders on their personal effectiveness to helping senior teams drive large-scale organizational change. Career/life coaching has aspects that straddle that spectrum. Although it has implications and benefits to the organization, it focuses primarily on the needs of the individual. The career/life coach is not an advice giver or a therapist. Instead, the coach is someone who establishes a long-term trusting relationship with a person who wants to make a change in their life or career, or, as is often the case, their life *and* career.

Why do successful people hire career/life coaches? They know that if they want to get extraordinary results, they must take the risks to grow. A good coach can help them do that by giving them objective assessments of where they stand, a clear perspective on the best way forward, and the tools and discipline to get there.

In this essay I want to lay out the approach I take to explain what being a career/life coach really means. Along the way, I hope to touch on some of the inherent dilemmas within that discipline, describe its overlooked value for organizations, and provide some guidance for selecting the right coach for a person's individual needs.

Developing the Whole Person

Executive development coaching is a young practice still forming its identity. Although it was born out of the leadership training movement, it shares many of the same viewpoints as the adult development and human potential movements. The coach is a teacher interested in the development of leadership potential, but the subject being taught is the development of the whole person.

The dilemma of career/life coaching relates to the complexity of the whole person approach. Executive coaching, much like psychotherapy, confers the privilege and responsibility of helping people develop on their own terms. That's a significant point, in my view, because it says that the client is the individual being coached, not the organization footing the bill.

There's no doubt that coaching operates within the constraints of contributing to the business. Typically, it is the organization that contracts with the coach and provides compensation. So it's understandable that the organization should expect to see some kind of benefit from that expense. Coaches who are concerned about continuing to be paid for their work rally around the behavioral or organizational impact of what they do. Nevertheless, when a coach finally talks to a coachee in confidence, the business concerns that were discussed at the front end of the engagement become life concerns as soon as the office door is closed.

If a coach teaches an executive to read a balance sheet or develop a strategic plan, it's easy to put a finger on the benefit of that work. If a coach helps a manager become more authentic and lead from their strengths, how should the benefits of that be measured? It can be done, but it's certainly more difficult. The reality is that many of the breakdowns in external behavior and organizational performance are created by internal issues. The reason why a manager can't function well as a team leader, for example, may be because they find it difficult to place trust in others. Although this might come across as an interpersonal or leadership performance issue, the root cause of that distrust may be an internal issue of personal authenticity.

The challenge to the career/life coach is in straddling that fine economic line. The coach must focus on the wants and needs of the individual while still being accountable to the overall system. As companies become further immersed in the knowledge economy, it will become even clearer that effective leadership is based more on trust and influence than on power and structure. When that happens, the contradiction of coaching the whole person in the context of the narrow demands of work will become less of an issue.

The Beginning of a Great Inventure

In my own career/life coaching, there are two approaches to the work I do. The first I call "Inventuring," which is a year-long process of working one on one with a leader to build their capacity to lead authentically. The second I call "Repacking Your Bags," which is a three-month process that offers a seasoned perspective on work and retirement transitions. Explaining how these work will shed light on what career/life coaching aims to do.

Our coaching starts with the core belief that people are born with a purpose. In fact, our firm's moniker is "discover your purpose" and I call myself a purpose coach. The essence of the idea is that people are not fully engaged and authentic until they begin to operate from their purpose. Both inventuring and repacking stem from that concept.

Inventuring is based on the belief that people perform better when they act in harmony with their authentic selves. Aligned with that is our belief in focusing on strengths rather than weaknesses. In our experience, effective leaders, effective teams, and effective organizations focus on strengths and manage weaknesses. Our coaching point of view, therefore, is to help a leader discover purpose and build on strengths while managing weaknesses.

We begin by creating what I call a leader map. Building the map is an intensive process of developing a full picture of a person's authentic leadership. Together, we define her purpose, vision, values, strengths, and goals. This provides an inside-out look at the core of who the person is as a leader, which will eventually reveal how that person will act. Discovering the "who" comes before working on the "what."

The leader map is used to help people develop daily practices. Like a professional athlete, if a leader lacks the discipline of practice, all the talent in the world will not lead to success. Once the map is designed and the practices defined, my role becomes similar to that of a personal trainer. I follow up to make sure the leader is practicing and to figure out what needs to be done differently should any breakdowns occur.

Repacking Your Bags is a similar process for executives who are trying to figure out what to do next. Either they're in a transition already, or they hope to be in one within a couple years. The repacking process helps clarify purpose and direction for the next step in their lives.

The repacking coach works with the coachee as a thinking partner, offering guidance, structure, and tools to make next steps. It accelerates the process of letting go and reaching for a new beginning. It also helps people and organizations avoid the drain of indecision. It often costs companies a lot of money when an executive is uncertain about the next stage in their life. It's a worthy investment to help him figure out whether he or she should stay, go, or engage in a new career or position.

In repacking, instead of using a leader map, we use a life map, built in words, images, and pictures. Following the life map helps the executive track progress and recognize when goals or objectives are reached.

Selecting a Good Career/Life Coach

I never refer someone to a career/life coach unless that coach has a statement of ethics. One of the ethical issues I look at is who the coach believes to be the client. To me, that's an issue concerning the boundaries of confidentiality. When a coach works with an executive, it is not uncommon for the boss or Human Resources to pressure for information about issues that emerge. The organization, after all, is paying for the services and may feel that it has a right to know. In my view, if the client wants to share any or all of that information, that is up to them; but I won't provide information as a matter of principle. I have seen the damage that can be done to a person's career with even an innocent comment about that person's capacity.

In evaluating a coach, I also look to understand her point of view. The question I ask is "What is your anthropology?" It's a concept that I adopted from Viktor Frankl, who tried to develop psychiatrists as doctors of personhood. To me, the question of a coach's anthropology goes deeper than philosophy or technique. It asks, instead, what that person believes about human beings. Where did we come from? Where do we find ourselves? Where are we going?

The core of my own point of view is that human beings have the freedom to choose how they are going to act or react in any situation they face. To understand the nature of that choice, I first work with a person to discover their core constants: the values, purpose, gifts, and talents, which never change. The power of leadership is in listening to yourself and listening to your constituents from the perspective of their core constants. Choosing starts with making your own choices and extends to helping others make effective choices as well.

Given those two fundamentals of ethics and anthropology, the process of finding a coach is a systematic one. I call it the six steps of shopping for a coach.

1. *Get real.* Getting real means you are going to have to share parts of yourself with a coach that may feel uncomfortable. A good coach, like a doctor, needs to do a thorough examination. I tell people that they shouldn't worry about being exposed as long as they are certain about a coach's ethics. A good coach sees many clients, many of them in worse shape than you.

2. *Get referrals.* Don't just hire the first coach you read about or meet. Get referrals from friends or colleagues who have worked with coaches. Pick one with solid ethics and credentials.

3. *Get specialized.* Check out your coach's specialty. No matter how highly recommended a coach comes, he or she won't be effective if you get one with the wrong specialty. Ask the candidates directly. Evaluate what they are good at. Some coaches appear to be successful at many things, but in reality they're nothing but good salespeople.

4. *Get the numbers.* Make sure the price is right and the payment schedule works. An ethical coach will tell you the fees right away. If the price isn't right, relax and think it over for 24 hours. Don't be afraid to shop around and see what others are charging. On the other hand, don't be too cheap, because you usually get what you pay for.

5. *Get going.* Set up a tire-kicking session. Remember, you're the one doing the hiring. Don't be afraid to ask questions. What's your specialty? How long have you been coaching people in this area? Are you certified? Can I talk to some people you have coached? Ninety-nine percent of coaching revolves around the issue of trust. You need information to create that groundwork.

6. *Get a board.* A corporation has a board that provides advice and counsel. I think executives also need a board, two or three people to check in with, to sound out ideas. At least one board member should be a good listener and another a wisdom keeper. This breaks the dependency pattern of coaching. You need to balance the point of view of your coach with those whose perspectives you respect, admire, and aspire to. If a coach is threatened by that idea, walk away.

There is no silver bullet in coaching. A person who will succeed and grow through the experience is someone who has a willingness to reflect and dig deep. Courage is also key since it is not only necessary to look deep within yourself, but also necessary to be decisive about the risks you must take to grow. Finally, commitment is the last remaining ingredient. Without committed practices, development will never take place.

Understand why you want to be coached, find the right coach through a rigorous evaluation of who fits your needs, and live up to the commitment you are making. There is no other way to benefit from coaching.

William Bridges

TRANSITIONS COACHING

 Dr. William Bridges is an internationally known author, consultant, and speaker who helps organizations and individuals deal more productively with change. He is the world's authority on managing transitions. The most recent of his nine books is *Creating You & Co.* a handbook for creating and managing a twenty-first century career. Today, Bill is one of the most widely read and quoted experts on what is happening to jobs in today's organizations and on the new strategies that individuals must use to find work. He can be reached by e-mail at Bill@wmbridges.com, via the Internet at www.wmbridges.com, or by phone at (415) 381-9663.

When large-scale organizational change occurs, the human side of that change rarely gets factored into the equation. Nevertheless, during mergers, reorganizations, downsizes, or shifts in strategy or leadership, it almost always becomes clear that leaders at multiple levels of the organization need help to be successful in their new circumstances. Typically, those leaders do not run into trouble over tactical issues such as implementing the new strategy or reconfiguring roles and responsibilities. Either they're skillful at managing those complicated challenges themselves, or they have consultants with the right expertise to back them up. Instead, the guidance they truly do need is in letting go of the old ways of doing things, while undergoing a psychological reorientation to focus on the new way.

Transitions coaching focuses on seeing a leader through their own transition and providing them with the capability to help others do the same. The event that caused the transition is the change, whether that be the promotion, the merger, the layoff of a few hundred people or the appointment of a new CEO. The transition is the psychological realignment of people to make the change work. A look at the phases of that journey will help describe the role of a transitions coach in making change successful.

Phase 1: Relinquishing the Old

Very few leaders know how to relinquish old ways of doing business; fewer still are good at helping others do the same. The first part of coaching a leader through a transition, or coaching that leader to help others through a transition, is to help the leader discover the behaviors and approaches useful in the relinquishment process, either personally or organizationally.

Much of the coaching at this stage involves giving up old realities. The leader's own former role is one such reality. A person transitioning from leadership of an independent organization to leadership of a joint venture, for example, has to relinquish a lot of assumptions about independence and autonomy. In that sense, although the leader may be doing inner work to manage that transition, there are definite organizational implications as well.

Ideally, the transitions coach should come in before the change has occurred, in order to plan for the transition that will be needed. Typically, however, the coach is called in when a change has been implemented but isn't going well. As the wheels fall off, morale plummets, and deadlines are missed. Leaders who thought they could manage change the way they manage any other challenge begin to realize that the human side of change is far more complicated.

Phase 2: The Neutral Zone

It would be much easier if a transition, like a change, could occur within an hour or two. To replace one leader with another, reorganize divisions and departments, or realign reporting relationships are all changes that can happen overnight. But the inner shift—the transition—does not happen as quickly as the outer shift—the change. We call that transitional phase, the neutral zone. It is a term that the traditional language of change doesn't recognize.

In the neutral zone, the old reality is gone but the new reality isn't functional yet. Even so, this may be a time full of activity. In a merger, for example, implementation teams are probably meeting around the clock, making decisions on everything from HR policies to reporting relationships. Conversely, this may also be an empty time in which not much is happening. A new CEO has taken over, but the CEO's imprint has yet to be felt, even though everyone is waiting to see what will happen. In either case, the neutral zone is a phase during which the future is not clear but the past is gone. The past may not be gone in a literal sense—the same people may still be around, the same letterhead may be in use—but the past no longer offers the answers.

Leaders have a special role to play in the neutral zone. They need to help people understand exactly what has ended with the relinquishment of old ways. Especially at operational levels, this is not always clear. Once people do understand what is over, there's still a job to be done determining how everyone is going to function while creating the new ways. What policies will be adopted in the interim? How will reassignments be managed before they are functional? Leaders need to work with their organizations to determine how everything will play out during a time in which the way things will ultimately play out remains unclear.

To understand the neutral zone, consider what it's like to move from one city to another. The move can happen so quickly that you may think there was virtually no neutral zone period. Yet it is likely that you felt weird even before you left your old city, before the change occurred. During that time your productivity was down, you were starting to grieve, and you were confused about the future. Long after you have arrived in your new city—after the change has happened—you are still not fully up to speed. In that sense, the neutral zone exists before the old situation ends and even after the new situation is in place.

Although that's an easy process to explain, it's a very uncomfortable one for leaders to manage, especially those who like crisp policies and clear strategies. In reaction, many try to put the new in place as quickly as possible, even though people aren't emotionally ready. But structure isn't the answer. Coaching in the neutral zone helps leaders understand what can be done, what should be done, why people feel the way they feel, and what people need, as well as what events signal that the transition is going poorly or well.

Phase 3: The New Beginning

The neutral zone is the area where the real transformations take place. At some point, imperceptibly, the neutral zone starts to do its work. During the neutral zone, the two merging companies, for example, start to act as one. It may be that the structural details of the company were clear on the first day, but it took time for the people to act accordingly. Individual roles changed, but people are responding only now. Working under a new leader, people are beginning to learn a new style of habits, what the new leader wants, values or likes. Although all of that comes into focus during the neutral zone, the new beginning doesn't start until people can identify with those new demands. The new beginning is a new identity and a new reality.

Transitions coaching helps people recognize the phases of transition and act in the best ways to make the changeover successful. Other forms of coaching do not touch on these issues. Developmental coaching, for example, looks at a leader in a situation and determines what new behaviors need to be adopted to be more successful. Although that is very valuable, it doesn't address (except accidentally) the critical issues necessary for navigating transition successfully. Given the amount of change that is occurring in the marketplace, transitions coaching is something that should be worked into projects more often.

Change is misunderstood because transitions are overlooked. When change occurs, what began in hope too often ends in frustration. New leaders may be unable to produce the results they were brought on to accomplish. Mergers may fail to realize the expected value. Start-ups may falter when evolving to a more established structure. Reorganizations may be unable to produce desired benefits. The problems that emerge in leadership, strategy, operations, and so forth are likely to be symptoms rather than root causes. A client should not engage a change coach if transition is the challenge. The failure of leaders to know how to handle transitions is a constant but often hidden factor in the underperformance of organizations, just as it is an underlying source of derailment in careers.

Beverly Kaye

COACHING FOR ENGAGEMENT

Beverly Kaye is a nationally recognized expert in organizational, management, and career development, and founder and President of Career Systems International. She is author of *Up Is Not the Only Way* and coauthor of *Designing Career Development Systems*, as well as a popular resource for national media such as the *New York Times, Time, Fortune,* and a variety of professional magazines. *Love 'Em or Lose 'Em,* co-authored with Sharon Jordan-Evans, is a bestseller that taught managers practical strategies (A to Z) that are key to engaging and retaining employees. Their new book, *Love It, Don't Leave It* (Berrett-Koehler, 2003) provides employees with similar A to Z strategies to find satisfaction right where they are. She is reachable through Career Systems International by phone at (800) 577-6916 or via the Internet at www.careersystemsintl.com.

> Behind every successful person, there is one elementary truth. Somewhere, some way, someone cared about their growth and development.
>
> —Donald Miller

Whether the economy is good or bad, organizations need the capability to retain their people and keep them engaged. Research into the retention of star employees shows that people don't leave organizations for money; they leave because no one is concerned about their learning and growth. Coaching is an excellent means to demonstrate that kind of concern in a purposeful way, while meeting pressing business challenges. In whatever form it is delivered—internal, external, or through the manager—coaching can be applied to develop and retain current employees while growing future leaders. It is also a highly effective tool for sustaining teaching and learning.

We believe coaching falls into two main areas, both centered around talent. We coach managers on developing their people; and we coach individual employees on how to take charge of their careers within the framework of the organization. These two forms of coaching are especially valued by organizations that are becoming more thoughtful, systemic, and innovative with their talent development and retention strategies. Both forms align with our belief that a good career is one that engages your passion in an organization that supports your learning and growth.

Managers have a huge impact in retaining and engaging people. Employees want a relationship with their managers. They feel engaged by their work and cared for by their organizations when they can have open, honest, two-way conversations with managers about their abilities, interests, and options. They need managers who listen to their perspectives, offer their own points of view and provide encouragement, guidance, and development opportunities.

We have identified five skills fundamental to managers who want to succeed as career coaches. Such manager-coaches need to:

- *Listen.* In order to engage employees, grow and develop them in a meaningful way, and maximize their potential, a manager must create an open dialogue with employees. The purpose of this conversation is to help employees identify their core values, work interests, marketable skills, and career concerns.
- *Level.* Managers must provide employees with honest, candid feedback about performance. They also need to suggest specific actions for improvement.
- *Look ahead.* A good manager, like a good mentor, helps employees look beyond the current situation to identify future opportunities in line with their aspirations. This means the manager is thinking about the development needs of the employee in those terms, and also helping the employee understand the organization's strategy, culture, and politics.
- *Leverage.* Managers help people identify options for development and career growth within the organization.
- *Link.* Managers help people develop detailed learning assignments and formal plans to move their career aspirations from vision to action.

When people feel that their managers care about their development, they also believe that the organization cares. It's the feeling of engagement, hand in hand with directed development, that is so valuable to organizations in getting the most out of people, while retaining and growing future leaders.

Despite the critical role managers can play in development, individual employees are ultimately responsible for their own career satisfaction. For that reason, we also coach employees on how to take charge of their professional destinies in line with the possibilities that exist in their organizations.

Employees, at any level, need to be proactive in managing their careers and development opportunities. We coach people to assess their own skills and behaviors, discover their aspirations, and link those goals with a development plan aligned to the organization's overall objectives. Some of that coaching is done online, some in workshops, and some through a process of collaborative development in which employees team up to support each other's career action plans. The purpose is to enable employees to go after their own job satisfaction and take responsibility for their lives.

This kind of coaching is effective in many different forms. Organizations can choose among various delivery strategies to meet their specific objectives. Some focus on training managers to become coaches. Others gain a better return on investment by developing internal coaches or hiring outside experts.

Regardless of approach, our philosophy is that organizations should recognize coaching as a tool that can be used with a broader base of employees than most people usually consider. Most coaches and most organizations typically focus only on high potentials. Doing so, they miss engaging, developing, and retaining those who are critical in supporting the stars.

There's a tremendous amount of buried treasure in organizations. Many employees (not on the hi-po list) feel ignored in the organization's headlong rush to focus on its stars. We think that managers and organizations should look wider and deeper in identifying their key employees. The definition of a star, in our view, is anyone the manager would miss if she should happen to leave the organization. Thinking in those terms, organizations should reconsider which employees provide a valuable contribution through top performance. If retaining those people is critical to your success, then you'd better find some way of engaging them in learning and development to experience deeper career satisfaction.

———⟫◆⟪———

David Allen

COACHING FOR WORKFLOW

 David Allen is an international author, lecturer, and founder and President of the David Allen Company, a management consulting, coaching, and training company. In the last 20 years he has developed and implemented productivity improvement programs for over a half million professionals in hundreds of organizations worldwide, including many Fortune 500 corporations and U.S. Government agencies. He is the author of the best-selling book, *Getting Things Done: the Art of Stress-Free Productivity,* and numerous articles in professional journals and periodicals. He can be reached by phone at (805) 646-8432, by e-mail at david@davidco.com, or via the Internet at www.davidco.com.

Every leader faces the same critical problem each day: how do I stay focused on the big stuff without losing my grip on everything else? Most people try to resolve that conflict by increasing the time and attention they spend on significant issues. The better answer is to free up more time and attention by handling both the big AND little things through a systematic organization of workflow.

My personal productivity coaching deals with this problem by creating customized implementation systems for organizing, managing, and negotiating the totality of people's commitments more objectively and effectively. In that sense, our coaching moves from the bottom up. Whereas most coaches start with vision, mission, and strategy before moving on to objectives and work, we start with what's in people's heads and piled on their desks, and overflowing from their in-boxes. Between the reason why a person is alive on the planet, and the 300 unopened e-mails in their Outlook program, there are many levels of importance to what gets our attention during the course of the day. By starting with what has our attention, often the more mundane and pressing tasks, we free people to move steadily up in level until they have the time and ability to take care of what matters most.

Although focused on the individual, workflow coaching has a great impact within organizations as well. If all employees manage their workflow, the organization gets to move on to bigger problems sooner. If workflow management is in bad shape generally, then it's likely that few people are really taking care of the bullet point they inherited when they walked out of the last meeting. Add that up across the board, and you have an organization with a lot of wind spilling out of its sails.

Peter Drucker said that the biggest challenge for any knowledge worker is to define their work. We make people actually do that. What's your work? Give me a list of your 67 different projects. Didn't know you had that many? I'm not surprised. Most people don't have a clue what their inventory of commitments actually includes. Between registering their children for summer camp, restructuring the department, hiring a new assistant, refinancing the mortgage, and researching a potential strategic alliance, there are probably 30 to 100 things on the plate of the average executive. Very few have that inventory clearly and objectively distributed outside of their head, in some sort of cognitive system where they can actually see it. Fewer still have figured out the action steps necessary to make forward motion on all those commitments. To do so, we get people to make those kinds of operational decisions, and become, in essence, their own Chief Operating Officer.

Essentially, we are providing martial arts training in knowledge work athletics. Most people make their knowledge moves instinctively and intuitively. They understand that at some point they have to make decisions about their commitments and action steps. But few have trained themselves to make those decisions on the front end and actually clear their minds of the commitments that are otherwise cluttering their thinking. This discipline is not automatic, but it is learnable. Once the discipline has been embraced, it can be improved, so that people move up in level as a martial arts student progresses steadily toward a black belt. In fact, the best and the brightest take to these ideas most enthusiastically. They know that they are already at a point where fine tuning their system will allow them to get home at 7 o'clock instead of midnight, or provide an extra 2 hours a week of really creative time instead of 18 hours a day dealing with mission critical dramas.

Our coaching is usually done as an intensive two-day installment of this methodology with occasional follow-up. I tell leaders, if it were easy, you wouldn't have stacks on your desk. Most people avoid making a lot of these kinds of mundane decisions. Smart, creative people are the most handicapped because they are afraid of closing off options and ideas. Workflow management is not a closing off but an opening up. We teach how to recognize when a commitment is distracting attention, and how liberating it is to make an action decision to move forward. People don't need perfect solutions; they just need forward motion. We make people collect their backlog of issues, practice making those decisions, and develop a customized process for how they are going to park their commitments in the future.

In other words, we get very down and dirty. It usually takes one to six hours to collect the inventory of open loops. Then, it takes 6 to 12 hours for people to go through and make all the decisions they've been avoiding. We actually guide people through that process until they've created a systematic approach that can be followed with practice. Even the most productive people are astounded by the liberating effects that fine-tuning can bring. When we bring this to teams and every member goes through the process, commitments get met, trust becomes deeper, and communication moves to higher levels.

People need to feel tremendous trust in their coach in order to deal with the many things they've been avoiding. For a coach to be effective at productivity improvement, they must learn that they can't editorialize about how somebody should do something. In other words, if I tell someone, "No, here's the way you should do it," they're going to shut down and lose their willingness to be vulnerable. Instead, coaches have to be very process-oriented. They need to point out the piles of magazines lying around the office and suggest that they be read, trashed, or filed. Anyone who thinks that's a mundane concern can't do this kind of coaching. For that reason, it's almost impossible to train internal coaches to do the job. By nature, they are politically invested in the people they are coaching. A good coach has to be elegantly noninflictive.

For people to benefit from this kind of coaching, they need to have an interest in having their world improved. People who are willing to stay in their comfort zone, who are not driven by inspiration or pain to be somewhere different, are probably not going to develop any of these new behaviors. Sometimes, that inspiration or pain is about becoming more effective in a leadership role, or giving more back to the world or the community, or spending extra time with the family to be there as children grow up. The inspiration or the pain is what made them hungry for whatever tricks they could find to make that happen.

I'm on a mission to teach the world that there's a different way and a best practice for managing knowledge work. Everyone can benefit from this capability because everyone has lives in which there are open loops that must be tracked. Most people still think that the mind is the best manager of their open loops, but the mind is stupid. It reminds us of things when we think of them, not when we need the data. The only way to free our minds is to develop an external system for dealing with our many commitments. By doing so, we off-load our brains.

Barbara Moses

CAREER ACTIVISM AND THE NEW EMPLOYMENT CONTRACT

Dr. Barbara Moses is the best-selling author of *What Next? The Complete Guide to Taking Control of Your Work Life, Career Intelligence*, and *The Good News About Careers: How You'll Be Working in the Next Decade*. Her *Career Planning Workbook* is a corporate best-seller and has been used by over a million people. She is a professional speaker on contemporary work issues, a frequent media commentator, and President of BBM Human Resource Consultants, Inc. (www.bbmcareerdev.com). She can be reached by e-mail at bbm@bbmcareerdev.com or via the Internet at www.bmoses.com.

The leading edge of what's being done in career planning today hinges on the tenets of the new employment contract. On the one hand, job security is dead, and traditional loyalty to the organization has died along with it. On the other hand, organizations still need to attract and retain talented workers. In response, savvy organizations emphasize employability over job security while providing workers with the skills they need to manage their own careers. Those same employees embrace that training, knowing that personal career activism is the only way to achieve any sense of security and control in their lives. It may be an uneasy truce, in the middle of a tense and uncertain economy, but in the best scenarios it seems to be working.

I help organizations respond to the career issues of employees. I think of myself as a coach, but I do my coaching by providing tools, information, and capabilities. Through my speaking engagements and the occasional workshop, I coach people at all organizational levels. I also work directly with human resource practitioners and line managers, responsible for career planning and programming in their organizations, to show them how to respond to and coach staff on contemporary career challengers. In the career planning sense, I coach them on how to coach.

My personal fascination is with the broad social trends that are expressed in the host of contemporary workplace issues. There are huge tensions today in employment. Work demands are relentless; lives are over-committed; organizations can be thankless. Everyone is grappling with work-life balance; everyone needs to take responsibility for their own employability by ensuring that their skills are up to date. People feel stuck. They're looking for a sense of direction, and they need to make decisions about the future. Even those who are happy with their organizations are often dissatisfied with the effect of work on their personal lives.

With career-planning programs, organizations need to be sensitive to the nuanced differences of individual needs, motivations, talents, and values. When people find themselves in work situations where they feel valued, and in which their work speaks not only to their personal values but also to their strengths, their satisfaction, authenticity, and performance levels are all much higher. They certainly know a good thing when they see it, and tend to stay or jump ship accordingly.

When I work with HR or line managers, the vehicle I often use is their own personal career planning. Everyone is eager to do it. After all, who doesn't recognize and enjoy the benefits of thinking more deeply about themselves in relation to their own career and future plans? But more importantly, receiving such counseling provides managers with a greater understanding of workplace trends and a deeper appreciation for individual differences, which will assist them in coaching their own staff.

Human Resources practitioners and line managers should not play clinician/counselor. Few are equipped or inclined; and fewer still have the time. That's where my tools come in. My *Career Planning Workbook* serves as the counselor by extracting information about desires, needs, skills, and aspirations. The manager builds on that data to promote career activism in the staff. In other words, the manager is not abdicating responsibility to the tools; rather the manager's role focuses on dialogue and action steps. This makes the manager more efficient and effective because their career planning duties can take place within a well-structured context.

The impact of this approach is often anecdotal but always clear. People call me up and say that employees were "really demoralized but now they're buzzing." "The teams are working more effectively together." Managers relate that although they are dedicating less time to career coaching, that time is "much more engaging and effective." Employees themselves have a feeling of greater self-reliance in managing their own careers, even as they have connected in a more satisfying way with their managers. A typical reaction from manager and employee alike would be: "I just had the most productive career discussion I've ever experienced."

There are degrees to which organizations make this enthusiasm come alive. For those that bring career activism to its full potential, it becomes part of the fundamental employment contract. It's an aspect, in other words, of their performance management system; it helps in recruitment and retention; and it creates a basis for work-life balance and health and wellness programming.

Because I coach a lot of coaches, among both internal practitioners and outside counselors, I've come to formulate some strong opinions about which experiences and viewpoints are actually valuable and effective. When you look at those who find themselves in the career coaching business, some are obviously very gifted, but many have been drawn to the profession because they had a powerful personal career experience and want to guide others toward similar revelations. Those in the latter camp tend to be like cheerleaders, often lacking a depth of knowledge of individual differences and personality characteristics or any real appreciation for the complexities of the contemporary workplace. They tend to hold a facile perspective, an "if you can dream it, you can do it" philosophy. Although that may be true in theory and ultimately a more authentic expression of self, it may also be unwise to encourage someone to quit their day job.

Another group of coaches includes those who have developed hard business skills, which they feel help them to understand the reality of work in an organizational context. They may have had experience leading a department or turning around a division. As a result, they have war stories, battle scars, and a certain degree of empathy for those dealing with the complexities of work and organizational change. That kind of perspective may help in coaching individuals or teams to better performance, but it's unlikely that such coaches will have a sufficient understanding of psychological issues to take a humanistic, whole-person approach.

To be an effective career coach, I think you need to be an applied social psychologist to some degree. You must combine an intimate understanding of the new workplace and its dynamics with an appreciation for its impact on how people feel and what they need. In other words, you must think in terms of the nuances of contemporary life as well as the nuances of individual differences.

For me, there are three principles in enabling people to be effective in the work world today. People need to know themselves and understand what they truly care about. They need to find work that speaks to their strengths and values, that is, their authentic selves. And they must be career activists to make both of those happen. A career coach is valuable to the extent that he or she guides and supports that set of capabilities.

Good work is not a privilege, it's a right. Yet the individual is responsible for making the decisions and choices that provide the right fit. There's a lot of repressed quitting going on in organizations today. People have put their work desires on hold because of the uncertain economy. I come across two kinds of organizations in that regard. There are those which really do treat their people with care and sensitivity, because they are concerned with attraction and retention. And there are also those that have very short memories. The latter organization allows the weather of the day to dictate its behavior toward employees. Although the war for talent has subsided in the short-term forecast, that will not always be the case. A turnaround will come, and the looming skill shortage is not going to disappear. When the ship is righted and conditions improve, people will pass clear judgment by voting with their feet on how well organizations live up to the terms of the new employment contract.

Brian Tracy

GETTING WHAT YOU WANT

Brian Tracy, Chairman of Brian Tracy International, is one of America's leading authorities on the development of human potential and personal effectiveness. He addresses more than 250,000 people each year on the subjects of personal and professional development. He has written 35 books and is the author/narrator of more than 300 audio and video learning programs. He can be reached by phone at (858) 481-2977 or via the Internet at www.briantracy.com.

My mission in life has been to liberate human potential by helping people set and achieve their most important goals. The coaching I do is designed to bring people through a rigorous analysis of defining those goals and determining appropriate action steps. Once we've programmed a goal into the superconscious mind, it works 24 hours a day generating ideas, attracting the right people to our side, and activating our particular context so that we see things we might not have seen before. The results are a wondrous thing to behold.

I concentrate primarily on entrepreneurs, business people near the top of their organizations, professionals such as doctors, architects and lawyers, and top salespeople. All currently earn a minimum salary of $100,000 a year—since that is a level, in my opinion, that indicates that a person has a strong sense of what she's good at and what she doesn't want to do. Our promise is that we will double that income while doubling time off. We work in groups, through a structured format, over a period of a year. The awareness that our coaching creates helps participants achieve their goals. It's amazing how many people have doubled their incomes and doubled their time off within the first 30 days.

The key to the success of our coaching is its structure. I developed it by considering hundreds of different sources. The emphasis is extremely practical. Our focus is not on instructing but on questions. We deal with four aspects of our clients' lives: first, their career, work, and income; second, their relationships; third, their overall financial situation; and fourth, how much they intend to be worth. We make a strong distinction between income and worth. There are three other critical parameters that we consider—personal and professional development, community and social involvement, and spiritual development. But we do not contemplate these as deeply because they are more personal and time consuming, and require a different level of coaching.

Instead, in each of the first four areas, we discuss how to organize our lives to reach a higher level of satisfaction. I call this the focal point process. Participants have come to the session having done prework on these areas already, the purpose of which is to get psychologically out of their existing space and force them to think through questions about who they are, what they want and how they're measuring up. Now, it's time to bring that initial thinking into greater clarity and action.

Working in small groups of five people helps generate a different level of creative possibility. This idea is related to the Mastermind concept in which the quality of your life is determined by the quality of the people you hang out with. When like-minded positive people come together to share ideas, amazing things happen. Sometimes, a great conversation with a really interesting person turns on all kinds of lights in our minds. In our program, we create a structured Mastermind in which everyone asks each other a series of questions and goes through a series of exercises. One such question is "What are the points of intensity in your life?" Intensity is defined as a point when you make a decision that has a multiplier effect on the actions or outcomes of many other people. For example, we ask: "What are the intensity points in your work?" Contemplating that, people reflect on whom they would work with, what markets they would get in or out of, and what skills they would need to be more successful. Once we've decided to learn a new skill, what kind of multiplier effect will that have on our lives?

Out of those questions comes one more, just as important: "What action will you take immediately as a result of your answers to the preceding questions?" I tell everyone to share and discuss the answers. The conversation is made rigorous by a series of consulting-type questions: "Why will you do that?" "How will you measure it?" "How will you know if you've been successful?" Out of those answers comes greater clarity and a further refinement of the goals and action steps. The results are written down on an action-planning form. Then, we go onto the next in the series of 12 thinking exercises.

The experience is like going around a darkened house and turning on the lights, one by one. By the time people have gone through the first session, all the lights are on. Suddenly, they are able to think clearly about the things that they are doing now that they wouldn't be doing otherwise. When they consider that question, there's almost always something in place that is a major clog in the drain of their lives. By the time they come back for the next session, they've broken up their partnership, started a new business, reorganized their lives, increased their income, and gotten rid of their headaches.

Once the drain has been unclogged, people are ready for the higher work. I have a seven-step process for examining the areas of their life, which we follow in logical sequence. First, we determine true values. People know that they have general values, but they also have values specific to areas of their lives. We have values with our families, with our communities, and with our work. We even have values specific to our colleagues and customers. Second, we look at personal vision. I encourage people to imagine that they have a magical wand. What would each area of their lives look like in perfect form in three to five years? People think of how much money they would be earning, how much time they would be spending with their families, and so on. Then, I ask people to think about their goals. Goals are tangible things that must be realized to achieve vision. Even though the soft side of life, such as relationships and family, is ultimately more important, I keep bringing people back to their business and work because I believe that it is more quantifiable and improvements in those hard areas lead to dramatic improvements in the softer areas.

After goals come skills. What specific skills will they need to develop or improve to achieve their goals? There's a skill connected to every goal. The reason people haven't achieved a goal is because they have not yet developed that skill to a high enough degree. Most people think, "I am what I am." I tell them to get over that. To allow yourself to be held back because you lack an eminently learnable skill is a terrible waste.

From skills, we move on to qualities or habits. What qualities will you need to develop these skills? In reality, all fundamental change occurs when we develop certain qualities. We might need to become more disciplined, functional, respectful, or patient. If these are qualities of personality and character that are absolutely essential, what activities would you need to engage in every day to develop them? The final area, of course, is action. Everything must always come down to the actions that should be taken.

By the time participants have finished 12 months of work, they've become totally different people. The key to their success is whether they have the ability to begin a program and stick to it. Many entrepreneurs and many successful people in general have extremely short attention spans. Nevertheless, most people are eager to pounce on these ideas and the process has been designed to generate tangible returns. If the ideas are used on a regular basis, the results are always extraordinary.

To be an effective coach in the area of human potential, it is critical to have the structure, credibility, presence, and maturity of a teacher or trainer. A good coach has a very clear structure because people have a lot going on in their lives and need the discipline to focus on what's critical. The credibility comes from having been there and done it, on a personal level. If someone wants to coach in the area of success, they'd better have a track record of success themselves. Presence is required to be able to carry the room. When a coach works with someone, he or she had better be a very powerful and confident person to enable the client to believe that the process is really going to help. And finally, a coach must have the maturity to be a caring and serious person. Ken Blanchard once said that he wanted to be known as a loving teacher. Our goal is for people to see us as a warm, friendly, supportive, and fully committed team, dedicated to making them become more effective. When people feel that, they learn better, laugh and talk more, and have the energy to work on the exercises we give them.

There are some people for whom coaching is a form of psychotherapy. There are others who focus on people's passion and the giant actions they must take to realize their dreams. In my coaching, we allow the structure and the action orientation to create actual results. If people follow the structure and commit to the work, the results will appear with the force of gravity, pulling you along whether you believe in the existence of that force or not. I promise that your whole life will change.

PRACTITIONERS

Shirley Anderson

Shirley Anderson is a master coach and confidante to influential people. Her training in social sciences and English—as well as being one of the pioneers in the coaching profession—have equipped her for working with today's top creative and business minds. Her bachelor's degree is from the University of Miami and her master's degree is from Nova University. Her coach training is from Coach U, the premier coach training firm, and she's been a leader in the field for 13 years. She can be reached by e-mail at shirley@coachmiami.com. Her web sites are www.coachmiami.com and www.coachingsalon.com.

Coaching executives and leaders is similar to an experience I had as a student pilot. I had returned from the practice area and entered the traffic pattern for Tamiami Airport at 1,000 feet. I was surprised to find myself in white puffy clouds at that level, and immediately lost both my orientation and my confidence to make the approach and landing. I called the tower with my airplane identification and told them I was in the pattern, but didn't know exactly where. The voice told me I was going north. I said, "I don't know which way is north." He said, "Okay, I'll put you on downwind; turn left heading two-seven-zero." I trusted the voice and followed the instruction. I was in and out of the clouds and very scared. I knew I could fly and land the airplane if I could just get reoriented to where I was in relation to the airport. The tower told me where I was and guided me into the landing pattern, and I landed safely.

I typically work with high-level executives, business owners, and authors whose expertise falls into the financial industry, management training, or professional services. They come to me because somebody they trust has recommended me. Generally, they are hugely successful people who've suddenly become stuck or found themselves struggling with something they've never struggled with before. My coaching works best when clients tell the truth about a situation as soon as they realize it; trust me to know (or to help them find out who knows) what direction to go; then let me put the controls squarely back in their hands.

In their hearts, they know what to do. I think what they truly want is another set of eyes. I have a knack or ingenuity for solving the left-brain/right-brain problem. What I love most about the people I work with is that they are not only brilliant thinkers, but caring and responsive people. They have a profound realization of the possibilities and opportunities for humanity—a very special combination in leaders. But sometimes, they have a blind spot when it comes to their own specialness. It may seem like a contradiction, but often such people have received so much external applause, recognition, or admiration that they lose touch with the part of themselves that nobody knows.

They want validation. They want help in looking for what is missing. They want to perfect it. They ask, "What am I not seeing here?" I am the innocent who can see what others overlook. I provide the piece of insight that makes it all come together.

My preference is to work by phone. Generally, I talk with people 3 times a month for 45 minutes to an hour each time. I'm also available whenever someone wants to bounce an idea off me. They might toss a simple question my way, and I respond with an observation. I even get e-mails and can engage that way, as well. I end up working with people for many years. In the best relationships, I am their coach for life. We may not always be working together, may even go a long time between that need, but I'm always there for them. I am the person who always sees their genius.

I don't push. There's an internal shift that occurs. In the most mature coaching relationship, coach and client are cocreative. The relationship lasts forever. There are no steps. The coaching flows from a continuous, creative conversation. Clients move effortlessly among ideas congruent to their projects. There's an energy that occurs, something electric that happens. Sometimes, it's something brand-new; other times, it's something the client forgot. We're tapping into the most brilliant part of their minds. If it's true that people use a mere 10 percent of their brains, then coaching taps into the other 90 percent. It helps clients connect to what they already know and make connections to what they want to discover.

I think that in the future coaching will evolve into a profession in which coach and client engage in a level of creative dialogue that can generate such revelations. Among the thought leaders and world leaders I know, people are searching for the ideas, connections and points of awareness they can use to benefit the world. A coach is someone who can help them seek out and recognize those things over a lifetime.

Joel Garfinkle

Joel Garfinkle is the founder of Dream Job Coaching, the top online resource for creating fulfillment at work. He has inspired thousands of people to reach personal and professional fulfillment and transformation. He is a successful coach, speaker, and author whose works are read in more than 25 countries. He works with individual clients and facilitates executive and group coaching. He is the author of *Land Your Dream Job; Love Your Work; Job Searching Made Easy;* and *How to Master the Job Search Process in as Little as 14 Days.* He can be reached by telephone at (510) 655-2010 or by e-mail at Joel@dreamjobcoaching.com. You can subscribe to his newsletter, fulfillment@work, which is delivered to over 10,000 people. His web site can be found at www.dreamjobcoaching.com.

Everyone is gifted with talents to reveal to the world. Everyone has something unique that is meant to be known. I help people reach the clarity they need to find their dream job, the work they are meant to be doing. I help people find work that fully utilizes their passions, taps into their innate gifts, and develops their full potential.

On the surface, this may seem like a tall order, especially in a tough economy. But lean economic times are actually a perfect time to find a dream job. You can have it all. A difficult job market provides the perfect opening to re-examine what you do for a living, bringing not only financial gain, but also personal and professional satisfaction on all levels. Plenty of people are finding themselves without work or have been shocked into reconsidering what work they want to do. When people enter this period of transition—where they are evaluating themselves and what they want to do with their lives—this searching is what draws them to me.

Many clients have been working in their current industry for ten or more years, have read numerous job books, seen career counselors, switched companies, or tried different positions within the same company. Still, nothing has worked. No matter when a client finally picks up the phone and calls, I always believe the timing is perfect. This may be surprising when you're feeling uncertain and lost, but it's true. Your emotions—whether you're feeling anxious or hopeful—are the fuel you need to commit to a process that ultimately is transforming.

My process focuses on three areas: (1) recognizing your true passions, (2) developing an understanding of your innate gifts and talents, and (3) removing the barriers that prevent you from knowing and acting on the first two discoveries (each of which can be difficult). All three areas are useful, but helping a client identify and remove barriers is particularly effective. There are always things that hold people back and create limiting perspectives. I teach people how to remove their layers of limitations and reach the essence of who they are.

As a dream job coach, I develop a holistic, encompassing understanding of each client. I don't do any standardized testing. I find that it's more valuable to ask tailored questions that are directly related to each individual client. Based on my work with thousands of other clients, I have a developed sense of what a client needs and why. Typically, my coaching services include 3 scheduled 40-minute telephone sessions per month, unlimited e-mail correspondence Monday through Friday, and a 24-hour response time. Ongoing and consistent contact provides my clients with the support they need and encourages them to discuss any concerns that might arise. They also have access to extensive tools and resources. Each month, there is adequate time set aside for clients to assimilate and digest the information they have learned.

Metaphorically speaking, I shake a person's tree from the trunk because we never know which falling leaf will provide the greatest insight. We review all aspects of a client's life, not just what happens at their desk. From that search, we uncover how their passions and innate talents can best be expressed in the work that they do.

A good career coach changes and adjusts to the needs of their clients. I have personally interviewed with more than 1,200 companies and worked with thousands of clients during the past 7 years. As a result, everywhere a client has been or is looking toward, I've already personally explored. This fresh and contemporary professional awareness greatly benefits clients, especially those who already have explored traditional career-planning options.

Coaches must intimately know the work world, but they also must know themselves. Self-awareness allows a coach to step aside from his or her own needs and be fully focused on the client. It's important, too, for coaches to speak the truth to the level that clients are able to hear it. I must be passionate and gentle, but my clients pay me to speak the truth. I can't hold something back. I must deliver what needs to be delivered. A coach must also develop an intuitive ability to understand clients. My process for gathering data allows me to reach the core of a person's passion or uncover a barrier that has been holding them back.

The best client is someone who possesses a willingness to know him or herself better. The more open clients are, the quicker they reach greater depths and transformation. Invariably, a week or two before people discover and land their dream job they experience a feeling of great resistance. Sometimes, they want to stop their sessions; other times, they simply go into denial or hide the truth from themselves. There's a level of fear that shows up, just before the future becomes clear. Because I've seen people experience this before and have explained from the outset that it would happen, I can encourage clients to keep going.

Ultimately, I recognize success when my clients find fulfilling work, including feeling passionate about your job, loving your work, being inspired at the end of your workday, getting paid well for work you enjoy doing and looking forward to going to work each day, even Monday mornings. I also measure my impact by how much a client personally gains: Are you more confident? Do you more easily show up and take a stand for yourself? Do you know yourself better?

My aim is for people to be actualized. I want them to be, if I can use the term, "actual-sized." I want them to show up each day, moment by moment, through the work they do. I want people to have a clear purpose. When work is aligned with our true and authentic nature, we impact the lives of those around us on a daily basis. I want people to become more engaged in their lives than they've ever been before. When that happens, we're more balanced and healthy. The talents and gifts we have show up in all areas of our lives, not just at work. That's the possibility that is available to each and every one of us as human beings. To the extent that I help others become able to touch that potential, I am living my own dream job.

Richard Strozzi-Heckler

 Richard Strozzi-Heckler, PhD, is President of Strozzi Institute, The Center for Leadership and Mastery. He has a PhD in psychology and a sixth-degree black belt in aikido, and is the author of six books including the national bestseller, *In Search of the Warrior Spirit.* He was profiled on the front page of the *Wall Street Journal* for the leadership program he developed for the United States Marine Corps. He can be reached by phone at (707) 778-6505, by e-mail at info@strozziinstitute.com, or via the Internet at www.strozziinstitute.com.

The body is central to my coaching practice. When I say "body," I use the term in the somatic sense of the word, which from the ancient Greek means the living body in its wholeness. This is not the sleek, airbrushed body on magazine covers or the Cartesian notion of body as beast of burden that ferries a disembodied mind to its intellectual appointments. Nor is it the mechanical, physiological body of modern medicine or the religious formula of flesh as sin. The body, in the somatic sense, expresses our history, commitments, dignity, authenticity, identity, roles, moral strength, moods, and aspirations as a unique quality of aliveness we call the "self." In this interpretation, the body and the self are indistinguishable. In my coaching, I work with the self, the whole person, through the body. I ask my clients to commit to practices that allow them to embody new skills and behaviors; this is entirely different from having an insight or a cognitive understanding.

I work with the premise that the self is the leader's primary source of power. I have seen time and time again that who one is as a person, that is, the self that one is, ultimately becomes the deciding factor in success as an exemplary leader. Clearly, intellectual capacity and specific technical skills matter, but they do not alone make a powerful, effective leader. When I speak about the cultivation of an authentic self, I'm not referring to self-esteem training, personality development, or self-improvement seminars. These are processes where one may feel better about oneself, but they may not necessarily lead to new actions or improved performance. Working through the body, I coach executives and senior management toward a leadership self that fulfills both business and personal commitments. They often feel more confident and self-assured through the somatic coaching, but the goal is not so much a psychological state as becoming someone who can take actions that were previously unavailable to them.

My clients generally fall into three categories: CEOs and senior management who see that their current style of leadership is keeping them from moving their teams and organizations to the next level. For example, they find themselves unable to mobilize their people or to build trust or speak in a way that motivates others. Although historically successful, they feel stuck at a certain level of leadership.

Second, I work with emerging leaders who are on a strong upward trajectory and are in a succession plan in their organizations. With these individuals, I build a strong foundation of leadership skills that helps them serve those they lead, and their organizations.

Third, I often work with the immediate teams of the individuals I have coached. This builds a culture of action in which team coordination, dignity, respect, and communication are enhanced.

Regardless of what category—CEO/senior management, emerging leader, or team—it is critical that the design of the program and the goals be decided through a mutual process. Through interviews, I find out what is missing or what breakdown they are facing. We enter into a conversation about their purpose and what they deeply care about. I then assess whether I can be of help. If it is in my domain of expertise, we mutually arrive at conditions of satisfaction for the work. I promise a set of outcomes, and they commit to a set of practices. Throughout the course of our work together, we routinely review our progress.

Through my 40 years in the martial arts (primarily aikido), my research in learning and performance as a psychologist, and as a track and field athlete who competed at the international level, it has become abundantly clear to me that mind/body/spirit practices are fundamental to a successful coaching practice. Furthermore, my coaching is based on a close, trusting relationship in which honesty, forthrightness, and courage are required. The following qualities and skills are among those my clients consistently report they have gained through our work:

- Centered presence of integrity and authenticity
- The capacity to listen with empathy to the concerns of others
- The ability to generate life-affirming moods
- The capacity to quickly build trust
- The capability to coordinate effectively with others
- The gift to authentically motivate others
- The strength to stay emotionally balanced in times of adversity and change
- The wisdom to know when it is time to act and when it is time to wait
- The strength to be a lifelong learner

These skills of leadership may seem obvious to the point of being elementary. Certainly, they are not novel or contestable in what are commonly seen as the necessary social skills for a leader. Yet after 33 years of working with people, it has become abundantly clear to me that we do not transform ourselves and our thinking through good ideas or hope. To make sustainable shifts in our behavior and way of thinking, we have to embody new schemas. The path to achieving such embodiment is established through a series of recurrent practices of mind, emotions, language, and body. This new embodiment is integrated by building new interpretations of meaning and future possibilities.

<hr />

Marian Baker

 Marian Baker is a certified professional coach whose clients experience breakthroughs in creating true fulfillment in life, livelihood, and leadership. Called "The Queen of Powerful Questions" by a leader of Coaches Training Institute, she is coauthor of the *Awakening Corporate Soul; High Performance, High Fulfillment* workbook and author of the upcoming book, *Wake Up Inspired: Create the Joyful Life You Are Meant to Live.* Marian has been featured in the *Chicago Tribune,* the *Chicago Sun Times,* and *Health* magazine. She admires her clients and is committed to fueling that rewarding mission each person is meant to express. She can be reached via e-mail at marian@marianbaker.com, by phone at (773) 509-9408, or via the Internet at www.MarianBaker.com.

Most clients come to me with some variation of the question "Is this all there is?" out of (1) a craving to make a change or (2) a calling to make a difference. Coaching helps each client discover or fuel his or her enthusiastic mission. By this, I don't mean that we go through the exercise of writing a pithy mission statement that languishes in a binder. I mean a mission that is alive and multidimensional. It may be a business, project, renewed vision, a career, or life adventure. Using a "Passion Meets Profit" matrix, we identify how the client's passions and talents intersect with what a relevant group (an industry, organization, team, clients, etc.) needs and "what others are willing to pay for." This leads to breakthroughs about new strategies, optimal uses of talent, effective communications and more. We also look at following a "joyful mission" as a way of operating so that each day is infused with greater focus and a sense of triumph.

As coach, I serve as confidential sounding board, life-watcher/colearner, brainstorm partner, and devoted champion. Not being friend, boss, spouse, and so on puts the coach in a uniquely powerful place of having no ulterior motives or inhibiting concerns. A great coach is optimistic, but not a Pollyanna cheerleader. Nurturing is balanced with healthy challenges and kicks in the butt. I've learned that clients can take and appreciate more tough love than we often assume. My approach focuses on future possibilities and on unlocking potential, not on past mistakes or correcting problems. I encourage clients to take a holistic approach—to access the compass of one's heart, fuel physical energy, and give birth to bold plans of the mind. We create provocative conversations that lead to sustainable positive changes.

I heard the following quip at a Linkage conference and have quoted it ever since. "In an encounter with a good coach, you walk away impressed with the coach. With a great coach, you walk away impressed with yourself." Let's assume that coaching training, credentials, and experience are a given. Beyond that, it's about chemistry and qualities that are salient to your unique preferences. You want a coach who has the ability to not just listen well, but to *listen for*. I am almost always on a treasure hunt, listening *for* underlying themes, values, patterns, strengths, possible new solutions, and so on. Clients say they feel pleasantly surprised at what we are able to draw out of them. You also want a coach who does not give advice, but shares wisdom. It's the coactive coach's oath to never tell anyone what to do. However, it's relevant that I've been a zealous student of adult development, whole health, and leadership for decades and worked with hundreds of clients by now. I share principles, an ever-growing collection of pragmatic tools and intuitive insights that could help a client become a better master of his own life/work voyage.

I always come back to that model of trusting that the client has the answer. You also want to feel genuinely accountable to your coach. You want to feel that she is in your corner, thinking of you, cheering you on (maybe inside your head between sessions), and expecting a report or other specifics from you. Lastly, I would want a coach to be playful, funny, smart, and great at brainstorming new possibilities.

Effective coaching should be a catalyst for you to arrive at insights, solutions, new ideas, and behaviors that you would not have achieved on your own. The question "how will we know if we have been successful?" is clearly established up-front. Progress temperature checks are taken throughout. I often use 0 to 10 scales to assess effectiveness. As an example, a Performance Plus Leadership Inventory asks clients (and other feedback partners) to score satisfaction/competence of factors such as being an *inspiring communicator, creating clear boundaries* or *empowering others.* Coaching supports the client in reaching his desired higher scores and authentic self-confidence. Depending on the coaching engagement (six months or six years and going strong), the measurements of success evolve. We never stop checking to ensure that the coaching investment is extremely worthwhile and the client feels a sense of deepened learning and forward movement.

CHAPTER 6

Coaching for Leadership Development

Thought Leaders

NOEL M. TICHY
ROBERT M. FULMER
KEN BLANCHARD

PAUL HERSEY
NANCY J. ADLER
ALBERT A. VICERE

Practitioners

JOHN ALEXANDER
JIM BOLT

DAVID GIBER
JIM MOORE

THOUGHT LEADERS

Noel M. Tichy

LEADERS COACHING LEADERS

Noel M. Tichy is Director of the Global Leadership Partnership at the University of Michigan Business School. Professor Tichy is the author of *The Cycle of Leadership: How Great Leaders Teach Their Organizations To Win*, *The Leadership Engine*, *Control Your Destiny or Someone Else Will*, *Globalizing Management*, and *The Transformational Leader*. He can be e-mailed directly at tichy@umich.edu.

Coaching is critical to the success of organizations. But organizations do not win by inviting a small army of external coaches to infiltrate their ranks or by ceding the coaching function to the internal consultant. Instead, it is the job of the leader to build coaching capability into the DNA of the organization. The leader does so by developing his or her own "teachable point of view" and cascading that throughout the line. When leaders coach leaders around that teachable point of view, learning and teaching are continuously exchanged in a Virtuous Teaching Cycle. This creates alignment and energy for the organization's values, vision, and strategy even as it generates the new leadership necessary for the future.

As a coach, my job is to help the leader develop and cascade his or her teachable point of view. Many great leaders are able to do this intuitively, but for those who are leading large companies, the teachable point of view must be deliberately designed, planned, and built into the social architecture of the organization. Otherwise, its impact will be lost. A look at the 90-day process by which that happens will further clarify the role that I feel external coaches should play.

First Month: Build a Senior-Team Teachable Point of View

The process starts with the top leader. A CEO cannot teach from a blank piece of paper. She needs a teachable point of view that articulates the ideas, values, edge, and energy that will make the organization successful. The coach works with the CEO to develop that clarity. What's the leader's business theory for ringing the cash register, that is, developing goods and services that win in the marketplace? What are the concrete values that support and shape those business ideas? What tough decisions about people, products, businesses, customers, and suppliers will the leader need to make for the organization to succeed? How can the leader best energize and motivate others to embrace the changes that are necessary? Some CEOs need little guidance to articulate and tell their story, while others must build their teachable point of view from the ground up. The coach questions, prompts, and helps shape the story until the coach has a rough focus that he can before the senior team.

Typically, the top leadership team—10 to 12 members at most—goes off-site for the serious debate necessary to refine and become aligned with the leader's teachable point of view. The coach is present to help the leader guide the process and facilitate the debate. Each member of the team shares his or her individual thinking, pushing and pulling at the strategy, ideas, and values, until agreement has been reached.

It can be difficult for a leader to finesse this process. The leader cannot have all the answers, nor can he or she expect consensus to emerge without the appropriate expression of power. Typically, leaders who fail at building support do so in one of two ways. Either they are autocrats, using a megaphone to blast a point of view without making anyone around them smarter; or they are abdicrats, allowing the democracy of ideas to become an anarchy of misalignment. The paradox of power is that it is top-down but interactive, command-and-control but participatory. As in the best coaching, learning is always two-way, although organized around a firm point of view.

Second Month: Leaders Coaching Leaders

A top leader understands that one of the most powerful tools is the calendar. That's why the leader mandates that each member of the senior team spend the requisite amount of time personally coaching and teaching the next leadership level.

In the beginning, the senior team leads 2-to-3-day seminars with 50 to 100 people at the next leadership level. Again, the teaching and learning is two-way, even as it is aligned to the top leader's teachable point of view. By encouraging open debate and sharing of ideas, the teachable point of view becomes real for each individual—something he or she can pass on to the next level in turn.

Third Month: The Virtuous Teaching Cycle

The top 50 to 100 people engage the next level of leadership in a way that replicates their own teaching-learning experience. It's as though 50 to 100 tennis coaches were teaching the same techniques and strategies at the same time, each to their own class of students. As the ideas, values, and energy of the teachable point of view cascade through the organization, they gain expression in the concrete ways each individual contributes to the bottom line. Because leaders are learning from their reports as well, a virtuous teaching cycle develops in which the organization gets smarter through the interactivity, even as it is energized and aligned. In this way, the teachable point of view is always evolving as strategy and the marketplace changes.

Coaching or teaching is an activity that takes place face to face and one on one. It's energizing, spontaneous, and two-way. In the best scenarios, however, structure is in place for this spontaneous interaction to occur. Teachouts are planned and organized. Leadership institutes are created. In such a way, an entire organization can be transformed, aligned, and continuously regenerated—from a senior leader's teachable point of view to the individual on the shop floor, even in an organization of 90,000 employees with 600 stores.

Avoiding Coach Dependency and Disarray

What do coaches add to this mix? In my view, 90 percent of coaching has to occur on the line. Otherwise, the organization does not gain the benefits of continuous learning and development, and may even be put in disarray. Executive coaches can work at cross-purposes without demonstrating bottom-line benefit. Management coaches are given incentives to create dependency, not capability. Even internal coaches can get in the way, acting more like go-betweens and career counselors than teachers, unless they are fully aligned with the priorities of the business.

Leaders should coach leaders. After all, who makes a better coach than someone with the incentive to help the coachee develop his or her own independent capability? U.S. Navy Seals don't use coaches to develop critical, life-and-death leadership skills; they rely on those whose lives are also on the line. Who trains a heart surgeon but another heart surgeon? In successful organizations, coaching takes place leader to leader, level to level, up and down the line. Only then does the organization have the alignment, energy, and smarts to win.

Robert M. Fulmer

BUSINESS CHALLENGE COACHING

Dr. Robert M. Fulmer is Distinguished Visiting Professor at Pepperdine University and also serves as Academic Director of Duke Corporate Education. He served as Director of Worldwide Management Development at Allied-Signal, headed two HRD consulting firms, authored four editions of *The New Management*, and coauthored four editions of *A Practical Introduction to Business*, as well as the acclaimed books *Crafting Competitiveness*, *Executive Development and Organizational Learning for Global Business*, *Leadership by Design*, *The Leadership Investment*, and *Growing Your Company's Leaders*. He can be contacted via e-mail at robert.fulmer@dukece.com or via the Internet at www.dukece.com.

Coaching individual executives or leadership teams, for me, generally involves tackling some type of business challenge as part of a leadership development initiative. Work with individuals is most likely to come from an assessment that the individual is not meeting his or her objectives or is out of alignment with the organizational values or strategy. More frequently, the coaching is based on the principles of action learning and is part of a corporate program that involves traditional education in leadership, strategy, or change. Particularly in my work with Duke Corporate Education, we try to combine content with a business challenge assignment and supplement that with team and personal coaching to improve effectiveness. In other words, the participants are learning for action as opposed to learning for knowledge alone; they are having a Just-In-Time developmental experience rather than a Just-In-Case one. The idea is to design an intervention that stretches the abilities of leaders and helps them reach a new level of effectiveness while solving a real business challenge.

I think it's important to design the intervention together with the client. Not only does that create buy-in, it also helps the coach to understand the perspective of the organization and the needs of the individuals. To get to that understanding, the first part of my coaching work involves a great deal of listening. My background in applied research, university executive education, HRD consulting, and worldwide responsibility for management development at a global corporation provides me with a broad perspective of what is best practice in the world. I draw from that experience as I listen to the client's challenges, and consider what I've seen or used in other circumstances that might fit this situation. Then, we work together to develop a customized approach.

How that occurs is actually less structured than it might seem when I describe it in stages. Nevertheless, drawing on the three major methodologies of action learning, gap analysis, and systems dynamics, I've broken down the process of developing an intervention into what I call the five A's. These are depicted in Figure 6.1.

The first A is *Awareness*. The process starts, as I mentioned, with a great deal of listening, and a certain amount of data collection, to gain a detailed understanding of the challenge at hand. I like to think of this awareness as being like the Roman perception of Janus who had faces looking to the past for understanding and to the future for strategy. The next A is *Anticipation*. This involves setting up the goals or objectives of where the client executive or organization wants to be in the future, with or without an intervention. With the first two components, we can identify the gap between where we are and where we want to be. The third A is *Action*. We use action as the arena for learning in order to push the executive toward that future goal. This may be individual coaching that has actionable objectives or part of a total cultural shift in an organization. The fourth A is *Alignment*. The fact that a real business challenge is being tackled helps make sure that individual objectives align with the team and the organization, in terms of values, culture, and strategy. Finally, the fifth A is *Assessment*. It's necessary at the end of the intervention to measure what we've done in order to demonstrate that progress has occurred.

I find that an engagement is successful when there's a commitment to change on the part of the client and a good fit with the coach. For example, when a project does not succeed, failure often boils down to the fact that the coach and client's personalities or approaches to business or life were not in synch. Generally speaking, if a degree of rapport develops in the initial interviews and both sides sense that values are in line, it is likely that chemistry will be good. If the coach sees, or the client is able to determine, that the problem or challenge is within the coach's realm of experience, that's further

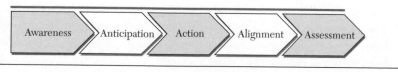

FIGURE 6.1   The Five A's

indication of the likelihood of success. If both sides have no troubles listening or respecting each other's perspective, that's the final stamp of approval.

My whole career has been spent in the field of learning. Learning is basically what my life is about. In most of my current work, I emphasize the ways in which leaders can learn by doing. My goal is to help people learn how to become what they want to be or help them do what they want to accomplish. A very effective way of managing that, I have found, is to coach executives while they are grappling with an assignment or a business challenge. That is key, I've found, to development that helps individuals achieve their goals in alignment with what the organization needs. The most successful engagement is when the individual shows actual progress, the team becomes more effective, and the organization becomes more successful.

⇒•◇•⇐

Ken Blanchard

THE SERVANT LEADER AS COACH

 Ken Blanchard is Chairman and Chief Spiritual Officer of The Ken Blanchard Companies and cofounder of the Center for FaithWalk Leadership. Ken is a visiting lecturer at his alma mater, Cornell University, where he is a Trustee Emeritus of the Board of Trustees. His phenomenal best-selling book, *The One Minute Manager®*, coauthored with Spencer Johnson, has sold more than 10 million copies worldwide and has been translated into more than 25 languages. He is reachable by phone through The Ken Blanchard Companies at (800) 728-6000. You can also visit The Ken Blanchard Companies at www.kenblanchard.com or the Center for *FaithWalk* Leadership at www.leadlikejesus.com.

Leadership is an influence process. Any time you're trying to influence the behavior of someone toward some goal, you're engaging in leadership. This is true whether you're a politician, a parent, a CEO, a teacher, or a reverend. Leaders coach because it is an effective style for moving people from dependence to independence in pursuit of a goal. In that sense, being a coach is also a form of leadership. Some might argue with me on that point because they hold that coaches facilitate or guide rather than lead. But to me, coaching and leadership go hand in hand.

I don't think you can lead people unless you have a sense of where you want them to go. Leadership is about going somewhere. If you don't know where you're going, your leadership doesn't matter. Once people know where they are going, the next step is implementation. That involves helping people to live according to the vision and direction. Leaders lead by setting the stage in terms of vision and direction. But they also work to get people closer to that destination, which is what coaching for implementation is all about. At that point, the leader or coach shifts from directing to serving people by guiding, supporting, and cheerleading them as their needs require. The coaches now become servant leaders.

In our company, we're trying to create a movement to uplift the human spirit by making sure that people-development gets put on an equal plane with performance. That's our vision and direction. As Chief Spiritual Officer, one of my jobs is to connect us to that mission every day. Each morning, I leave a voice mail message for the more than 250 people in our company. I talk about three things: people tell me who ought to be prayed for; people tell me what praising others should get; and I end the call with an inspirational message. The prayer and the praising are part of the care and support we all need. As a company, we have to check in on ourselves, make sure everyone is doing okay, and cheer for those who are doing the work to make our vision and direction happen. The inspirational message touches on those things and reminds us of what we're all here to accomplish.

For example, one day I talked about profit being the applause we get for taking care of our customers and creating a motivating environment for our people. I emphasized that our company is all about relationships. First, we want to create raving fan customers—people who are so excited about us that they want to brag about our work. These people become part of our salesforce. To create that, we need gung ho people—associates who are so committed to our company that they're willing to go the extra mile for our customers and each other.

Coaching and leadership are about focusing on what's important in life. What are our values? What are we trying to accomplish? My own personal coach, Shirley Anderson, helps me figure out what I want to work on. We talk about what issues I have, what's bugging me, what's not working. We sort through all of that and identify strategies that can help me become the kind of leader I want to be.

As a coach, knowing what needs to be done is only half the job. You also need to get people there. If coaching or leadership fails, it may be that you've done a lot of up-front work on directing people toward a goal and even laying out the path, but you didn't finish the cycle. The important thing isn't what happens when you're there, but what happens when you're not there. To move people from dependence to independence, you need to see them through a Situational Leadership journey that raises their levels of commitment and competence to the point where they no longer need your direct guidance.

People start out as Enthusiastic Beginners, high on commitment but low on competence. They need information, expertise, and direction from their coach or leader to get them started. The work doesn't stop there, though. What happens next is that people often find the goal more difficult than expected, and become what we call Disillusioned Learners. This means that they have some competence but are low on commitment. They are dependent on you to dialogue with them in order to work through their concerns. In other words, they still need direction but they also need tender loving care.

The third level of development is Capable but Cautious. By this point, people are able to follow the path and see the benefits, but they don't have full confidence in themselves. They need you to be a supportive cheerleader for a while longer. The final level is Self-Directed Achiever, meaning they own what they are doing and only need you to delegate and cheer them on.

It takes will and determination for a leader or coach to fulfill the vision and direction to the point where people become Self-Directed Achievers. It also takes humility. The traditional hierarchy is fine for setting vision and direction, but it's lousy for implementation. To move people to independence, you need to turn the pyramid upside down. Suddenly, the ones who developed the vision and direction are now at the bottom of the hierarchy as cheerleaders, supporters, and encouragers. This is where servant leadership kicks in.

A major part of my work right now is involved in a Lead Like Jesus movement around the country. Our mission is to challenge and equip people to lead like Jesus. We're not trying to evangelize. What we want is for people to behave differently. We want leaders to serve rather than rule; to give rather than take. The goal is to become—as Jesus mandated—a servant leader.

Servant leaders understand that leadership is not about them; it's about what they can do to help people live and develop according to a vision. But that only exists through humility. People with humility don't think less of themselves; they just think about themselves less. They don't deny their own power; they just recognize that it passes through them, not from them. To develop humility you have to recognize a higher power or something that is your source of unconditional love. Where else could you expect to find the wisdom and openness to lead or coach another person through growth and change?

Paul Hersey

COACHING IS THE MANAGER'S JOB

Dr. Paul Hersey is founder and CEO of the Center for Leadership Studies. He is author of the popular book, *The Situational Leader,* and the textbook model for situational leadership, *Management of Organizational Behavior.* He is reachable by phone at (800) 330-2840 or via the Internet at www.situational.com.

Twenty years ago, if you'd asked managers to describe their most critical tasks and responsibilities, coaching would have made it to nearly everyone's top-five list. Today, few include it among their priorities. How did this shift happen? It took place almost unnoticed, I believe, as managers became transitory in their careers and switched organizations more freely. At some point, the sense of obligation managers felt for investing in people long-term seemed to fall away. In a sense, our work in the leadership development field is dedicated to rebuilding coaching capacity in the line by putting that obligation back onto the manager's plate.

Simply put, we consider leadership to be the process of diagnosing the individual or group in terms of their readiness to perform; and providing them with the direction, guidance, or supportive behavior necessary to enable them to take the ball and run with it. As might be expected, this takes place in many different ways in an organization. All of us are responsible for coaching those who report directly to us. There are also many occasions in which we help others internally, as happens, for example, when we are part of a team. In working with the people who report to us, we coach down with personal and positional power. When we are members of a group or team, we influence and coach through personal power. The dynamic may change, but the end goal remains the same. People are coached to help maximize their potential. If the coaching is successful, they eventually become self-directed rather than leader-directed.

If this sounds like a natural activity for managers, it should. So why aren't they doing it? We train trainers to go back into their organizations and work with managers from executive to supervisory levels. We start at the top if possible, but we have a philosophical conviction that the change we advocate can begin from anywhere. For a manager to fulfill his or her leadership capacity, being a coach means passing that capability along. If the manager gets it, who are they giving it to in turn? Are those who are being coached coaching others as well? How are those people doing? Are they pushing it deeper still? That's how the impact of leadership gets measured, and that's how legacies are created. The process can begin with any single manager at any level.

Organizations rise and fall based on how effectively they use their human resources. The individual manager is in the most powerful position to make the most of that potential.

◄═◆═►

Nancy J. Adler

THE ART OF LEADERSHIP: COACHING IN THE TWENTY-FIRST CENTURY

 Dr. Nancy J. Adler is a foremost authority on cross-cultural management and women's global leadership. She is a Professor of International Management at McGill University in Montreal, Canada. She has authored over 100 articles and published the books, *International Dimensions of Organizational Behavior, Women in Management Worldwide, Competitive Frontiers: Women Managers in a Global Economy,* and *From Boston to Beijing: Managing with a Worldview.* Also a visual artist working primarily with watercolor and Japanese and Chinese ink techniques, she currently teaches seminars on "The Art of Leadership." She can be e-mailed at nancy.adler@mcgill.ca.

At some time over the next fifty years or so, the word *manager* will disappear from our understanding of leadership, and thankfully so. Another word will emerge, more alive with possibility, more helpful, hopefully not decided upon by a committee, which will describe the new role of leadership now emerging. An image of leadership that embraces the attentive, open-minded, conversationally based, people-minded person who has not given up on her intellect and can still act and act quickly when needed. Much of the wisdom needed to create these new roles lies not in our empirical, strategic disciplines but in our artistic traditions. It is the artist in each of us we must now encourage into the world, whether we have worked for the Getty Foundation or for Getty Oil. We must bring our visionary artistic powers into emancipation with our highly trained empirical powers of division and deduction.

—David Whyte, poet[1]

How do leaders shift their thinking into the realm of possibility? As we struggle with the dynamic challenges of today's very complex world, how can we move to a twenty-first-century definition of leadership that is free of the constraints of twentieth-century vocabulary and image? In our desire to create a better future, how do we change the focus of our leadership, as Frances Hesselbein has said, from success to significance?

For a quarter century, I have conducted research, consulted, and coached on global leadership and cross-cultural management. As the world's interconnectedness and the demands on leadership have intensified, I have come to understand that the movement from successful to significant leadership cannot and will not happen inside our current leadership vocabulary. The twentieth century's words, concepts, and approaches just don't stretch far enough for us to be able to see today's reality, think possibility, and communicate powerfully.

Often, when I work with individual leaders, I ask them to assess their leadership by considering a very simple framework comprised of three realms: What are you very good at doing? What do you passionately love to do? And what's the world's greatest need.? I then ask, "For you, where do these three realms intersect?" For all too many leaders, one or even two of these realms have been ignored in their professional life. Many bright and talented executives feel lucky to be born in an era that rewards them for the things they do very well. In the glare of recognition for what they are good at, they never ask, "What am I passionate about?" or they split their lives between doing what they are good at in their professional life while saving what they care about for "after hours." Considering the world's greatest needs and their own passionate concerns becomes limited to the time remaining for their personal lives. Because real leadership resides in the intersection of the three realms, I push executives, especially those who have been most outwardly successful, to see the possibility of their contribution and efficacy coming simultaneously from their competence (what they are really good at), their passion (what they love doing), and the world's greatest needs (their potentially most significant contributions). See Figure 6.2 for a graphic representation of these three realms.

Earlier this year, I presented the overlapping realms of significant leadership to executives at the University of South Africa's Business Leadership Institute, the University where Nelson Mandela received his degree. Managers from throughout southern Africa travel to the Institute twice a year. With years of experience and an average age between 35 to 40, they include the full range of twenty-first-century managers—male and female, black and white, African, Asian, and European descent—a diversity unheard of in most twentieth-century groups of similar leaders. The questions "What am I good at?" "What am I passionate about?" and "What's the world's greatest need?" were hugely important to these executives because current African business and societal challenges are so large. No one in the room could escape

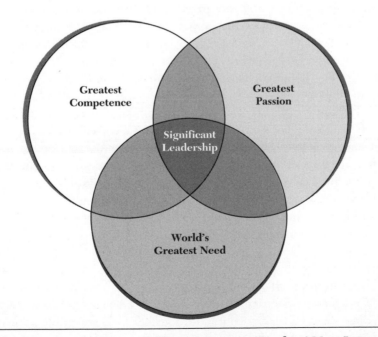

FIGURE 6.2 **Significant Leadership: Supporting Leaders' Most Important Contributions**

the reality that neither the companies they lead nor their society will make it unless they bring the very best of their skills and passion to the most critically important challenges.

The discussion was intense and authentic. At one point, I suggested that no one is truly a leader who engages people primarily through coercion; that they could not consider themselves leaders unless their people would be willing to work for their companies as volunteers. I was not suggesting that salary and benefits are unimportant, but rather that true commitment is always rooted in something beyond money. In a quiet but definite voice, an Afrikaans executive thoughtfully responded, "That's true for some industries, but not all." His statement was not hostile, but rather profoundly sincere and personal. I held my ground and repeated that the idea applied to all industries. Everyone in the room sensed the tension as the executive continued, "I'm in the mining industry, and nobody would ever go down into a mine unless they absolutely needed the money."

Despite my worst images of the horrendous conditions in many mines and my desire to shout my agreement—"Yes, you're right, it doesn't apply in your industry!"—something in the man's authenticity made me insist that yes, it also applied to his industry. "You're the expert in your industry," I responded, "I can't say exactly how it applies to your industry and to the mining operations you direct, but it does. Maybe your mine can offer the best health and safety conditions. Or maybe it can offer the best education for miners' children, so that every day when miners descend into the mines, they know their children will never have to do the same." The words hit home. The man's face changed. He knew, along with everyone else in the room, what had just happened. Perhaps for the first time as a leader, this Afrikaans mining director realized that he did not have to be a bastard to succeed at his job.

Einstein reminded us that "a problem cannot be solved at the level at which it was caused." You have to jump a level to find the right answer. Although I know I can't solve the problems others face, I also know we can do much better than we're currently doing. As a coach it's my goal to help executives see, think, and communicate from the perspective of possibility.[2] To do so, demands courage, specifically:

- The courage to see reality as it actually is—to "collude against illusion"[3] even when society and your colleagues reject your perceptions.
- The courage to imagine a better world—to imagine possibility even when society and your colleagues consider such possibilities naïve, unattainable, or foolish.
- The courage to communicate reality and possibility so powerfully that others can't help but move forward toward a better future.

Our twentieth-century management and leadership vocabulary, with its now-antiquated images based primarily on military, hierarchical, and production-line concepts, has become too impoverished to allow us to see reality, think possibility, and communicate with significance. A leadership workshop for women executives provides a case in point. I opened the week by inviting the women to define "power" and their relationship to it. Each group's discussion immediately descended into an overwhelmingly negative vortex. These senior executives saw "power" as masculine, manipulative, Machiavellian, and overly hierarchical. As the group verged on the edge of rejecting entirely their leftover notions of misused twentieth-century power, one very senior executive from a prominent global organization confronted her colleagues: "Unless you can tell me that the world is perfect, your company is perfect, your community is perfect, and your family is perfect, don't tell me that you're not interested in power."

For this group of executives, the vocabulary of leadership had become so corrupted that we couldn't discuss one of the central tenants of leadership: power and influence. To shift from the limitations of twentieth-century perspectives to the type of vocabulary we need to discuss and enact twenty-first-century leadership, we need to shift our very understanding of core words and concepts. Without such a shift, seeing reality, thinking possibility, and communicating significance would remain impossible.

For me, one highly effective means for creating that shift is by using the arts and artistic processes. For example, after my initial failure to create a twenty-first-century discussion of power using the traditional approach—words—I decided to try an alternative approach: visual images. This time I started by writing the word "Power" on a flipchart and asking everyone to respond with what first came to mind. The now-expected barrage of negative connotations ensued. Next, I invited them to use new tools, a mountain of art supplies, to create their own image of power. The only rule was that the process had to be nonverbal. They could neither talk during the exercise nor use any words in their artwork. After completing their power images, I asked them to sign their name, as artists, so they would own their visual definitions of power.

As we discussed each image, the most robust, positive, and owned definition of power emerged that I have ever witnessed. By changing the vocabulary—from traditional words to artistic images—we had changed the nature of the conversation, and with it, our very understanding of each leader's relationship to power.

Most coaches are well versed in chaos and complexity theory because it has been so helpful in allowing us to understand the turbulent, not completely knowable world in which we live and work. Using those principles, we coach executives to understand that learning organizations need to be flexible, inclusive, innovative, and quick in dealing with an unpredictable future. Yet rarely do we give executives the new behavioral capabilities we say they need to deal effectively and spontaneously with rapid change.

Unfortunately, the words of even the most brilliant lectures, while definitely increasing leaders' understanding of turbulent environments, often fail to improve those same leaders' actual capability to lead when confronted by chaotic, rapidly changing situations. By contrast, improvisational theater techniques demonstrably increase executives' capabilities to lead in such twenty-first-century environments.[4] To excel as an improv actor, you must respond instantly to what's going on around you; you can't rely on preplanned strategies or lines. When I introduce managers working in international joint ventures, for example, to improvisational theater techniques, it immediately shifts their understanding of how leadership, teamwork, cooperation, and flexibility really work.

In one classic improv exercise, the managers tell a story by having each individual rapidly add one word to the narrative in turn. Typically, the first attempt at building a story is painfully dry, nonsensical, and completely lacking in leaps of creativity or surges of energy. The reason is simple: between turns, each person is focusing on deciding which word to add, rather than listening to their colleagues. By the time the narrative reaches them, their carefully chosen word no longer fits.

Only by letting go of preplanned strategies and focusing on the flow of the unfolding story can each manager become able to contribute to the story in a way that brings it to life. As the story becomes more coherent, surprising, energized, and fun, the executives viscerally understand what they need to do differently. Being successful in a spontaneous, chaotic, interdependent, team-oriented environment requires observational, listening, and input skills, much more than our traditional talking, doing, and more output-oriented skills. Leading effectively in turbulent environments requires a mode of teamwork that cannot be learned except through direct experience.

Leaders are most intensely out of their comfort zone and into a learning zone when areas of leadership are explored that draw heavily on artistic and creative processes, reflection and the symbolic aspects of leadership. Poetry can hold ambiguity and paradox in ways that our dehydrated business vocabulary cannot. David Whyte, often referred to as the poet of the corporate world, reminds us that: "Poetry is the art of overhearing ourselves say things from which it is impossible to retreat."[5] Similarly, with music, Benjamin Zander, conductor of the Boston Philharmonic, teaches us: "A symphony is about getting all of the voices sounding together, which is what leadership is really about. It is not about winning or losing—but about sounding together."[6] Exceptional leadership demands a level of inspiration, perspective, courage, understanding, and commitment that transcends day-to-day management; twenty-first-century leadership demands approaches that transcend the accepted practices of twentieth-century organizations.

Artists and leaders face similar challenges: to see reality as it is, without succumbing to despair, while imagining possibilities that go far beyond current reality; to have the courage to collude against illusion while articulating possible futures previously unimaginable; and to inspire people to surpass themselves, individually and collectively, for the benefit of all. The world needs better leadership, and the people within organizations and communities are hungry for the change. They no longer want the narrow, circumscribed leadership of the twentieth century, nor its outcomes. And yet those who choose to truly lead in this journey should not dismiss the risks. Whenever a paradigm shifts, those who have the most to gain from the old ways hold on extremely tightly.

━━⇒•◆•⇐━━

Albert A. Vicere

COACHING FOR LEADERSHIP DEPTH

Dr. Albert A. Vicere is Executive Education Professor of Strategic Leadership at Penn State's Smeal College of Business and President of Vicere Associates Inc., a consulting firm whose clients span the globe. He is the author/editor of several books, including *Leadership By Design* and *The Many Facets of Leadership,* and more than 80 articles on leadership development and organizational effectiveness. His article "Leadership in the Networked Economy" won the Human Resource Planning Society's 2002 Walker Prize for the most influential article of the year. He can be reached by phone at (814) 233-1120, by e-mail at a.vicere@vicere.com, or via the Internet at www.vicere.com.

Over the years, I have had the great fortune to work with scores of business organizations and to spend time with their leaders. The best of those leaders share at least one very similar perspective—that the essence of their job is to get results and at the same time to build commitment to the organization's culture and values. But there is little doubt that today's leaders must carry out those responsibilities in an incredibly complex environment. The current business climate challenges leaders to fulfill their responsibilities while directing their organization's movement into a new economic order. This often requires not only the development and deployment of new strategies and business models, but also reformulation of corporate culture and values.

My clients tend to be business and HRD leaders from organizations like Cisco, 3M, Aramark, and Merck that are looking to build relevant leadership development initiatives to meet the challenge of today's complex competitive environment. I work in partnership with those clients to design, develop, and sometimes deliver initiatives that help their organization to get results, shape culture, and develop leadership depth. As challenging as this work can be, there is nothing more inspiring or exhilarating than working in tandem with a team of clients to build momentum, ratchet up performance, and inspire renewed leadership commitment across an organization.

The number-one critical success factor in my work is having a team of clients—on both the business and HRD side—that is visibly committed to leadership development as a driver of organizational performance. It really helps if the team is comprised of both business leaders and HRD experts. Early in the engagement, I try to facilitate discussion and build consensus within the team around a number of issues that are at the heart of effective leadership development processes. The goal is to have the team:

- *Clarify core objectives for development based on the strategic imperatives of the firm,* including discussions around targeting key audiences for development; defining critical competencies and capabilities; creating networks to share knowledge and leverage performance; enhancing communications and teamwork; refining organizational culture; and implementing business strategies.
- *Select methods and approaches to be used for development, ensuring consistency with the company's strategic imperatives and the overall learning/development objectives of the initiative.* This could include action learning projects, leader-led learning, classroom education, and other methods for promoting individual and organizational effectiveness.
- *Build and maintain strategic partnerships with resources to help in initiative delivery.* I am a strong advocate of leader-led processes in which client company executives play major roles in any initiative. But

I also know the value that fresh eyes can bring to the table. My goal is to help the client team build a network of outstanding, committed partners for program delivery from both within and outside the company. We work together to develop processes for recruiting and coaching people from within the company who are selected to be teachers, mentors, or coaches themselves. We also develop processes for identifying, engaging, and managing the involvement and performance of external resources that bring critical expertise and outside perspectives to the development initiative.

- *Align leadership development processes with the organization's human resource management systems.* I work with the client team to ensure that the leadership development initiatives are tightly linked to the organization's performance metrics and human resource management infrastructure, including reward systems, recruitment and selection procedures, and succession and executive resource planning processes. This final step ensures relevance and impact for any development initiative.

In my experience, members of an effective client team must have a commitment to moving the organization from where it is to a desired future state. They need to have vision, to see the pattern of where the organization was, where it is now, and where it is going. They need a real feel for the people, the culture, and the political climate of the organization. And they have to know how far you can push and how hard you can push the people.

My most effective clients are patient and persistent, have a clear vision of the role leadership development can play in the organization, and are willing to be an active part of the process. Clearly, it helps to have senior executive sponsors who believe in leadership development. Without that level of support and involvement, it is hard to maintain the credibility and momentum of the process. But even so, my most successful engagements have been those in which a core team of motivated individuals have made a commitment to make leadership development a key driver of business success.

From the experience I have gained while coaching teams to build high-impact leadership development initiatives, I have learned that success in leadership development starts with a commitment at the top. The initiatives are tightly linked to the company's strategic agenda. They are viewed as a lever for communicating strategy, focusing behaviors, and driving change. They provide next-generation leaders with an opportunity to learn, practice, develop, and grow. And when done well, they drive business results, the best measure of success that I can imagine.

PRACTITIONERS

John Alexander

John Alexander is President and CEO of the Center for Creative Leadership, an international, nonprofit educational institution devoted to research and teaching in leadership and leadership development. As a participant in the Center's coaching network, John gives feedback in the Center's flagship Leadership Development Program and periodically serves as a coach to senior executives. Organizational highlights during John's tenure as president include two number-one rankings in the Leadership category in the *BusinessWeek* nondegree executive education survey and a Top 20 ranking for nondegree executive education providers worldwide in a *Financial Times* survey. In 1979, John was a finalist for the Pulitzer Prize in editorial writing. John may be contacted at CCL's headquarters in Greensboro, NC by telephone at (336) 286-4002, via e-mail at alexander@leaders.ccl.org, or on the Internet at www.ccl.org.

At the Center for Creative Leadership (CCL), we specialize in coaching that concentrates on leadership and personal development. It is feedback-intensive, behaviorally focused, and results oriented. It can stand alone or be integrated into a larger developmental initiative, either as a one-to-one experience or in group or team settings. Whatever the situation, we devote a lot of time to two aspects of coaching—the overall process and the actual content and conduct of the coaching sessions.

Process includes things such as organizational context and support for the coaching experience, appropriate pairing of coaches with coachees, design of the coaching program, assessment of client needs and desired outcomes, and postprogram evaluation. The importance of these factors cannot be overemphasized. Too often, not enough time is spent assessing the purpose and desired outcomes of the coaching, the readiness of the coachee and fit with the coach, assumptions of organizational sponsors, and the organizational context in which the coaching takes place.

Coaching experiences are, of course, as varied as the leaders and coaches who participate in them. At CCL, we have developed a core framework of coaching that provides a helpful structure while allowing the infinite diversity of coaching experiences to unfold. That framework consists of three elements:

the relationship between coach and coachee, a leader development model, and a results orientation.

What are the factors that coachees rate most important in a coaching relationship? A CCL survey of more than 100 respondents indicated that the top-rated quality is that the coach be trustworthy and honest. Good interpersonal and communication skills were also highly rated. Although men and women coachees concurred on these first two items, men rated "straightforward feedback/willingness to challenge assumptions" next, while women selected "creates a developmental and nonthreatening environment." Two sides of the same coin, perhaps? There is no evidence that men and women have significantly different expectations or requirements in a coach. In either case, it's important that the coachee select a coach with whom he or she feels rapport, who is a good listener and facilitator, and whose repertoire of skills and experiences is a good match for the desired outcomes of the coaching experience. In the end, the successful coaching experience is a collaboration between coach and coachee, an exquisite pas de deux between partners in learning.

The CCL model of leader development that forms the basis of the coaching experience encompasses three components: Assessment, Challenge, and Support (ACS). *Assessment* means that the coach will work with the coachee to assess the situation in which the coachee is working, and identify the specific behaviors that are either helping or hindering his or her effectiveness as a leader. The process of assessment can entail interviews with the coachee and others, including coworkers and family members; 360-degree feedback instruments; surveys; observations by the coach; examination of performance appraisals; and the like. A good coach will help the coachee sort through this data and identify key behavioral themes and patterns. Time is profitably spent on trying to identify the internal drivers, such as personal beliefs and feelings, which lead to these observable behaviors. Understanding internal drivers can contribute to greater success in changing behaviors visible to others. CCL draws a line between this type of exploration and a more clinical intervention. Coaching is not therapy, although coaching can sometimes lead to a referral to a health care professional.

From this assessment, the coachee typically selects one or two concrete goals on which he or she wants to work during the coaching engagement—a personal learning agenda. It is extremely important to avoid goal creep. Coaches can and should help their coachees avoid the temptation to select too many goals or goals that are too broad or ambitious. Smaller victories build confidence and facilitate learning; overreaching typically leads to frustration or failure.

After an action plan is set, the coachee is *challenged* to explore alternative courses of action and to select those that will allow him or her to most successfully demonstrate the desired new behaviors. This challenge creates disequilibrium by addressing gaps between the current state and desired state described in the action plan. Challenge can come from the coach, from the coachee's own self-assessment, or from external factors such as a new job assignment or stretch organizational goal. The key for the coach is to maintain a balance—to create conditions for change without overwhelming or demoralizing the coachee.

An appropriate level of *support* can ameliorate the stress that challenge creates for the coachee. This is where the coach's emphasis on small victories is helpful, or where mistakes made during the learning process can be analyzed and put in proper perspective (because mistakes will be made), or where the long-term goals driving the coaching experience can be called out during difficult times. Real change, based on real learning, is hard work. It is the successful coach's job to pace the mixture and flow of assessment, challenge, and support with the coachee to maximize the opportunity for long-term success.

How do we at CCL know whether the coaching experience has had a successful result? The most obvious answer is to determine whether positive, observable behavioral change has been achieved over a sufficient period of time. This can be done through informal means, such as asking the coachee and others around him or her whether there has been change; or through a more formal process of postprogram assessment, using written surveys and interviews. Such temperature taking is typically done at least six months, and sometimes a full year, following completion of the coaching experience. But lasting behavioral change, although very important, is not the only positive result. Surveys and interviews do not often capture the sometimes profound insights that coachees gain about their long-term career goals, personal developmental goals, and individual learning styles.

After all, if coaching is to help the coachee over a long period of time—long after the coach has departed—it must help him or her learn how to continue to adapt and grow in response to changing work and personal environments. That is the ultimate and enduring achievement, for coaches and the clients they serve.

Jim Bolt

Jim Bolt is CEO and founder of Executive Development Associates (EDA), a leading consulting firm specializing in the strategic use of executive and leadership development. EDA custom-designs executive development strategies, systems, and programs that ensure clients have the top talent needed to achieve their strategic objectives. EDA's clients have included 50 of the Fortune 100 companies and many other leading organizations around the world. Jim was recently selected by the *Financial Times* as one of the top experts in executive/leadership development. He is the author of the book *Executive Development: A Strategy for Corporate Competitiveness.* He can be reached by phone at (415) 399-9797 or by e-mail at jbolt@executivedevelopment.com.

I coach CEOs and their senior management teams on how to build great systems and programs for developing the leaders and leadership capabilities they need to successfully execute their business strategy. Basically, my job is to coach them through the process shown in Figure 6.3.

Together, we need to understand the global forces and trends that impact the organization, both today and in the future. Also important are their critical marketplace challenges, and of course their company's vision, values, and strategies. Once these are identified, we should be able to pinpoint their business priorities. The end result should be clarity about the organizational and leadership capabilities they need. Naturally, we then have to determine how the needs match up with the capabilities that currently exist so that we can be crystal clear about where the gaps exist. These gaps provide the

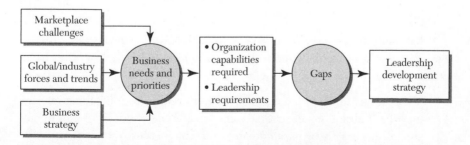

FIGURE 6.3   The Leadership Development Strategy Process

agenda for the custom-designed leadership development strategy and programs we create.

For this process to work well, the client has to have some special qualities, which often work against their natural instincts:

- *Let me be the expert.* They have to trust that I'm the expert on leadership development—not them. I've found that leadership and leadership development, is like sex and marketing, that is, everyone thinks they're an expert. They have to let me do my job. They have to be willing to let go of control, and that is something they aren't typically used to. We make a deal: I don't tell them how to run their company, and they don't tell me how to create high-impact leadership development systems and programs.
- *Suspend judgment.* Many CEOs and other senior executives have to forget what they think they know about executive or leadership development. Many have a poor schema based on their own experiences. Few have actually experienced leadership development that was strategic. If they did happen to have attended a university executive education program, it most likely didn't have anything to do with their company and therefore has little to no relevance in this context. Moreover, many have never participated in a well designed, high-impact, customized internal program that was directly linked to their business strategy and produced measurable results.
- *Let go of having all the answers.* It's important for the client to be willing to make herself vulnerable and to be open to learning and admitting she doesn't have all the answers. This is important throughout the process, but especially after the new leadership development system and programs are put in place, and when the client is exposed to leaders in a program or workshop setting. If the CEO acts like she or he knows it all, then the subtle message is: "What do they need all this other great talent for?" They need to be willing to attend the learning events just like everyone else: as students.

What qualities are crucial for me as a coach? Well, after 20 years in this line of work, these are the things I believe are most important in order to be a trusted advisor to top management:

- *Deep listening.* There is no substitute for really deep listening and for making it absolutely clear that you've heard the client. This can be accomplished easily by paraphrasing what you just heard to confirm it, by asking a question that is based on what you heard, by summarizing your meeting in writing, and so on.

- *Courage.* You have to be willing to say the unpopular, unpleasant thing. Most people in the organization won't tell the CEO the truth if it might endanger their careers. You have to be willing to get fired as a coach or advisor. You have no value to the CEO if you can't be brutally honest and candid. Of course, it helps to do so in a way that allows her or him to hear you.
- *Fight your own arrogance.* After 20 years, it's mighty easy for me to think I know everything there is to know about leadership development and to stop learning because I'm the expert. I have to fight with myself constantly over this. If I stop learning, I'm of no use to my client and a lousy role model to boot.
- *Flexibility.* I have proven, time-tested methods for doing things. I know they work. It's easy to get into a "it's my way or the highway" frame of mind with a client, and that can be dangerous. Sometimes, there are other ways to get things done that may not be perfect from a technical standpoint but may work fine (or even better) in that organization, given its culture or circumstance. Thus, I try to remind myself to know when to back off so that I don't get too stuck in my ways.
- *Keep promises and keep your mouth shut.* Perhaps this is all too obvious, but I still have to keep it at the forefront of my thinking. I must do what I said I was going to do, and when I said I would do it. Secondly, I have to keep confidences. It is very seductive to be in the know, and when you're in the know, it's even more seductive to want to let others know you're in the know. This is a potential death trap to a coach or advisor.
- *Know when to say no.* It is very tempting to say yes to everything, but I learned a long time ago that a client really appreciates it when I turn down business. The clients I don't take on are pleasantly surprised, and my credibility goes way up, when I tell them that I'm not qualified for a job they offer me and recommend someone else who is.

When I sat down to write this, I didn't intend for the list of qualities for me as a coach/advisor to be twice as long as the list for the client. The lists just came out that way. In retrospect, though, it seems appropriate, in that I think I bear the bulk of the responsibility for making a coach-client relationship work.

David Giber

David Giber, PhD, has served as a coach to leaders and executives for over 20 years. He is Senior Vice President of Leadership Development at Linkage, Inc., an organizational development company whose specialty is leadership development. David has designed and implemented leadership programs worldwide. He is the editor of two top-selling books in the field, *Best Practices in Leadership Development Handbook* and *Best Practices in Organizational Development and Change.* He can be reached by e-mail at dgiber@linkageinc.com.

In many ways, coaching is the interweaving of two stories—the coach's and the person being coached. The coach must understand the experiences or stories of his or her clients, but also help them connect the drivers and lessons from their lives to the future stories they need to write.

I use the idea of life stories and themes to guide my work and approach. Often, my clients emerge because they are in a transition, either moving from one level in an organization to another, or resolving some problem between the fit of their current skills and abilities, and the demands of their job. Many times I see people struggling with what I call leadership paradoxes such as balancing concerns about people while still driving results; thinking strategically while finding new ways to monitor the operation; and defining one's own vision and direction while simultaneously learning to empower others.

Coaching people through these dilemmas requires that the coach understand the evolving life story of the client. Who are they trying to become? What life problem are they searching to solve? I make extensive use of the leadership story exercise, which I learned from Noel Tichy at the University of Michigan. I ask people to write an autobiography of two pages or less, and ask them to think about those people and incidents that have had a big impact on them. Having executives draw out the high and low points of their lives and careers, and the lessons and values learned from them, is a tremendously useful exercise in helping them connect better with others. One senior vice president used this exercise to understand how leaving home as a teenager and working his way through college in menial jobs had affected his overdemanding standards for others and his own lack of life balance. As a coach, I try to help clients learn from both positive and negative experiences by identifying what they took out of those incidents and considering how those lessons affect their behavior today.

In coaching leaders, I aim for depth in exploring their life issues as well as their approach to business. I draw on my own business knowledge and experience to help business leaders translate their feedback into practical action. I also use several tools that aim at many of the common dilemmas of my business clients.

One approach I use is to have clients develop a leadership agenda. It is challenging and enlightening for leaders to articulate their key goals and plans. Often, I have them map these to a balanced scorecard format where they look at their system/process, financial, people, and innovation goals. The purpose is to help them test the clarity of their communication about their own vision and direction to others.

Another coaching exercise aimed specifically at the area of strategic thinking is to have clients write a future business scenario. A typical question is "If you were head of this business, what two actions would you take that would dramatically improve results over the next two years?" I often exchange these scenarios between people I am coaching or have them reviewed by senior business leaders. This leads to new insights on risk taking or new development plans for how to improve and expand that person's external perspective on the business.

I use 360-degree feedback in my practice. I find, however, that providing verbatim comments is sometimes the most useful part of the data provided. Typical questions we ask are "If you were to give this person one piece of advice what would it be?" or "What is one thing you most admire about this person?" I have increasingly found that connecting this feedback to validated personality inventories, such as the NEO-PIR or the Hogan Personality Assessment, makes it much more powerful. Many of the leaders I coach are what I call successful introverts—people whose personality scores reveal that they would rather connect to small groups or spend time alone than be occupied with socializing or reaching out to others. Such leaders have trained themselves to accept the social part of their roles; however, they need to be mindful of a tendency to withdraw from others. Often, they receive feedback that they don't recognize others enough or do not provide enough feedback themselves. For such leaders, connecting personality feedback to the behaviors rated in a 360-degree instrument is essential.

Even more important is the follow-up to feedback provided to leaders. My fellow coach, Dick Gauthier, speaks of the fact that 360-degree feedback is "just data; you need to talk to people to turn it into real information." I spend a great deal of time working with leaders on how they will react to feedback they have received, how they will ask others for further clarification without getting defensive, and how they will signal their sincerity to follow through on the changes they need to make.

More than any of these techniques, the coach's most powerful tool is who he or she is as a person. As a clinical psychologist, I have not only been through therapy regarding my own psychological issues but also had intensive feedback (a whole class of psychologists watching me work from behind a one-way mirror) that has formed my consciousness about what I do. Although coaching is not psychotherapy, I recommend that those without psychological training find supervision or peer support to monitor their own behavior, especially with clients who may evoke deep emotional reactions from them. I also think that coaches need to be grounded in personality theory, have an understanding of organizational structure and dynamics, and be experienced in career development, especially around the issue of career enhancers and derailers.

What is success? In leadership coaching, the true standard is for the coach and client to have made clear changes in behavior and performance that can be measured. The biggest downfall in coaching is focusing so much on the side of client confidentiality that the client's manager and the sponsoring company fall out of the loop. Many coaches wish to avoid reporting back to the company at all costs. I believe this to be a mistake for all sides involved. Leadership coaching requires the willingness of leaders to be accountable for making changes and raising their positive impact on others. It also requires some amount of self-disclosure. Leaders must be ready to take a risk by going public with not only their shortcomings, but also their goals for improvement. The coach's role is to support this courageous journey by providing tools for self-knowledge, anticipating the rough spots, and connecting a development plan to the demands of the leader's work and role. At its best, leadership coaching is a powerful means to help individuals translate their values into practical, positive action.

———⊰◆⊱———

Jim Moore

Jim Moore is currently an independent consultant working with the Alliance For Strategic Leadership Coaching & Consulting, where he helps clients build leadership development strategies and programs. His expertise includes the design of succession planning systems, leadership models, and customized executive education programs that help companies achieve their strategic objectives. He has led executive and leadership development organizations at three major corporations. He spent the first 20 years of his career on the doing side of the business as a line executive in the former Bell System. He holds a Masters in Electrical Engineering from the University of Louisville, Speed Scientific School. He is reachable by e-mail at jmoore@a4sl.com, by phone at (650) 328-7897, or via the Internet at www.A4SL.com.

My coaching/consulting practice is centered on helping clients create leadership development strategies, systems, and programs that support the achievement of business goals. My client is usually the head of Human Resources or the head of Executive/Leadership Development at a large corporation.

There are two key ingredients that ensure a successful engagement: the approach I use and the client. Of course, each engagement is different, and there is some art associated with success; however, over the years, I have developed the following guidelines to deal with each of these ingredients:

- *Start with the business.* The only reason a company should invest in leadership development is to positively impact the business. Therefore, leadership development processes, systems, and tools must be grounded in the business. Leadership development strategy creation should start with an analysis of the business—the business strategy, the marketplace challenges, the current performance issues, and so on. Linking leadership development to the business is the right thing to do for the shareholders, and it will help ensure organizational and financial success.

- *Be clear about the purpose of leadership development before designing a solution.* This sounds obvious; however, clients have hired me to help design a program without a clear understanding of why they were doing it. If the purpose is to build bench strength and a pipeline of talent, then the focus should be on creating a first-class succession planning process that identifies the highest potential talent, providing excellent development plans for those selected leaders, and managing their job experiences. If the purpose is to support the transformation of the company, it is critical to identify the specific transformations that need to be made and then touch lots of leaders in a high-impact way. If the purpose is to improve current operations, it is critical to conduct a thorough needs analysis to identify the critical knowledge and skill gaps and then touch as many leaders as possible in a high-impact way.

- *Produce cool-looking solutions AND help insure execution.* It's not enough to develop an elegant leadership development product that gets "oohs" and "aahs" when presented to other HR people at Linkage Leadership Conferences. (Although that does feel good!) If the leadership development product doesn't get implemented and benefits received over a sustained period of time, the effort cannot be considered a success, except for what was learned from the failure. Producing elegant leadership development products has almost become a commodity. There are many consultants and firms that can produce leadership development products that are as elegant as or more elegant than the products I help clients create. I don't try to differentiate myself by the elegance of the product. Studies at GE that led to the creation of their CAP model demonstrated that the failure of projects to achieve the desired benefits resulted more from a failure to consider the acceptance and support for the project rather than failures of design. I work with my clients to focus on building a supportive environment for the product as much or more than I work with them on the design of the product itself.

Some of the principles I use in building acceptance include the following:

- *Involving line managers in developing the product.* Line managers, when successfully integrated into the design process, can help ensure acceptance of the product when it is released. The concept is described in the phrase "If they build it, they will come."
- *Testing for simplicity, practicality, and focus.* Many of my clients are well educated in the behavioral sciences but have never held a line assignment. I am forever biased by my more than 20 years as a line manager and user (or sometimes victim) of HR products and services. Often, during the design process, I ask myself, "What would I have thought about this product in my line manager role?" Sometimes, I conclude that I would have called it "HR foo foo" or something even more obscene. When that happens, it's time to go back to the drawing board. The key questions I ask, to see if it passes the test of a line

manager, are "Does it help me do my job? Do I understand it? Does it matter if I do it right? Who cares?"

- *Branding.* Some clients find branding or marketing a product distasteful or even unprofessional. "The product should stand on its own merits!" I don't agree, and I shamelessly advocate putting bells and whistles around a leadership development product. Certainly, overhyping a product can backfire, but most of my clients err on the side of underhyping, or they want to surround the product with superficial words rather than a clear branding strategy.

- *Engaging the CEO.* People pay attention to and support what the CEO pays attention to and supports. I have found that many of my clients are reluctant to engage the CEO in the leadership development process. One reason for this reluctance is the barriers that organizations put around CEOs to protect them from access by people lower in the organization. Another is the HR person's fear of the CEO or his or her inability to communicate in language the CEO understands. I encourage my clients to blow through these barriers. Most CEOs are eager to get involved in leadership development activities, and when they are engaged, success is highly likely.

- *Using a common language for leadership.* As my colleague Marshall Goldsmith has said on many occasions, "Nobody fails to be a good leader because they fail to understand some complex theory of leadership." Everybody gets it. It's the doing that's hard. In addition, although most people understand the concepts, they use different language to describe it, making it difficult to focus the organization on specific leadership themes. I encourage my clients to develop a common language around leadership (a leadership model or profile) and reinforce it in multiple HR processes and tools.

- *Understanding the political environment.* A coach can be helpful to the client in helping him or her identify the people and actions that could derail the project and develop strategies to prevent this.

- *Creating the image.* This is the art of leadership development. How do you create an environment where executives are banging on your door to take advantage of your leadership development services? There is no prescription here. It means designing the whole experience including rewards, punishments, exclusivity, and so on. One of the best pieces of advice I ever received in my corporate leadership development life was from a line executive who told me that if the folklore is positive, the program will have a life of its own, but if the folklore is negative, it's over!

- *Making the client successful, not the coach/consultant.* Sometimes, it's easy to forget that the hero or heroine of a successful design should be the client, not the coach or consultant. It is important to involve the client in all aspects of the project and instill a feeling within the company that it is his or her work, not the work of the coach/consultant that made it successful.

There are also some factors critical to the client:

- *Access to senior management.* Because of the importance of CEO engagement in the final product, I prefer to work with clients who are either (1) positioned in the hierarchy to access the CEO, or (2) comfortable around senior executives by virtue of their senior-level perspective, or (3) a junior-level person who is not afraid to interact with senior-level people or demand access to them.
- *Willingness to push the envelope.* A conservative solution rarely has impact. To change a leader's behavior, it is usually necessary to take them out of their comfort zone. This requires some willingness to take risks on the part of the client in producing innovative and effective solutions. This can be a challenge, because after the engagement is over the client hopes to remain in the organization while the coach or consultant moves on.

As a first principle, success should be measured in the eyes of the client. Within the Alliance for Strategic Leadership Coaching & Consulting practice, we have a clear reminder of this principle. We tell clients that if they are not happy with our coaching or consulting efforts, they don't have to pay. So, one measure of success is whether I got paid or not.

In addition, I work with my clients to establish a set of metrics that will help them judge the success of our work. I have found that many clients struggle with identifying measures of success. They too often want a single, financial return on investment number that is elusive and requires many assumptions. Short of this ultimate measure, I help clients identify indicators of success that are easily measured and have credibility with line managers.

CHAPTER 7

Coaching for Organizational Change

Thought Leaders

PHIL HARKINS

W. WARNER BURKE

SALLY HELGESEN

R. ROOSEVELT THOMAS JR.

GIFFORD PINCHOT

DAVID DOTLICH

Practitioners

STRATFORD SHERMAN

GARY RANKER

LEIGH FOUNTAIN

BRUCE PFAU

THOUGHT LEADERS

Phil Harkins

GETTING THE ORGANIZATION TO CLICK

Phil Harkins is the President and CEO of Linkage, Inc., a global organizational development company that specializes in leadership development. A recognized expert on leadership and communications, Phil is the author of *Powerful Conversations: How High-Impact Leaders Communicate* as well as *Everybody Wins,* a book on the growth story and strategy of RE/MAX. Phil shares the chairmanship of Linkage's *Global Institute for Leadership Development* with Warren Bennis. He can be reached by e-mail at pharkins@linkageinc.com.

It's not easy shifting an organization to a new direction. No single leader, no matter how visionary, driven, or persuasive, can mandate such change to occur. Whether the shift derives from a change in the leadership team, a new capability, a reorganization, a product launch, or a next-generation information system, success hinges on the organization's willingness and capacity to execute. To secure the commitment and drive of others, the leader's relationship with his or her team must be high-functioning; diverse perspectives and agendas must be aligned with a common sense of mission; and passionate champions throughout the organization must be enlisted in the cause. It's a complex set of dynamics that few can manage unassisted. Enter the coach who helps the organization hit the ground running.

Unlike traditional coaching, which is typically one on one and focused on performance improvement, coaching for organizational change concerns the capabilities and relationships of any number of leaders and teams. The effective coach is part social psychologist and part organizational development expert with a sound business orientation and an acute understanding of what it takes to build alignment, teamwork, and trust. The objective is to get the organization onto the same page, singing from the same hymnal, charging in the same direction. Because so many people are involved and so much is at stake, doing so can seem like an overwhelming challenge. But in my experience, the essence is simple. It all comes down to creating a sense of click.

Understanding what it means to click on a personal level is easy. We need only think about our most energizing conversations to realize that those were the times when we were truly open, authentic, optimistic, and forward-directed. That same feeling is present in the best teams and highest functioning groups. In such cases, trust is implicit and unquestioned, and communication occurs at high levels. As a result, lengthy meetings and formal conversations are rarely necessary, while the focus is always in next steps. In the best circumstances, team members can anticipate each other's moves, ideas, and opinions while operating in the flow of the game, allowing for faster response times, more consistent alignment and creative leaps. As an organizational change coach, I try to instill that sense of click as widely as necessary. Imagine the power when such conversations and relationships are occurring across an organization in pursuit of a common objective.

The Role of the Coach in Organizational Change

The organizational change coach operates like a free safety—a football term for the player who can move freely around the field as the play requires. In other words, the coach must be able to work when and where the need arises, in order to facilitate the shift that is taking place.

First and foremost, the coach works behind the scenes with the leadership team to help them achieve their strategic objectives. The coach's role is not to assist in formulating the strategy so much as provide help in facilitating the strategic discussions and seeing that the agreed-upon strategy is then implemented. The coach works with the team to sift through the options and come to agreement around primary goals and best approaches. The coach then helps the team drive that strategy throughout the organization.

This is the fundamental distinction between coaching and traditional consulting. The consultant is expected to perform as part of the team, setting the strategy, designing the work plan, drawing up the realignment, or creating the product line for the organization to adopt and execute. The coach, on the other hand, works with the leadership team on its own agenda to maximize its capabilities. The coach stays in the background and shadows the actual players. Rather than being the focal point of the process, the coach seeks out the cracks and gaps by doing the prework, the in-between work, and the after-work needed to keep the organization on the move.

Sometimes, this means the coach is facilitating various teams. Other times, the coach is working one on one with key leaders—the CEO, general manager, product director, or other person in charge of the IT or M&A

implementation, for example. No matter what level the change initiative is being driven from, there's a wide gap between the strategy and the organization's capacity to get up and running. Frequently, the people within the organization find it difficult to perceive the true nature of their situation and the real barriers to change. An outsider with the right expertise can quickly size up those conditions and encapsulate them for others to be able to grasp. The coach provides the blueprint for that journey by defining current realities, laying out the desired future, identifying critical barriers, and plotting the way forward. The coach gets the leaders to face up to reality, identify the challenges that exist, and build attack plans for getting beyond the barriers.

The coach is there to create momentum, while keeping the organization motivated and energized toward the end game. To accomplish that objective, the coach creates alliances with passionate champions to spread the word from the vantage of key leverage points in the change process. The success of the intervention is measured not by the credit or recognition heaped on the coach, but by the achievements of the team or organization as a whole.

Credibility, Trust, and Click

Understandably, the organizational change coach must be able to develop rapport with a wide cast of characters. Different job roles, responsibilities, personality types, communication styles, and competence levels will be found among the key people. Although it may be impossible to be all things to all people, the organizational change coach must be flexible and fluid enough to create click within these situations. The background and skill set of the coach are critical in this regard.

First of all, the coach must have technical credibility. He or she needs a solid understanding of the overall business model as well as knowledge of what each part of the organization is doing. If the change initiative is occurring in a manufacturing environment, for example, the coach who has no experience in that business may find it difficult to gain traction. Similarly, for the organization that has just purchased an enterprise resource planning or supply chain solution, the coach who lacks an understanding of knowledge and workflow will be challenged to empathize with the difficulties that are being encountered.

The ideal organizational coach has worked in a functional organization, preferably one that has mass, meaning that he or she has experience with the complexities of various functions, roles, and responsibilities. In addition, the coach has studied organizations widely and understands intricacies and complexities, while also having a wellspring of benchmarks to compare and contrast what works and what doesn't. Although organizations are more similar than dissimilar in their functionality and dysfunctionality, certain sectors such as health care or financial services have distinct vertical qualities. In the health care industry, for example, although physicians may have many of the same competencies as their colleagues in engineering or research, the nature of their work and training creates a unique situation. Indeed, physicians are generally not experienced working in teams—and teaming is a critical competency in health care today.

Secondly, the coach must be highly skilled at communication. The best coaches are effective listeners, able to ask probing questions to obtain new levels of information. Over a series of many such interactions, the coach adds tremendous value. Understanding where each critical player is coming from and how they all perceive their role and benefit in the change enables the coach to facilitate with greater impact.

Obviously, confidentiality is a key concern in this regard. The difficulty, however, is that what is private to one person may be considered part of the normal flow of information to someone else. With that in mind, I always ask each person to tell me what is confidential and promise not to share whatever is private. Still, in many instances, people who discuss matters without reservation could be harmed if the specific details of those conversations were ever revealed. I make it a point in my own communication style to never make reference what another person has said. When presenting group information, I always declare what I am saying to be derived from the aggregate perspective.

It helps to have a contract or charter in place. The ground rules and conditions must be clear. Who is the client? Who makes decisions? Who should be approached for authorization? Having clear milestones and metrics in place also makes the job easier. If significant problems arise, what is the nature of the coach's mandate or authority for surfacing those obstacles? There are probably more people within the organization resistant to the change than those who are passionate about the vision, while many others become unwittingly mired in the swamp of day-to-day imperatives. To handle those kinds of challenges in the spirit of confidentiality, I make it clear to everyone that organizational objectives supercede individual ones, while promising to never divulge what someone tells me about another person, incident, or circumstance.

The organizational change coach is under constant review from multiple angles. Many are assessing how much that person can be trusted with every new situation that arises. It shouldn't be surprising. Much of what holds organizations back from change is fear and threat. The organization must be able to trust in the leadership and the coach before that fear and threat can be transformed into enthusiasm and commitment.

Trust is the foundation of any successful coaching engagement. The quality and impact of what emerges is directly related to the quality of the relationship. In one-on-one coaching, trust is established through open and honest communication. The organizational change coach is ultimately a facilitator of that trust on a larger scale. By acting as a roving go-between with a clearly defined mission, the coach is constantly working to uncover hopes and fears, to surface hidden dialogue, and to engage in critical conversations that lead to a shared agenda, deeper commitment, and greater alignment. In a sense, the coach is trying to engage the organization in a single powerful conversation that will produce a sense of click—the feeling that everyone is onboard, that all obstacles have been acknowledged, and that forward momentum is unstoppable.

Trust also must be validated in the long run. The coach is also there to make sure that the promises and commitments made around the change are fulfilled. It's all too easy for such lofty goals to be lost in the distance between vision and reality. But an organization will not sustain the impact of change without making sure that those promises are met.

The Learning Agenda

The future of coaching for organizational change is linked to the new pressures that organizations are experiencing. Five years ago, the emphasis was on rapid growth, total quality, leadership development, and customer intimacy. In the last three years, organizations have dealt with a radical downsizing of their strategies and development plans, which, in some cases, came at the expense of earlier initiatives. As we enter a new and hopefully smarter period of growth, many leaders are concerned with developing the organizational discipline to convert ideas into action. They want to get better at generating innovation while increasing productivity. In other words, the goal is to develop ideas that are sustainable, where the benefits can be reaped for a long time.

Organizational change coaches are well suited to facilitate success in this new direction. By definition, they work at providing long-term capabilities, not quick fixes. Indeed, sustainability is a hallmark of their success. To achieve that sustainability, the coach knows that it is not just the change that is valuable, but the learning that occurs along the way. Every conversation the coach has with the members of the leadership team and the passionate champions throughout the organization is geared toward three goals: deepening the relationship, creating alignment around a shared agenda, and furthering the learning process. In fact, it's the learning that serves as the true guidepost for how well the organization is progressing and how meaningful were its efforts.

<hr/>

W. Warner Burke

THINKING STRATEGICALLY DURING CHANGE

W. Warner Burke is the Edward Lee Thorndike Professor of Psychology and Education at Teachers College, Columbia University, and a Fellow of the Academy of Management, the American Psychological Society, and the Society of Industrial and Organizational Psychology. He is the author, coauthor, editor, or coeditor of 14 books, including *Organizational Development: A Process of Learning* and, most recently, *Organization Change: Theory and Practice*. He can be reached by phone at (212) 678-3831 or by e-mail at burke1@exchange.tc.columbia.edu.

Whether implementing a change or trying to deal with change that has been mandated, the job of the modern executive is fraught with complexity. People are inundated with conflicts around the decisions they must make. As soon as one set of demands has been made, another conflicting set emerges. Those conflicts may revolve around values or resources, or simply the speed with which new demands keep coming.

As a coach, I work with people in leadership positions who are trying to manage or bring about organizational change. Naturally, there are larger strategic issues in what the change is all about. My coaching is therefore to help those leaders make sense of the strategic implications of change in a way that enables them to deal more effectively with the pressures they are under. In doing so, I focus on the person, not the role or job. In my view, there's no such thing as a person playing a role or conducting a job. You need to understand who the person is, what his or her personality is all about, and how that affects the role that the person is in—and vice versa.

The first thing I do is help the client understand the priorities of the demands he or she faces. Together, we look at the bigger picture in terms of the external environment. Depending on the client's job, the external environment may be the corporation itself. From there, we go to mission and strategy, then to culture and leadership. On an individual level, we start with goals, then go to roles and responsibilities, procedures and relationships, until we understand the context of the client's position in line with objectives and strategies.

A client who is driving change may find him or herself in a strange position within the organization. Although the CEO may designate that person with power, formal authority does not necessarily come with the job. The role of change agent may demand that he or she functions in new ways as a politician and persuader in lining up other executives to back the cause. Other people find themselves dealing with formal roles that have changed because of larger organizational changes or even a change in customer. Still others may need to bolster their position and organize their team and resources to do their job well. The job of coach is to help those people sort out these multiple demands and determine the part they play, while keeping in mind the change strategy of the organization.

Along the way, I seize moments to teach. I don't call it teaching, but I do believe that a good teacher is a coach and a good coach is a teacher. If there are issues we encounter that can be dealt with more effectively, I take just a few minutes to explain something or tell a story that the person can use as a concept, framework, or model to think through a problem and alleviate some of the pressure.

It's important to be able to listen. Although that may be a given for a coach, it is certainly not sufficient for success, and is an absolute necessity to be able to do well. Empathy is part of that. Can I put myself in another person's shoes? When I work with someone, I am always asking him or her, "What are the pressures you are experiencing? What are the forces that are coming in on you?" These pressures and forces could be coming from the boss, the customers or internal clients, for example. I want the person I am working with to describe to me what that is like, and how he or she feels about it. Doing so helps me open the client up and understand their perspective, and gives me important information and a feel for what it is they are going through.

I try to establish a personal relationship with the client. Being a psychologist is helpful in that regard. I rely on therapeutic techniques to assist with my coaching. Therapy training allows me to ask questions, confront and push with a certain level of expertise. I am trying to move the person to try or do something that is different from what he or she is doing now. But there must be a comfort zone within which risks can be taken. A keen awareness of the psychological implications of personal and organizational change is valuable in that regard.

Just as the pressure on leaders has intensified greatly in recent years, so too the expectations for coaches have risen as well. Much of that pressure comes in a form that is antithetical to effective coaching. There are time constraints that do not always meet the needs of good coaching. There is a demand for progress that may fit the time line of organizational plans, but not the time line of behavior change. It is a challenge for coaches to do that well and with integrity. Yet that is the reality of the pressure that organizational change places on us all.

━━◆━━

Sally Helgesen

COACHING ANTHROPOLOGY

 Sally Helgesen is the author of *The Web of Inclusion: A New Architecture for Building Great Organizations,* in which she explores how innovative organizations make use of the talents and ideas of all their people, learning lessons in transformation in the process. She is also the author of *The Female Advantage: Women's Ways of Leadership.* She can be reached at sally@sallyhelgesen.com.

My coaching is done in the service of driving organizational change. To accomplish that, I engage in a deep, narrative study of how the leaders in the organization do their jobs, in the context of the organization's culture. Out of that understanding, I analyze how well that leadership style is suited to the change that is desired. I have come to think of my approach as similar to the way in which a cultural anthropologist does field research, with one significant difference. Although an anthropologist aims to preserve a culture or leave it as undisturbed as possible, I am helping the culture adapt to new technologies, new economics, new markets, more globalization, or the need for faster response times. It goes without saying that such issues are rampant in businesses and institutions today.

My skills in coaching anthropology grew in part from experience researching *The Female Advantage: Women's Ways of Leadership.* For that book, I conducted diary studies of women who are leading organizations. Henry Mintzberg had done the classic study of management in *The Practice of Management,* using diary studies as well. But Mintzberg's method was very quantitative. He recorded when a manager got into the office each morning, how much time was spent in meetings, how many decisions were made each day. Rather than apply a similar quantitative study to women leaders, I took a much more narrative approach by following them through their daily work lives. I recorded very specific and detailed notes about what they did; how they managed and interacted with people; how they scheduled, organized, and structured their time; and how much of their job they devoted to internal versus external issues. By focusing so precisely and concretely on details and behaviors, I was able to develop a full conception of how their leadership style impacted the culture of the organization.

By developing diary studies of both male and female leaders, I use that same anthropological approach when I work with organizations driving large-scale change. Whether the organization is a consumer products company, an industrial manufacturing business or a quintessentially modern NGO (Non-Governmental Organization), I look at how leadership style impacts personal interactions, strategy, and the capacity to change. Through that analysis, I capture the distinct strengths, issues, or challenges the organization faces in terms of its leadership. The organization uses that topographical map as the basis for necessary changes to its structure, training, approach, and strategy.

An actual example of some work done in the international, not-for-profit sector will help clarify the value this approach has for today's organizations. Recently, I was brought in by the United Nations Development Program (UNDP) to help it adapt to a major shift in how development is done. The UNDP is a geographically dispersed organization, with local offices in every country in the world. Those offices were structured and led in a way that reflected the UNDP's traditional role of working closely with host country governmental hierarchies. In recent years, however, NGOs have arisen as a means of bypassing traditional hierarchies and power structures in meeting the needs of local populations. As the primary coordinator of international development aid, the UNDP had essentially undergone a change in its client base, with significant implications for its own culture and approach. Specifically, NGOs, run in a very networked and inclusive way, are effective in using decentralized technology, and are open to strategic ideas from leaders at all levels. The UNDP had little experience with this decentralized, grassroots style, and needed to adapt in order to be an effective service provider to this growing constituency.

I was brought in to meet with the leaders (known as resident representatives) and staff of 10 country offices, which would serve as centers of experimentation for the kind of leadership shift the UNDP needed to make. My initial job was to lay out the changes in thinking, style, and training that would help the leadership become more flexible and networked in their approach. We did some initial training around those ideas. A year later, I followed that up with an in-depth anthropological observation of multiple centers of experimentation to determine how effectively the transformation was taking place.

The offices were in Pakistan, Zimbabwe, and Egypt. I lived in each of those countries for several weeks, shadowing the leaders of the country offices and doing diary studies of their ways of working. Following that, I interviewed the people around those key leaders extensively, as one might do in a traditional 360-degree survey. Then, I went into the field to spend time with the primary NGOs the country offices were coordinating. Out of that research came a major report that was highly specific in detail and fairly profound in its evaluation of the traits of leadership that reflected the culture of the UNDP country offices. The strengths of these traits measured the progress that the UNDP had made in transforming to meet its new reality, while the weaknesses indicated the work that had yet to be done.

Rather than an academic or theoretical model, I think of such reports as narratives describing the real story of an organization. The value resides in the articulation of how things work in practice and what that feels like on a day-to-day basis. Organizations are rarely able to observe and analyze why they do what they do. Despite whatever strategy, mission, or values may formally be in place, most are operating by the seat of their pants, without the time and mental space to consciously deliberate on the gaps between perceived direction and reality.

Although bottom-line orientation can make some organizations resistant to an open, searching analysis of culture and leadership, I have found that there are significant and lasting bottom-line results to the approach. In particular, large organizations are recognizing, in these economically challenging times, that they need to attend to their core businesses or core customers with more precision and focus. Articulating leadership style in the context of the culture helps people get in touch with the nature of that core. It can demonstrate whether subsidiaries fit with the culture or whether a particular market is in line with the overall strategy or how various internal service providers fit into the mix. This method also addresses what I have found to be a buried issue in many organizations, namely the fear of losing identity in a world in which the customer, the market, and the competition are always top of mind. An anthropological approach has the potential to provide a way for the organization to listen more closely to customers and key stakeholders, without losing touch with identity and purpose. Drucker talks about the importance of having a clearly defined mission; I would add that it is equally important to have a clearly defined culture. It allows the organization to think and act freely in an ever-changing world, without losing its orientation.

To be a coaching anthropologist in the service of organizational change, I think one must have several key attributes. First, it is necessary to have an aptitude for what academics call appreciative inquiry, meaning the ability to dig deep on an issue, while keeping one eye out for optimal solutions. Second, one must have an interviewing talent that allows the conversation to take off from any predetermined questions and explore the areas and dilemmas that surface. This ability, I'm afraid, is more art than science, although it certainly grows with experience. It is also one of the aspects that make coaching an exciting interpersonal journey rather than a methodical management science.

There are attributes that predispose the client to being successful as well. When I selected my interviewees in the *Female Advantage,* I looked for people who could fully articulate why and how they did things. Similarly, with organizations, I look for clients who do not give mere lip service to change. When the gap between ideology and practice, or word and deed, is too large, it can be difficult to make headway. I find that it is also difficult to work with organizations that aren't inclusive by nature. If the organization is not open-minded about drawing ideas from a broad platform of employees, that heads-versus-hands orientation can indicate a split in the culture. No matter how much I work with such leaders, I doubt that the efforts have much impact on the culture at large.

Finally, I look for organizations that are interested in building a sustainable culture. We have witnessed too much flash and glitz in recent years from companies that lacked sustainability. It is my belief that economic development at a community and country level is impacted by the sustainability of its larger organizations and institutions. Coaching anthropology done in the service of organizational change is in-depth, painstaking work. I see the value in those efforts as greatly enhanced by the organization's interest in sustaining its own development over time.

———⟫◆⟪———

R. Roosevelt Thomas Jr.

COACHING FOR STRATEGIC DIVERSITY MANAGEMENT™

 Dr. R. Roosevelt Thomas Jr., CEO of Roosevelt Thomas Consulting & Training, Inc. and President/Founder of the American Institute for Managing Diversity, has been at the forefront of developing and implementing innovative strategies for maximizing organizational and individual potential for over two decades. He is the author of four published books: *Beyond Race and Gender: Unleashing the Total Power of Your Workforce by Managing Diversity, Redefining Diversity, Building a House for Diversity,* and *Giraffe and Elephant, A Diversity Fable.* He can be reached by phone at (404) 212-0070, by e-mail at rthomas@rthomasconsulting.com, or via the Internet at www.rthomasconsulting.com.

Coaching is usually considered to be a very personal endeavor, a kind of sorting through an individual's decisions and options in line with an agenda. The coaching that I do is typically with a group of leaders struggling with an organizational challenge related to diversity. Although my coaching focuses on the organization instead of the individual, the sense of working through decisions and options in line with a strategy remains very strong.

I think of diversity differently from most people. I define diversity as the differences and similarities that can exist among the elements of a mixture. The greater the number of differences relative to similarities, the more diverse the mixture. The greater the amount of similarities relative to differences, the more homogeneous the mixture.

What does this mean with respect to workforce diversity? For starters, diversity does not refer to brute statistics around how many minorities or women are represented in the workforce, but rather to the differences and similarities that exist among all members of the workforce. Those differences and similarities can be with respect to race, educational background, work experience, age, tenure with organization, gender, sexual orientation, and/or geographic origin—just to name a few possibilities. Diversity, in other words, can occur along an infinite number of dimensions along which people can be different or similar.

There also can be differences and similarities among other workplace mixtures; such as, acquisitions/mergers/joint ventures, customers, brands, lines of business, functions, suppliers, headquarters/field, and strategic alternatives. Strategic Diversity Management™, then, becomes the process of making quality decisions about any collective mixtures with strategic implications for the organization. Stated differently, Strategic Diversity Management™ is the process of making quality decisions in the midst of differences, similarities, and tensions. I am convinced that if you have diversity of any kind, you will have related diversity tension. The objective of Diversity Management is not to reduce or eliminate the tension, but rather to develop a capability for making quality decisions in spite of tension. In the context of how I define diversity, the acquisition of a Strategic Diversity Management™ capability usually requires a mind-set shift.

Typically, when I am brought into an organization, I initially meet with a group of senior executives, frequently the CEO and his or her direct reports, who are grappling with the organizational implications of what they consider to be a diversity issue. After I clarify my views on diversity in an executive briefing, I lead the senior team through an exploration of the Strategic Diversity Management Process™ and its key concepts and how this framework can benefit their organization. Typically, this exercise takes place in what I refer to as a Strategic Thinking Session. Once an executive team gets the mind-set shift, this new perspective allows those leaders to view the concept of diversity in terms of their overall mission, vision, and strategy.

If organizational leaders have been thinking of diversity in the context of race or gender, the mind-set shift empowers them to broaden their contemplation of diversity management to other mixtures that may also have strategic significance. An organization may, for example, have a diversity issue with two functions that are strategically critical. It may need better integration between two divisions. It may have a problem between corporate and field, with each segment focusing on its parochial agendas, despite continual alignment efforts. Or a corporation's growth-through-acquisitions strategy may suffer because of an inability to cope with cultural diversity. Failure to excel in Strategic Diversity Management™—the making of quality decisions in the midst of similarities, differences and tensions—can greatly hinder a company's effectiveness in many arenas.

Sometimes, it can take months for the implications of the mind-set shift to sink in. As a coach I am there to talk through that transition. If I'm working with an individual who is struggling with the corporation's adoption of Strategic Diversity Management™, then I provide encouragement, suggest points that can provide greater leverage, and explain what I have seen work before and how those ideas can be put into action and generate Strategic Diversity Management™ capability. The importance of that support should not be underestimated. It takes courage, intellectual resources, and strategic readiness to go against the grain successfully. And Strategic Diversity Management™, as I define it, goes against the grain of how most managers traditionally have thought about diversity.

Although I believe clarity about the business rationale is critical if sustainable progress is to be made with Strategic Diversity Management™, as coach my role is not to develop the business case. The leaders of the organization themselves must identify the critical diversity mixtures that are unique to their circumstances and offer opportunity for strategic gain. The question should be "Where can I enhance our bottom-line through application of the Strategic Diversity Management™ framework?"

Often, I am engaged to help bring the process to the implementation stage. A major component of that work focuses on diagnostic research to determine the location and causes of diversity tensions, and also the nature of the organization's culture roots and their compatibility with the leaders' diversity aspirations. These research findings become the context for intervention planning, which could involve changing culture, systems, or policies, as well as training and education. The latter, it should be noted, is different from training. Education is about mind-set shift, not skill sets. If Strategic Diversity Management™ is to succeed, mind-set shifts will need to occur not just at the top of the organization but throughout the hierarchy as well.

When leaders consider hiring a "diversity" coach, they should be clear about what they mean by "diversity." Sometimes, leaders are interested in helping people who are different navigate better. In other cases, executives are looking for someone to design an affirmative action program. An increasing number of others are seeking coaching in dealing with differences and similarities in general. Diversity is an issue that can mean different things to different people. Executives definitely should seek a coach who matches their diversity focus and aspirations.

Before you can select and accept a Strategic Diversity Management™ coach, you have to recognize that there's a game called Strategic Diversity Management™. For example, leaders have come to rely on leadership coaches because they accept that there is a domain called leadership. Only a few short years ago, the idea of educating senior executives was an alien one. Now you would be hard-pressed to find anyone who does not subscribe to that idea.

Once the game of leadership gained legitimacy, the logic for coaching evolved. If continuous learning can really occur, and is in fact necessary for leaders to be successful, then it would be nice to have a coach to turn to during the middle of the game and ask, "What do you think? Do you see something that I'm doing right or wrong? What kind of feedback can you give me?"

Similarly, with respect to Strategic Diversity Management™, as it gains credibility as a field, senior executives will seek Strategic Diversity Management™ coaches. It has been only in recent years that I have been asked to coach. This is a result of leaders deciding that Strategic Diversity Management™ is a legitimate game. And, once again, I stress the distinction between Strategic Diversity Management™ and diversity. As more executives decide that there is a game, more will determine that it is one worth winning.

<hr />

Gifford Pinchot

COACHING INNOVATION LEADERS

Gifford Pinchot leads Pinchot & Company, a firm that helps companies to reduce bureaucratic obstacles, and to design and implement more effective and sustainable business practices. He is also Chairman of the Bainbridge Island Graduate Institute, one of the first business schools to focus on sustainable business practices (www.bgiedu.org). His best-selling book, *INTRAPRENEURING: Why You Don't Have to Leave the Corporation to Become an Entrepreneur,* defined the ground rules for an emerging field of enterprise: the courageous pursuit of new ideas in established organizations. He can be reached by phone at (206) 780-2800 or via the Internet at www.pinchot.com.

Coaching innovation leaders is a whole system task. The issues in a single assignment may range from personality issues, through dealing effectively with the organizational immune system, to dealing with a tough competitor.

Business strategy and personal leadership style, the individual and the team, psychological issues and organizational one, are all intertwined.

We coach five types of innovation leaders:

1. Inventors
2. Intrapreneurial leaders
3. Intrapreneurial teams
4. Sponsors of innovation
5. Climate makers

Inventors

Inventors often come with built-in headwinds when it comes to getting their ideas implemented. Either they must become intrapreneurs themselves, which is a major transition in viewpoint, or they need to learn to enroll and work with intrapreneurs who can bring their ideas into commercial reality. Normally, inventors are not given coaches, so we end up coaching them informally as part of some other assignment. However, in some cases, a particular inventor will be so prolific and important to a company's success that they are given their own coach.

Intrapreneurial Leaders

Ideas and inventions go nowhere in a large organization unless someone takes on the entrepreneurial role of making them happen. We call those who behave like entrepreneurs inside a larger organization intrapreneurs.

Coaching innovation leaders generally includes helping them bring out and/or manage the entrepreneurial side of their nature. Intrapreneurs tread a narrow path between expressing the impatience needed to overcome the lethargy of an established firm and the need to avoid being rejected as foreign to the culture. The coaches of intrapreneurial leaders support the courage to act boldly and choose ways of behaving that will cause fewer political problems. They have to encourage both a participatory leadership style that gets the most from the team and the ability to make quick decisions and rapid reversals when something is not working. The best coaches for intrapreneurs have struggled with these dilemmas themselves. They have been entrepreneurs or intrapreneurs long enough to have a deeply rooted understanding of the issues.

When we are asked to coach an intrapreneurial leader to remove dysfunctional behaviors that are getting in the way of business success, we do not overfocus on what's wrong; we spend more attention on increasing our client's behavioral options. The end goal is to help intrapreneurs make the most of their strengths. In focusing on getting their strengths to be more effective they can explore alternatives to the behaviors that are getting in the way and learn to delegate things they don't do well. People can let go of what's blocking them more easily if they are feeling good about moving ahead with strengths that are already working.

There is a certain conspiratorial tone in intrapreneurial coaching. As coaches, we are on the side of our intrapreneurial client. This often finds us siding with our client in opposition to the systems and people who are trying to block the new idea. This gives us the leverage to work on the behavioral issues as a friend rather than as a representative of "the system." On the other hand, we are often peacemakers, helping the client to see others in a more positive light so that they can collaborate rather than fight. The goal when coaching intrapreneurial leaders is to help them become more effective in turning ideas and technologies into profitable business success.

Intrapreneurial Teams

We do a lot of work with the whole intrapreneurial team as well as with their leader. These teams are developing something new for a company and struggling with how to make it happen. We coach them in everything from business strategy to personal leadership, from managing the immune system to personal development—all the issues involved in launching a successful business.

Breakdowns in teamwork are one of the two most common causes of innovation failure. If the team is not fully functional, we coach them on team work, sometimes focusing on how the members of the team are behaving relative to each other, sometimes taking the leader or a team member aside if a particular behavior is a central concern. We also use performance challenges with teams, to help the team to "catch themselves in the act of being themselves." Once they see how they behave under stress and the consequences in terms of team performance, they establish new team operating principles and gradually learn to live by them.

Sponsors of Innovation

Every intrapreneurial team needs sponsors, higher-level managers who protect and guide them. Many managers and even executives have very little idea what effective sponsorship looks like. They underestimate the time commitment and see themselves mainly as funders. Equally critical is their role as coaches. We have to help sponsors learn to be good coaches without taking over the team's ability to make its own decisions. An individual with high status can ask an innocent question and be interpreted as having issued an order. We also help sponsors to recognize and foster the intrapreneurial spirit. This helps them to make better decisions about what to fund and to be more effective in coaching the teams they are sponsoring.

Climate Makers

A number of our clients are working to create a general environment that brings out cost-effective innovation. Their most innovative people are also troublesome and challenging to manage. Some of their people are routinely blocking innovation. Some aspects of the culture make the innovator's job too hard. Even some of their own actions and ways of thinking are inhibiting others' ability to innovate. We help them find and build on the positives that exist and to work on a few high-leverage changes that will create space for innovation to flourish.

We often find that our climate maker clients face significant challenges. Repeatedly, money has been spent, staff assigned, and yet the innovation projects keep falling way behind schedule. How do we make innovation pay off? What is holding things up?

Perhaps, the client has already put in place a formal system and processes to drive innovation. These systems are often counterproductive to cost-effective innovation. Innovation in particular is almost always driven by the informal rather than the formal organization. Unless it already has the support of the informal organization, an innovative idea that arises at the bottom of the organization has little chance of getting up through the formal decision system. We coach climate makers on how to fix the formal systems so that profitable innovations are more likely to get through in a timely manner.

In these cases, we are working with senior leaders above the level of intrapreneurs and even many sponsors. We begin with their mental model of an innovative organization. Does it fit the somewhat chaotic way in which innovation actually happens? As we are invited to do so, we also coach them on their behavior and the behavior of their direct reports. How are they affecting the organization? We talk about the ways in which the organization supports the five roles of innovation, including inventors, intrapreneurs, innovation teammates, sponsors, and climate matters. Senior leaders want to understand how the strategies, policies, actions, and management styles can support the organization's ability to innovate.

A Good Client

A good client is serious about innovation. Many people pretend to be, but really aren't. We can help them realize how much risk they are willing to take and to align what they begin with what they are likely to finish. It helps if they have courage and are coming to the challenge from a safe base in both a psychological and an organizational sense. It's counterproductive to coach someone to take on the risks inherent in innovation if they are inherently fearful of mistakes or objectively in a position of great career risk. To innovate, innovators must make many significant decisions for which there is not good data. They have to trust their intuition, and chances are that it won't always be right.

A Good Innovation Coach

A good innovation coach needs business acumen, based on direct experience. Innovation is not just about process. Coaches need to be able to recognize a good business proposition when they see one and to help shape it in the direction of greater success. They need to see the weak points in a strategy and ask the specific questions that challenge the parts of that proposition that need toughening up.

Psychological acumen is also a critical success factor. The coach must be able to see what's going on in terms of the effect the client is having on the team, other parts of the organization, and those they are selling to. The coach helps the client move to the next level of effectiveness. This is not a routine process. A good innovation coach must act in the teachable moment to point out the options when something is happening that makes the issues clear and available for learning.

People struggling with innovation are facing whole system challenges. Finding a coach with the appropriate business and psychological acumen is not easy. On top of that, sustainability is emerging as a core strategy for creating new opportunities and getting the jump on coming business challenges. Striving for sustainability stimulates creative thinking and engages intrapreneurial passion. Knowledge of sustainability gives the innovation manager another tool that can guide people to opportunities that will serve the company well in both the short and long-term. A good innovation coach brings experience, humor, and excitement to the challenges that clients face.

—————◦◦◦————

David Dotlich

CREATING A THEORY FOR CHANGE

David Dotlich, CEO and Managing Partner of CDR International, a Mercer Delta Company, consults to executive committees, CEOs, and senior leaders in the areas of leadership, business strategy, and executive coaching. Prior to founding CDR International, Dr. Dotlich was Executive Vice President of Groupe Bull, and Corporate Vice President of Human Resources for Honeywell International. Prior to that he was a professor on the faculty of the University of Minnesota, teaching in the Business School and the Department of Speech-Communication. He is the coauthor with Peter Cairo of three books: *Why CEOs Fail: The 11 Behaviors that Can Derail Your Climb to the Top—And How To Manage Them; Action Coaching: How to Leverage Individual Performance for Company Success;* and *Unnatural Leadership: Going Against Intuition and Experience to Develop Ten New Leadership Instincts.* With Jim Noel, he coauthored *Action Learning: How the World's Best Companies Develop Their Top Leaders and Themselves* and the forthcoming book, *Head, Heart, and Guts.* He can be reached by e-mail at David.Dotlich@CDR-intl.com.

Despite the number of books that have been written about change, few leaders have developed their own theory for how change happens. A lot of the coaching I do is to help people elicit, form, or create their own theory for making change occur in their work, their organizations, or their lives.

The people I coach fall into three broad categories. Most are CEOs or senior leaders of Fortune 50 companies or global organizations. A coaching engagement with someone at that level is rarely limited to a single issue or challenge. Instead, we move back and forth together, covering organizational and business challenges as well as personal and life issues. A second kind of coaching that I do occurs with executives engaged in action learning programs. These are shorter relationships designed to link behavior to business requirements. The third area of coaching is with line executives and heads of Human Resources driving organizational change by linking business strategy with learning initiatives.

Before we begin, I discern whether the people I am coaching know what they want to accomplish and where they want to go. Although they usually know what they need to achieve or develop, they often lack an understanding of how change happens. Sometimes, however, we need to back up and develop clarity about where they want to take the organization or determine the defined objectives they want to meet. From there, we develop a theory for how that change will take place, and we discover the critical action steps needed to travel that path.

All coaching is a process of dialogue. When coaching for change, the coach elicits the individual's implicit and explicit understanding of the challenges that will get in the way. These can include forces of resistance, systemic or technical issues, internal politics, the dynamics of power, and the organization's own embedded values. Once we've surfaced all potential blockers, we do some analysis of the systemic elements of the change process and put a change plan in place. Although I am agnostic about change models, I am particularly fond of John Kotter's, Noel Tichy's, Meg Wheatley's, Warner Burke's and David Nadler's methodologies for driving change. Usually, the person I am coaching ends up subscribing to one of those approaches in his or her own words.

There are four levels, or coaching goals, at which a coach can work with someone during the change process. The first level is self-awareness. A coach can be very helpful in giving an individual, especially at senior levels, a perspective that others in the organization can't or won't provide. This involves developing an understanding of strengths and weaknesses, motivations and the general makeup of emotional intelligence—essentially holding a mirror for the individual to take a good look at him or herself. Although valuable, a lot of coaching starts at this level and goes no deeper.

The second level of coaching is improvement. Improvement concerns moving from self-awareness to a higher performance level. This movement can be measured in any number of ways from major metrics like revenue growth and operating profits to individual goals such as a change in communication habits, a longer attention span, or an improvement in the level of personal engagement.

The third level of coaching is about breakthroughs. Good leaders such as Jack Welch and others have taught us that it really is possible to reconceptualize what we're doing in a truly radical way. In coaching for breakthroughs, much of what I do is provide information about what leaders are doing in the field. I ask provocative questions and help people think about things differently. I might ask: "Why *not* cut inventory by 40 percent?" or "Why *can't* you run three shifts instead of two?" In my experience, simple, provocative questions and ideas can sometimes seem inconceivable to a person who comes from within the system.

The fourth level of coaching for change is about transformation. Transformations are rare and difficult, but always significant. They can involve a transformation of the individual, the organization or the way the leader thinks about things. An executive may move from being a functional manager to a general manager, and require an entirely different outlook or approach.

An organization may shift from product-driven to bundling services, requiring a transformational change in systems, skills, and strategy. Coaching for transformations involves helping people to reconceive themselves, their roles, or their organizations in a whole new way.

To be a successful change coach, I think it's less important to have a personal theory about change than it is to be able to recognize and embrace a good one. It also helps, I believe, to have an understanding of power and how power does or does not drive change. A coach needs to be adaptive and flexible in order to understand where the client is going and the uniqueness of his or her situation. Certainly, the ability to provide nonjudgmental listening goes a long way. It may be an old counseling technique, but it's amazing how many people in senior levels simply need to talk and be heard by someone without an agenda.

So much of a successful coaching relationship is based on chemistry and trust, and how quickly that can be established. The coach needs the capacity to get on the individual's wave length, to understand their business drivers, to intuit their culture, and to really see who they are. To do so, the coach need to cut through all the trappings. This takes a certain amount of personal clarity and self-awareness. I think senior executives can smell caution, ambivalence, or confusion in a coach and can sense how grounded he or she is as a way of evaluating how the coach can help ground the client in turn. A coach also needs a certain sense of detachment. As someone who follows Buddhist principles, I really believe that detachment is critical in helping people understand how their own attachments create suffering and pain, particularly during change.

My own coaching journey has involved a number of stages. I started out as an academic, then went on to business, then went back to academics and moved on to consulting. Much of my philosophy and point of view is based on having lived and worked in different systems, experiences that have helped me a great deal. I think it's important to always consider carefully who the client actually is in any coaching engagement. When I was in graduate school many years ago, I studied with Jack Sherwood. His advice to me was to "remember that the client is always the system." Although that may be easier said than done, I try to think in those terms when I enter into a coaching relationship. Coaching does not begin or end with the person you are coaching. The client may not be the person you are working with directly but may in fact, include the direct reports, the person paying the bill, the shareholders, or the organization itself. Sometimes, these interests are contradictory, and a good coach needs to consciously sort through his or her loyalties. I don't have a rigid set of rules in this regard, but I do think it's important to reflect on the question if only to realize that the change you are working toward may be viewed differently, depending on the stakeholder group.

PRACTITIONERS

Stratford Sherman

 Stratford Sherman brings world-class expertise in leadership and organizational change to his work as an executive coach. Strat's coaching helps successful senior executives and high potentials expand their capabilities and responsiveness in the context of change—*any* kind of change. During the early 1990s, Strat earned his global reputation with the publication of *Control Your Destiny or Someone Else Will,* the first serious study of Jack Welch's transformation of GE and a bestseller that is still taught in top business schools. Strat has lectured extensively, delivered seminars on six continents, taught at GE's Crotonville School, and appeared as a commentator on many TV shows, including *The News Hour* and *Charlie Rose.* Strat is a Senior Vice President of Executive Coaching Network, Inc. His coaching clients include Pitney Bowes, Oracle, and Coach Inc. A Harvard graduate, Strat is married and lives in Connecticut with his wife and two teenaged children. He can be reached by e-mail at stratsherman@excn.com, via the Internet at www.excn.com, or by phone at (203) 778-5481.

My coaching practice is dedicated to helping successful senior executives and high potentials expand their capabilities in the context of change. The skills of adaptation and responsiveness are critical success factors in a fast-moving, intensely challenging business environment. The most successful executives are the ones most likely to face new challenges, often through promotion. Business combinations and/or reorganizations occur ever more frequently. At the same time, economic, technological, and competitive conditions require endless adjustments. Developing adaptive skills, however, requires more sustained focus and effort than many active executives can muster by themselves.

Coaching can provide the structure and stimulus needed for the improvement of adaptive skills. My approach is based on the Executive Coaching Network's Strategic Executive Coaching Process, described on www.excn.com. It synthesizes at least three categories of understanding: business dynamics; organizational change; and individual development.

The first requirement is a clear, objective understanding of the present situation. Corporate executives benefit when coaching is grounded in the business imperatives governing the organization, and in the specific variables that define the operating environment—from cash flow to the temperaments of colleagues. Just as important, in dynamic situations, is the coach's familiarity with the predictable patterns and stresses of organizational change. Finally, it is essential to acknowledge and honor the individual nature—the humanity— of the coachee.

For such coaching to be meaningful and produce sustained benefit, it must facilitate a closer alignment of the individual coachee and the employing organization. Alignment is important, because most of us achieve results through relationships with others. To support success, the alignment must be genuine, deeply grounded, and conscious. Once alignment is attained, it becomes easier, at times even effortless, for the executive to respond to rapid, large-scale change in harmony with the organization.

No less important is personal integrity. This does not mean socially acceptable behavior or compliance with rules. Integrity is a matter of integration, becoming whole. It depends on recognition of the requirements of one's inner nature and on consistently behaving in accord with them. A professionally qualified executive who embodies integrity, and also is aligned with the goals of the organization, is capable of limitless achievement.

This coaching occurs at a level deeper than behavior; its concern is with the impulses that cause behavior. The coaching process takes time: rarely less than 4 months, usually between 6 and 12 months. The coachee and I will meet in person for at least a couple of hours, not less than once per month. The standard contract provides unlimited access throughout the coaching period, including shadowing, attending meetings, and communication through phone calls and e-mail. At the end of two months, if the chemistry isn't working, either party may opt out of the coaching relationship without penalty.

We begin with information. In addition to the usual 360-degree evaluation and personality tests, which I can conduct if they are not already available, I prefer to interview key stakeholders in the coachee's career. I present the feedback to the coachee, placing it in context. Next, we develop a plan of action. Each coaching engagement is focused on a very specific, actionable intention. The intended outcome must be important to both coachee and employer, and it must be definable and observable. Then we get to work.

It is marvelously difficult to describe what goes on behind closed doors between coach and coachee. Most of what happens is alert inquiry, usually related to specific business challenges, always in the context of our shared intention. We look for patterns, and when we find them, we try to understand them at the source. We explore areas of conflict, difficulty, and obstruction. We explore areas of strength, confidence, and certainty. Above all, we do our best to see the complete picture, putting each element in context and striving to make sense of the whole. We define specific responses to challenges, test them in action, and carefully review results. We learn as we go along, improving our understanding of how to realize integrity, alignment, ease, and adaptation.

The coachee does nearly all of the work; the coach serves as an informed, supportive ally who facilitates the coachee's development of understanding. By acquiring understanding, coachees empower themselves. They tap their own resources more fully and effectively to reach their defined goals. What a coach can bring to bear in this process is brains, sensitivity, experience, objectivity, commitment, heart, and—on good days—wisdom. Homework assignments rarely require much investment of time, focusing instead on building awareness and testing ideas in action.

Usually, it is obvious when the engagement is complete. When coaching is successful, the coachee has integrated new understandings and skills into daily behavior, and has learned methods of self-monitoring, self-correction, and ongoing development. The coach becomes redundant and departs. A successful coaching process promotes integrity, confidence, and ease with change. It produces clarity and objective understanding about the interplay of the coachee's nature with the organization and the larger business environment. It powerfully enhances the conscious alignment of personal and business imperatives. The measurable result of the coaching is a beneficial change in the coachee's attitude, behavior, and work product, a change that is noticed and appreciated equally by the individual and the organization. A formal 360-degree evaluation process can validate this result, but the impact of successful coaching should be perfectly obvious: The coachee has become more effective, in ways that everyone can see.

Gary Ranker

Dr. Gary Ranker is a pioneer in the field of coaching. Since the late 1980s, his specialty has been helping clients to analyze their corporate political environment and develop concrete strategies to achieve goals. Gary's prior senior management experience includes serving as the CEO of major international companies for Hallmark Cards and Textron. *Forbes* magazine has listed him as one of the top five executive coaches. He is based in Manhattan and can be reached by phone at (212) 244-8540 or by e-mail at granker@aol.com.

I got my first coaching assignment in 1989 at the suggestion of a friend, Steve Kerr. At the time, Steve was the dean of faculty at University of Southern California's School of Business, where I was teaching. He began working as a consultant to Jack Welch at GE. In my interpretation of Steve's role at GE, he was brought in to monitor and facilitate the changes Welch was driving through the company. To do that, Steve went to the different business units and talked with people about the change agenda.

In the process, Steve found that some valued managers felt ill-equipped to master the new style that was being asked of them. As top people, they had put a lot of time and effort into GE over the years, and GE had a lot invested in them. Yet they were unlikely to thrive in the new culture without making significant behavioral and style changes. Steve's idea was that I could help a few of these people manage that shift by working with them one on one.

My first coachee was a very senior and respected high-profile manager whose communication style was causing significant problems in his business unit. Why Steve asked me to work with that individual has a lot to do with the background and interests that led me to become a coach.

I grew up in a family that was very psychologically oriented, where we were encouraged to talk about why people do things. As a college student, I had a strong interest in international business and a deep desire to see life through the eyes of people from different cultures. To that end, I lived and worked in Europe for many years, assuming ever-broadening levels of business responsibility while learning a number of languages. Eventually, I came to work as a top manager on four continents, an experience that heightened my awareness of individual differences and prompted further interest in a trend that I saw occurring across many cultures and organizations.

Wherever I worked, I recognized a yearning among people for more participation in decision-making processes. Just as frequently, I saw resistance on the part of managers who did not understand or sympathize with that desire. I thought of this trend in broader terms as the kind of empowerment shift typified by the changing status of women, for example, or the movement in Central and Eastern Europe toward democratic capitalism. My desire to research that friction between value sets brought me to obtain a PhD and eventually into coaching at GE.

I was very curious about what was taking place at GE because of my interest in culture, change, and empowerment. That interest supported a number of qualities that had the potential to make me a successful coach. For instance, through my family upbringing and the fact that I had lived in a number of different countries, I had an ability to recognize patterns across cultures and a sensitivity to the effects that individuals have on one another. Unlike most coaches, who have formal backgrounds in consulting or psychology, I had also been very successful as a senior manager and knew my way around a business unit. And I had an ability to generate an extremely deep level of trust in a short time frame.

The manager Steve paired me up with was eminently respected for his technical skills, but had never valued the social side of managing, nor considered the negative costs of his communication style. I was very fortunate to work with him, however, because he truly wanted to change. My first task was to get him to trust that I was there to help him. He accepted that help and allowed me to stick around for an extended period and observe and contribute to what would unfold. In the process, I learned a great deal about what it means to coach, and established a pattern of working with managers that remains very consistent today although it has been refined over time.

I had no formula at my disposal then, but realized instinctively that if I was going to help this manager change I needed to understand how he was perceived through the eyes of those around him. In what was a very customized 360-degree feedback process, I interviewed people around the manager extensively, collected that information, and presented it to him. In those early days, I didn't realize the importance of prioritizing, so I overloaded him with behaviors to change. Nevertheless, what happened was a remarkable shift. As this manager came to understand the negative costs of his communication style, he was able to internalize that awareness and change the way he worked with others. Because I was there to observe those changes I could encourage the people around him to be supportive. In the end, his efficiency and effectiveness as a manager improved dramatically.

Because of that success, I was asked to do more and more coaching within GE. My work in companies outside of GE has held to the same pattern. Typically, I am brought into a business unit to work with a senior person who either has a behavioral issue or has taken on a new level of responsibility. If it's a remedial issue, then the manager is valued enough by the organization that it is preferable to spend money on having them make changes than go through the cost of replacing them. If the manager is in a new level of responsibility, they need to figure out how to squeeze more from themselves to meet the increased demands of their new role.

Different organizations play it different ways. Sometimes, I am a centrally provided resource, either directly assigned to a person or told that my job is to convince a manager that there will be value in working with me. At other times, the approach is more subtle, and I am asked to get to know a particular manager, develop a relationship and gradually turn that into a coaching intervention. After I gain the trust of one senior manager and work with him or her on changes that increase effectiveness, I rove around and develop coaching relationships with others who want or need the same kind of intervention.

The critical challenge lies in convincing top managers to recognize the fact that there is value in relating to the people around them as individuals with individual needs. Many successful leaders are comfortable with a consistent style of how they come across. They see no point in modulating that style to the needs of others. If pushed, they'll say, "That's just who I am." It's a logic that's difficult to argue against. After all, they make significant salaries and function at high levels of responsibility, visibility, and power—proof that their way works. My job is to help them see that by becoming aware of their own pluses and minuses, as well as how they are perceived by others, they can reach even higher levels of effectiveness.

Additionally, people in significant positions serve as role models for others and to a large extent set a tone that affects more than just themselves. Through my observations, I come to an understanding of the complex connections that such person has with him or herself: what they can offer in the context of the organization, what they are being asked to do, what they are comfortable with doing, and how they can contribute more efficiently to meeting the needs of others. This can be difficult to grasp and accept, but I'm very good at locking into people in an intense way, so that they feel safe and have an increasingly positive view of what will happen.

After establishing the beginnings of trust, I keep pushing, insistently and with determination, yet in a way that doesn't offend. We define the change priorities and how we can make them occur. The focus is very pragmatic.

Together, we determine where the manager shines and how they can gravitate toward doing more of that. We also look at mitigating their deficiencies by finding other people to buttress those weak points or at shifting to roles where the manager will be judged less on what they can't deliver.

During the process, I help the people around the manager come to understand what is happening. Through the conversations I have with those individuals I develop a level of trust that allows me to become a spokesperson or salesman for the person being coached. The very fact that I am coaching someone ends up heightening people's awareness of that person's need for change. In the case of a manager, this puts them in an extremely vulnerable position. My job is to avert the inclination to take pot shots at the one in charge by convincing people that their manager is someone who deserves respect for seeing change as a positive.

When I work with several people at the same time, it's easier because the manager's own changes end up being less emphasized in the context of widespread change among other managers. I realize that it's rare for a coach to choose to work so intensely, one on one, with a number of senior people in the same organization, but it's a style and approach that makes the most of my own skills and abilities. I have become confident in my coaching style over the years. I choose not to do shorter interventions, finding that quick fixes don't have the kind of impact I like to deliver. I am after profound, lasting change, preferably by a critical mass of change agents within an organization.

Working among many different leaders allows me to coach to the organization's culture in a way that maximizes my impact. Although I remain an outsider, I become trusted to the point where my ideas about what the culture can be are valued and embraced. As my usefulness to the organization spreads, I end up working with all the senior people and affecting that organizational change, one manager at a time. Eventually, a critical mass emerges, and the organization's change in culture and typical behavior is strong enough that even others notice. I feel profoundly fortunate to work as a change agent coach—the role pulls together the best of what I have to offer for my clients.

Leigh Fountain

Leigh Fountain is President of Life Force, LLC, a consultancy with laser focus on strategy, communication, and leadership. Prior to Life Force, LLC, Leigh worked on Wall Street in senior global management roles as head of human resources for institutional sales, leadership and organizational effectiveness, and sales staff development. He began his career coestablishing an educational and organizational consultancy group that grew to 275 staff. Leigh has both academic and clinical training in coaching and counseling. For more information, Leigh can be reached by e-mail at LF@Life-Force.net, via the Internet at www.Life-Force.net, or by phone at (888) 480-4242; outside North America dial +1 (973) 218-0885.

The areas of strategic and organizational change foster a strong debate on a demarcation separating consulting from coaching. As someone who works in a holistic way in each area, I combine both approaches, sometimes at the same time. In the late 1980s, I began calling the blended aspects of consulting and coaching Embedded Coaching™—a natural outgrowth of a learning or consulting activity where coaching occurs with the individual you are working with and/or becomes part of your work with others in their span of control. It can be short in duration (a coachable moment); but often becomes part of an ongoing and structured coaching arrangement due to the trust in place.

My organizational change work has spanned consulting and coaching in internal and external roles, and impacted groups into the tens of thousands. The situations have been as varied as helping a business leader drive change with their staff or a management team drive divisional or company-wide change. I've also worked globally in both local and cross-border environments.

At the macro level, coaching for organizational change centers on the systems and people; at the micro level this is inverted and focuses primarily on the people issues. Once the overarching themes are set it is the alignment of systems, behavior, communication, and culture that brings about sustainable change. All too often, people misjudge the time and intricacies involved in change. Coaching can help frame the process and provide the support to achieve it.

To illustrate, let me provide some examples. In an external role, I worked on an eighteen-month cultural, product, and production model change with a global electronics manufacturer. In this case, a new product was developed and built while the factory was shifting to a team-based focus. The consulting aspect focused on the changing environment (of work and people). The coaching centered on supporting the senior manager and organization on shifting team dynamics and policies. I also did individual and group coaching for supervisors and associates that were being asked to work in a new way. Another effort, this time in an internal role, occurred during the merger of two global financial firms. In addition to setting up a merger integration team to focus on people and organizational issues I provided coaching to managers and teams working through issues related to change and new work structures that blended the two organization's people and processes.

A tool I have developed to help people understand the strategic and tactical interrelated issues tied to organizational change is the Star Model for Change©. The Star Model for Change© provides a one-page visual, a simple model elucidating the complexity of issues for folks undertaking change. I tee off with this in many meetings to show the landscape and start a dialogue to bring clarity to important issues surrounding the change effort. Often, executives decide change is important for one of many significant reasons—competition, business environment, Wall Street expectations (or the global equivalent), client shifts, and so on—they get the "burning platform" and are motivated to drive change. Below them, there begins a potential wobble: people don't move fast enough and don't understand why there's a change. They see confusion/incongruent behavior across the leadership team, and the change seems like extra work with no benefit, especially when their paycheck still arrives at the same time each month. Simply put, they don't see the issues through the same lens. This creates an organizational drag at best; at worst, it can derail much of the anticipated change benefits (e.g., a great example is the statistical research on the proposed synergies of mergers that dynamically fall short of their stated goals—the outcome of the bulk of merger efforts). The Star Model for Change© does three major things to lever a systems/holistic view of organizational change, it:

1. Brings to light the "other" areas a leader/manager needs to ensure they and their management team are considering and planning for
2. Provides a template or road map that can be completed and can later serve as a framework to build aligned goals
3. Serves as part of an organizational communication tool to help educate people and build commitment toward shared goals

Simply looking at the Star Model for Change©, one could take the view that it's simply an organizational development model—which it is—and, yet, it is more. The Star Model for Change© actually provides an assessment to determine where to focus coaching energies. When considering coaching for organizational change, the diagnosis and next steps are just as important as the landscape of issues can be broad.

To be successful, I think the coach must push for clarity of the goals— achieving quick results and increasing communication. It's also important that the coach ensure that everyone is walking the talk, meaning that everyone is living up to commitments even while demonstrating a willingness to be flexible when appropriate. Throughout the change, business results must still be a focus. It also helps if rewards and development that support the goals are in place. Resistance, whether emerging from the business, the client, or the industry, must be acknowledged and handled.

A good coach is a fast study of the firm, industry, and client base. There's no other way, really, to ensure that the effort is aligned to clear business goals. I think a coach, especially in the area of organizational change, must have a systems/holistic way of looking at the interrelated aspects. Out of that awareness, the coach can provide or help to craft a plan to vet out a road map toward the goals. On the other hand, a good client is one who leverages the coach to his or her maximum potential by being thoroughly open about the issues that exist. It also helps if the client is aware of and takes into account the complexity of the change. The client should know that those who lead the change will always be steps ahead of those being impacted by the change. Both coach and client benefit from self-awareness as much as understanding of what others are going through. Out of such awareness comes the flexibility they will need to be successful together.

As William Bridges says in his book *Managing Transitions*, "It isn't the changes that do you in, it's the transitions." Coaching for organizational change is an exciting aspect of the coaching profession, one that focuses on multiple channels of activities and communication throughout the business organism. To me, it's about working with a living breathing structure of people.

Bruce Pfau

Dr. Bruce Pfau recently joined KPMG LLP as Vice Chair—Human Resources. Prior to that, he was National Practice Director of Organization Effectiveness at Watson Wyatt Worldwide and is an internationally recognized expert in the areas of employee motivation, corporate culture change, and organization measurement. He has written and spoken extensively on aligning human resources practices and business performance. Dr. Pfau has made numerous contributions to professional journals; has been quoted in the *Wall Street Journal,* the *New York Times, BusinessWeek,* and *Fortune;* and has been an invited speaker for various organizations, including The Conference Board, BusinessWeek Executive Programs, The Business Roundtable, SHRM, and the HR Planning Society. Dr. Pfau can be reached by phone at (201) 307-8333 or by e-mail at bpfau@kpmg.com.

For more than 20 years, I've worked with groups of executives at some of the world's largest companies to undertake significant organizational improvements and culture changes. These goals have become increasingly more challenging in recent years amidst a wave of increased competition, an uncertain economic climate, and an intense level of accountability for management. Throughout my experiences coaching leaders, I've learned that one of the most important things an organization can do to elicit change is tap into its most valuable asset—its people.

Organizations seek change for a variety of reasons—to improve operating efficiencies, boost morale, spur growth, or facilitate integration. Ultimately, this is all to create financial value. My work centers on human capital management, which, at its core, leverages the skills, talents, and creativity of a workforce to create high-performance organizations.

When I partner with a team of executives to help them successfully bring about change, my goal is to get them to recognize the importance of human capital, and harness its inherent value. One of the most effective ways I've been able to demonstrate the critical role of human capital (and its effect on change) is to emphasize its impact on the bottom line.

In 1999, I led a groundbreaking Watson Wyatt study, the Human Capital Index® (HCI), which did just that. The HCI study confirmed a positive correlation between the quality of a company's HR practices and its economic results. We developed a simple set of measures quantifying exactly which practices and policies had the greatest correlation to shareholder value. Using those to assign a single HCI score to each surveyed company allowed us to deliver conclusive results. Where there are superior HR practices, there is higher shareholder value. Those HR practices are grouped into five categories: recruiting and retention excellence; total rewards and accountability; a collegial, flexible workplace; communications integrity; and focused HR service technologies. By properly implementing them, organizations can help bring about change and improve their bottom line.

The 2002 follow-up HCI study took the data one step further, showing that superior HR practices are not only correlated with improved financial returns, but are, in fact, a leading *indicator* of increased shareholder value. We analyzed the correlation between 1999 HCI scores and 2001 financial performance (and then, conversely, the correlation between 1999 financial outcomes and 2001 HCI scores) and found that effective human capital practices drive business outcomes more than business outcomes lead to good HR practices.

Another important tool I use from the HCI research is the more counterintuitive finding—namely, that some complex, process-driven programs don't reap their intended results. For instance, 360-degree feedback—once considered a revolutionary way to communicate with employees and affect change—can actually lead to a decrease in financial value if it's not aligned with strategy and executed properly. Other practices, such as developmental training and implementing HR technologies with soft goals, should also be implemented with great care.

I work with clients every day to identify specific actions that organizations can take to affect desired culture change—and then help them understand and implement those actions. It's often difficult. The best leaders come to understand that corporate culture (the collective normative behavior, values, expectations, and attitudes of an organization's people) develops and maintains itself as a direct result of an organization's leadership, policies, practices, systems, structures, and staffing. They realize that culture can be changed only by altering these factors.

To initiate a culture change, I encourage clients to consider three elements: organizational consequences; expectations, goals and attitudes; and employee behavior. Organizational behavior is met by organizational consequences (such as feedback/recognition, pay, and career opportunity). These consequences set up certain expectations, which then lead to the next set of behaviors. But culture is tenacious. Changing one person's behavior is hard enough—altering the entire culture within an organization requires multiple interventions.

First and foremost, leadership must display the desired change in the values and management style of the organization. There also needs to be frequent, clear communication about the target culture. The organization must recruit employees with the desired personality and motives, as well as the specific knowledge and skills to achieve the desired culture. It then needs to put into place the right staff, structure, and systems.

Perhaps most critical, there has to be consensus regarding the target culture. That might seem obvious, but unless it's spelled out by the management team and universally agreed upon, a great deal of ambiguity can creep in.

Woodrow Wilson once said, "If you want to make enemies, try to change something." Although not the most optimistic approach to change, his words hold a great deal of truth. Organizational change is about understanding human capital and corporate culture, and then implementing appropriate human resources practices to bring about the change. The executive teams I've worked with have been most successful when they've conducted appropriate human capital due diligence, committed to change (and secured other senior management's commitment), and remained open to new ideas. In the end, it's their enthusiasm and hard work that allows me to succeed.

CHAPTER 8

———◆———

Strategy Coaching

Thought Leaders

C. K. PRAHALAD
VIJAY GOVINDARAJAN
CHRISTOPHER A. BARTLETT

FARIBORZ GHADAR
MICHAEL HAMMER
JOEL BARKER

Practitioners

NIKO CANNER
JULIE ANIXTER

BILL DAVIDSON
JUDY ROSENBLUM

THOUGHT LEADERS

C. K. Prahalad

THE COMPETITIVE DEMANDS ON TODAY'S LEADERS

C. K. Prahalad is Harvey C. Fruehauf Professor of Corporate Strategy and International Business at the University of Michigan Business School. Dr. Prahalad is a globally known figure and has consulted with the top management of many of the world's foremost companies. His research specializes in corporate strategy and the role and value added of top management in large, diversified, multinational corporations. He is the coauthor of more than ten articles in the *Harvard Business Review,* three of which won the McKinsey Prize, and coauthor of *Competing for the Future. BusinessWeek* called him "a brilliant teacher at the University of Michigan, Prahalad may be the most influential thinker on corporate strategy today." Selected as one of the top 10 teachers in the world in the *Wall Street Journal's* Report on Executive Education, Dr. Prahalad can be reached by phone at (858) 759-8948 or by e-mail at ckp@umich.edu.

In the area of strategy, two trends are shaping the need for coaching today. First, at the CEO level, there is probably more churn than ever before. Newly appointed and possibly even new to his or her organization, the CEO must quickly develop a point of view about how the organization will compete in the future. Second, although the markets once granted CEOs several years to deploy and execute this point of view, the CEO is now expected to start producing measurable results for shareholders and customers right away. Doing more of the same is probably not going to be the right answer going forward. The complexity of the competitive environment, coupled with the collapse in the time frame of expectations, adds urgency to the need for rapid development of a meaningful competitive strategy.

The strategy coach is hired to be a trusted partner of the CEO during the strategy building and deployment process. Why does the CEO need a partner from outside the organization? Besides the critical thinking, experience, and strategy-building expertise that the coach brings to the table, there is also the inherent loneliness of the CEO's position. Who inside the organization can the CEO turn to in working through ideas that will shape the direction of the company? Many of those ideas simply cannot be discussed internally because they involve the future of the key individuals in the group that reports to the CEO. Meanwhile, former colleagues or new reports are trying to reposition themselves for power and influence. Interests may conflict. Skeletons may be hiding in closets. The traditional recipe for success may have become a dangerous orthodoxy. If the CEO wants to develop strategy in a thoughtful, objective, and ultimately successful way, then a coach who is credible, experienced, and trustworthy totally will be a valued partner.

Although not all strategy coaching is done with new CEOs, a look at that circumstance will help explain the strategy coaching process. Along the way, the challenges I describe will clarify some of the attributes of a good strategy coach while describing the nature of a successful coach-client partnership.

Developing a Strategic Point of View

Whether the company is a troubled one or not so troubled, the newly appointed CEO is immediately under the gun to produce value for shareholders and customers. The temptation to engage in cost cutting is strong because it buys time while generating profits. But although layoffs or divestments (or even the acquisition of a competitor as a creative means of cost-cutting) may all exist within a zone of comfort, they probably do not constitute a successful long-term strategy. When the profit increases eventually taper off, people will figure out that they have been watching a one-time, unsustainable improvement.

Prepare before Taking Charge

Ideally, in today's time-compressed climate, a strategy coach should be brought on board before the appointment takes effect, say 100 days, so that the CEO can gain a running start. Although the changeover may not be announced yet, the CEO has been picked, the board of directors is in agreement, and the job has been accepted. It's time for the CEO to survey the portfolio of the business, the financial situation, the culture of the organization and the competitive landscape to understand the opportunities he or she will have in order to make a distinct impact.

A strategy coach first helps a new CEO develop *a point of view* on exactly what he or she has inherited. This point of view is developed not so that it can be imposed on the organization but so that the CEO will be able to listen in a discerning fashion and calibrate what he or she is hearing. Even if the CEO comes from within the organization and already possesses a lot of direct knowledge, a rigorously developed point of view is still a must. The CEO position is a totally different one. The world is now seen from a different and higher perch. The world looks different. Fresh thinking is needed to identify and exploit the competitive opportunities that exist or can be created.

The process of developing a strategic point of view can take up much of the first 100 days. It involves hard-core analysis, number crunching, and critical thought. The coach works with the CEO to do a diagnostic of the *potential of the portfolio* as distinct from the current performance of the portfolio. Is the portfolio the appropriate one? What is the performance of each business, and what is its history? Are there businesses dragging down the performance of the whole? If so, is it a bad business or a badly managed one? If it's badly managed, get rid of the management. If it's a bad business, get rid of the business. Is the break-up value of the portfolio higher than the corporate value and why? Although these questions are fairly straightforward, it may be difficult to come to terms with the answers. Nevertheless, the decisions need to be made fairly quickly.

The coach, at this stage, helps the CEO think radically differently and challenge current wisdom. The most important task of strategy development is to understand the roots of the dominant logic of the company. Stated simply, it is about understanding why we believe what we believe about (1) competition and competitors, (2) our products, (3) relationships across business units or the logic for the portfolio, and (4) our sources of competitive advantage. It is introspection and understanding ourselves as a company. The next step is to explicitly examine the emerging competitive landscape to assess the continued relevance of our beliefs and practices. Past successes often tend to be codified into the dominant logic. There is a thin line between outdated orthodoxy and the dominant logic that may be the source of future success. The coach works with the CEO to understand those orthodoxies in the company and the industry, and lays that over the emerging competitive landscape to see what to preserve and what to change.

Build a Coalition of the Able and Willing

In developing a strategic point of view, the CEO comes to understand the value of the business, the pattern of innovation that is taking place within the organization, the capacity to execute, and the pace and rhythm of the culture, all while determining what needs to be changed. This knowledge does not form in a vacuum, however. Around the CEO, much jockeying for position is taking place. It can be difficult to separate who is telling the CEO what and why, where skeletons are hidden and where opportunities are waiting, as well as which ideas are part of the organizational politics and which are being put forward as genuine strategic opportunities. There is a lot of noise overwhelming nuggets of opportunity.

The CEO must build momentum for the future direction of the company without killing the natives or going native himself. During this phase, *strategy coaching and personal effectiveness coaching* become very intertwined. Having a strategic point of view allows the CEO to work deftly with his or her leadership team, asking discerning questions, listening in a nuanced way, and challenging assumptions without necessarily threatening the people affected by those beliefs. It is, after all, very difficult for people to question the ideas that made them successful. Nor do senior managers rush to tell the CEO, "If I were you, I'd shut down my business." The coach helps the CEO develop processes that allow people to begin changing their own dominant logic as a means of coming on board.

Strategy, at best, is nothing more than a coalition of the powerful and the willing who all share a point of view on how to compete. Building that coalition requires a great deal of personal effectiveness. But personal effectiveness without strategic understanding does not create value for shareholders.

Deploying the Strategy

Within six months, the typical honeymoon period, the CEO must build a coherent theory on how to compete and create a consensus with senior leaders and managers who now form the coalition of the able and willing. That consensus—the corporate strategy—must then be translated into divisional and business unit strategies. The concepts must be deployed throughout the organization and made operational at all levels.

During this phase, *coaching for strategy and coaching for organizational change* come together. Tactics are needed for deploying the strategy and making it real. What are the implications of the strategy to individual divisions and individual managers, all the way up and down the system? Eventually, all individuals need to make sense of what the strategy means to them within the context of the overall scheme.

Creating Vitality

An organization is energized when its people are empowered and autonomous within the broad framework of where the company is going. During the vitality phase of strategy deployment, the organization attains the ability for self-renewal, not just in terms of people and processes, but also in terms of how to compete. If the individuals in the organization understand the strategy and are empowered to succeed under those terms, they will be able to adjust tactics as needed to meet new challenges.

The strategy belongs to the organization and is unique to it. Unlike a strategy consultant who may push a generic model of competition on an organization, the strategy coach works with the organization to build a strategy from within. The coach wants the organization to be successful and helps the leader guide the team. The CEO, like the captain of that team, takes a leadership role in the game. But it's the players who play the game and determine the organization's success.

Principles of a Successful Coach-Client Partnership

When the game is won, the coach can reflect on the glory of that victory, but the credit belongs to the organization. The focus of the strategy coach should always be on the organization winning, yet it's imperative that he or she not become overly involved in the game. The coach must be detached and involved simultaneously and never confuse his or her role.

Here are some principles, based on over 20 years of coaching CEOs, that I think form the basis for a successful coach-client relationship in the area of strategy coaching:

- *Keep pet theories out of the mix.* The coach is a valuable resource of knowledge and experience, but the coach needs to use that knowledge to help uncover what is right for the organization, within its own context. Imposing generic theories or one's latest ideas will not help build a meaningful strategy or make the CEO successful—even if it does make the coach look smart.
- *Make sure the coach and the CEO have good personal chemistry.* Since the coach and CEO have to work together to challenge deeply held assumptions, trust is fundamental. Both partners need to know that they won't be second-guessed by the other. My personal starting point in any coaching engagement is to spend time one-on one with the CEO followed by dinner together. If, by the end of the evening, we trust each other, then we shake hands and get to work.
- *A belief in each other's desire and willingness to be world class.* If the CEO is only interested in cosmetic approaches like cutting costs or other forms of window dressing, I doubt she will value or appreciate

my coaching. I'm not against what she wants to do but I don't think it requires strategy coaching. It would only be a waste of energy for both of us.

- *A willingness to be thoughtful about ways to change the company.* There are all kinds of ways to change an organization and the easiest is through brute force. Whether the CEO wants to be a butcher or a surgeon is a fundamental choice. Being a surgeon requires the kind of training, thoughtfulness, and nuanced understanding that coaching can support.
- *The maturity to be engaged without being overly involved.* The CEO of a large company is in a position of great power and influence. Once it is known that the coach has the CEO's ear, many will be eager to gain access. The coach must learn the lay of the land and be sensitive to the politics of the company, while never, ever getting personally involved.

I have likened my role as coach to the drop of water on the lily leaf. The water droplet has a distinct identity, and at the same time it is part of the leaf. A strategy coach must be self-aware enough that he or she can maintain a distinct identity while fully engaged at an intellectual level. The coach succeeds by seeing the client succeed while never putting his or her personality ahead of the players.

—————◆◆◆—————

Vijay Govindarajan

COACHING FOR STRATEGIC THINKING CAPABILITY

Vijay Govindarajan, known as VG, is the Earl C. Daum 1924 Professor of International Business at the Tuck School, and Founding Director of Tuck's Center for Global Leadership. VG's area of expertise is strategy, with particular emphasis on strategic innovation, industry transformation, and global strategy and organization. He was ranked by *Management International Review* as one of the "Top 20 North American Superstars" for research in strategy and organization and was named by *BusinessWeek* as one of its "Top Ten Business School Professors in Corporate Executive Education." One of his papers was recognized as "one of the 10 most-often cited articles" in the entire 40-year history of the prestigious Academy of Management Journal. He has written more than 60 articles and was the coauthor, most recently, of the book *The Quest for Global Dominance*. He can be reached by phone at (603) 646-2156, by e-mail at VG@dartmouth.edu, or via the Internet at www.vg-tuck.edu.

I work exclusively in the area of strategy with the CEO and top management team. My coaching tends to be with that small group, rather than one on one, and focuses more on business issues than behavioral ones. The need for strategy coaching has become increasingly critical over the last 30 years. In my view, there are four primary reasons why the kind of work that strategy coaches do has become so valuable to organizations.

First, the world has become very complex. In line with that, the half-life of knowledge has rapidly shortened. In a complex, fast-changing world, an idea has only a finite life. Even if the CEO had the best idea in the industry 10 years ago, that idea is probably no longer of great worth to the organization. The necessity for generating fresh ideas is so great that people who do research and stay on the edge of what is innovative are increasingly valuable.

Second, organizations do not need answers to their particular problems; instead, they need frameworks that will not only answer today's questions but perhaps tomorrow's as well. Those frameworks must be simple but effective, grounded in research but powerful in practice. Strategy coaches develop frameworks to apply tomorrow's landscape to today's opportunities.

Third, strategy coaches, because of their experience with more than one organization, provide the opportunity for sharing best practices. It has become very important for companies to understand knowledge, not only in academics but also as it exists in companies on the leading edge. If I work with five companies in technology and entertainment, the sixth company gets the benefit of what I know from working with the other five. This is not a competitive issue; the strategic insight may, in fact, be better coming from another industry. Consider the competition between Encyclopedia Britannica and Funk and Wagnall's. Both had the same business model, and studied each other's moves closely. Neither saw the advent of the CD-ROM or the Internet as paradigm-shifting developments that would transform their industry. One of the strengths a strategy coach brings is world-class practices from other industries. Over time, the coach collects more and more of that knowledge.

Fourth, it is very difficult for a CEO to have an open, candid, and free conversation about strategy. For one thing, it's difficult for a subordinate to disagree with a CEO, for fear that the CEO may keep it in mind. The CEO in turn will wonder if that person has an axe to grind. That's why CEOs like to develop a kitchen cabinet that includes people from outside the company to talk about strategy. If I disagree with the CEO, that's the only reason I disagree. I have nothing personal to gain and no axe to grind, and I am certainly not hesitant to contradict. As a result, the CEO feels comfortable talking with me about those issues.

A strategy coach must have the ability to ask the right questions as well as tremendous listening skills. The coach is trying to piece together many different points of view and bring them forward. She must have a broad base of knowledge to bring to bear on the challenges the organization is facing and a distinct point of view about strategy. The coach is thought of as a thought leader because of this point of view and the knowledge he or she has about best practices from inside and outside the organization's industry.

Strategy issues are far too complex for any one person to solve. CEOs need a multidisciplinary kind of team to manage them. One of the skills that a strategy coach brings is facilitation across the top management team. It's very difficult for members of that team to talk candidly. When two people are disagreeing, the coach's role is to try to make sense out of that and creatively solve those tensions.

What I don't do is solve their problems. I don't know their business as well as they do. There's no way I can tell them what their strategy should be. I can inform them about the best thinking on strategy today and provide them with frameworks they should be using to ask the right questions. I can facilitate an open and candid conversation with the top team. I can push them and prod them. I can help them self-diagnose their strategy issues and self-discover their solutions. In the end, my job is to provide them with strategic thinking capability.

A good client has a deep desire to rethink the strategy of the company in a five-year time frame. Many people mistake strategy for the plan they prepare for next year. Although such a plan may be important, it is not strategy.

I think of the things that companies do as belonging in one of three boxes. Box 1 is about managing the present. Box 2 is about selectively abandoning the past. And Box 3 is about creating the future. Most organizations spend most of their time in Box 1 and call it strategy. Strategy is really about Box 2 and Box 3.

For instance, in the last two to three years, many organizations have focused on cost reductions and improving margins. Strategy is not about what the organization needs to do to secure profits for the next two years, but what it needs to do to sustain leadership for the next seven years. Organizations that engage in cost cutting as though it is strategy are basing their tactics on a series of critical assumptions. They are assuming that technologies will stay the same and customers will remain in place. If they are making improvements, that is all very valuable, but those improvements are only linear and do not take into account nonlinear shifts in technology, customers, demographics, and lifestyle, to name a few variables.

If an organization is following the trajectory of continuous improvement, it is likely that it will one day wake up and realize that its business model is no longer valid. Either someone or something has completely disrupted the model currently in use; or that continuous improvement no longer provides the aggressive growth needed to reach targets and compete effectively.

Even if the organization's strategy is based on outstanding analysis of how the world is going to behave in the next five years, those insights are still only assumptions. First, the day the strategy is introduced into the organization is the day it starts to die; the only question is how fast. Second, company's strategies are almost entirely transparent today to competitors and potential customers; the ease with which strategy can be imitated and commoditized makes it possible to stay ahead of the game only by staying innovative.

Part of the job of the organization's leadership is to make money with the current strategy. That is the challenge in Box 1. Part of the job is to make up for the decay and commoditization of strategy. That is the challenge in Boxes 2 and 3. As much as possible, the leadership team wants to make up for the decay as it goes along, not when it has advanced too far.

The process of coaching for strategy will not look much different in the next 10 years. It will become even more critical, however, as the pace of nonlinear shifts continues to grow. Consider what the future looked like only a few years ago. Who could have predicted the collapse of the NASDAQ, the drop of the Dow, the bankruptcy of Enron and WorldCom, 9/11, and war with Iraq? What will the next few years bring? The only safe answer for an organization developing its strategy is that the future is going to be even more interesting. The leaders of that organization had better develop their strategic thinking capability, or they will be in for a big surprise.

⇒◆⇐

Christopher A. Bartlett
COACHING THE TOP TEAM

Christopher A. Bartlett is the Thomas D. Casserly Jr., Professor of Business Administration at Harvard Graduate School of Business Administration. He has published eight books, including *Managing Across Borders: The Transnational Solution*, named by the *Financial Times* as one of the "50 most influential business books of the century"; and *The Individualized Corporation*, winner of the Igor Ansoff Award for the best new work in strategic management and named one of the Best Business Books for the Millennium by *Strategy + Business* magazine. In addition to his academic responsibilities, he maintains ongoing coaching, consulting, and board relationships with several large corporations. He can be reached at cbartlett@hbs.edu.

If there is a continuum between consulting and coaching, then coaching is much less about providing the answers than it is about asking the right questions—and in the process, helping management find the answers while developing their own skills and personal capabilities. Most company leaders are smart, knowledgeable people stretched by sometimes overwhelming demands, and operating in organizations that are incredibly complex. Sometimes, it takes an outside eye to stand back from that complexity and see that below the surface-issues lie deeper questions or more embedded problems that may otherwise remain unrecognized or even taboo. And for the outsider, it is often easier to challenge the conventional wisdom and question the embedded truths that block creative new thinking.

I have another strong bias about the role of a coach at the highest levels of an organization. In my view, an effective coach must build a long-term trusting relationship not just with the top leader but also with the senior-level executive team. Since the CEO is the most influential person in the organization, some might argue that a coach should focus solely on that position. But by working with his or her direct reports, the coach can help the leader harness that key group to achieve two benefits. By gaining access to the diverse views and perspectives of the senior management, the coach can better serve the CEO through a richer understanding of both the strategic and organizational opportunities and constraints. And by becoming a resource to the top team, the coach creates value by helping to build its capability and alignment with the leader's objectives and priorities.

The greatest skill a coach can bring to the task is the ability to listen actively. When coupled with trust, careful listening yields information and insight that can be used to develop the organization's own understanding. Essentially, the coach's role is to hold up a mirror to help the organization see and evaluate its current position and future options, and to decide what path it should align around moving forward. The strategy coach should not be seen as the guru with all the answers; this is a role more often adopted by strategy consultants who may bring diagnostic frameworks and prescriptive models to analyze the company's competitive position and to develop strategic options and priorities. In my experience, however, most organizations are awash in strategic initiatives and operating imperatives. The problem more often is that their strategic ambitions far outstretch their organizational capabilities, a fact that gives the more organizationally focused, implementation-oriented coaching model its leverage.

But I'm not suggesting that the coach is a blank slate. There is always a reason why an organization approaches a particular coach. In my case, that reason relates to the research and writing I've done around the strategy and organization of multinationals or, more recently, the impact of transformational change on the roles of management throughout the organization. Like other strategy coaches, I've also had the benefit of seeing more than a few companies through global reorganizations or strategic realignments, experiences that would be once-in-a-career events for many managers. Although the nature of my research and experience lends itself to providing concepts, frameworks, and models to my thinking, as a coach I don't lead with these. I don't want to come into the organization with a hammer and bang away at something that requires a screwdriver. Instead, I listen carefully, ask questions, challenge, and provide feedback.

In my experience, the most common problem facing today's top managers is that they have inherited an organization designed so that strategy was set by a top-down process of allocating scarce financial capital across the competing needs of the business. This organizational model is typically reinforced by a set of sophisticated planning and control systems created to drive capital requests, strategic plans, and operating budgets upwards to top management so that it could allocate and control capital effectively. And supporting all this is a corporate staff whose whole purpose is to manage this flow of flow of information up and down.

But as we've moved into an information-based, knowledge-intensive service economy, capital remains important, but it is no longer the scarce, constraining, and therefore strategic resource for top management to control. The new strategic resource is the information, knowledge, and expertise required to develop and diffuse innovation. That information and knowledge exist in people's heads and in organizational relationships. It can no longer be hauled to the top to be allocated and controlled by the CEO. The task of developing and diffusing innovation is fundamentally different from allocating and controlling capital. This change has driven a decade of delayering, reengineering, and empowerment that has transformed the modern corporation and fundamentally altered the role of top management.

In this environment, most organizations are far too complex for the CEO to be conversant with everything. Critical to the success of any organization is obtaining the alignment and commitment of the top team. Almost all organizations hold a regular top management meeting, and one of the first things I will typically do as a coach is to sit in on a few, listening and observing to absorb the state of the business and the dynamics of the team. It's astounding how many such meetings serve as show and tell presentations of information that could be obtained by simply reading the accompanying reports. There's huge value added even just in getting the agenda of those meetings right by balancing operating review items with key strategic issues and development opportunities.

There also may be some intraorganizational tension or problem that is causing difficulty in the top team's effective functioning: a dysfunctional person who needs to be removed; an unresolved dispute that needs to be resolved; or an unspoken concern that needs to be explored. It helps to have fresh eyes and ears observing the work of the top of the organization. As an outsider, my role is to gain sufficient confidence and respect that I can question, challenge, and coach the CEO and senior team, and help them see how they can become more effective individually and together. It's a process that I think is enormously helpful in building the capability of the most pivotal part of an organization, the CEO and his or her top team.

I regard a coaching engagement with an organization as a long-term relationship rather than a one-time project. Most consultants are hired for specific change initiatives or strategic shifts. But these events often become a series of unconnected programmatic changes when the organization needs an overall systemic review. A coach who is there for the long run can be helpful in keeping the focus on that systemic change—and, equally important, can ensure that it is management who develops and implements it. The coach can provide the advice, encouragement, and sometimes discipline to keep working toward the big organizational goals and prevent a drift back to day-to-day operating requirements.

Most managers are very smart, capable people. I work with them recognizing that they know their industry and business better than I do. I'm there to understand what they do. Then, I'm going to question and challenge. If things seem blocked, I'm going to apply the naive questions of an outsider to try and pry it open. As trust and comfort grow, I can challenge and push the top team with more skill and precision. From my perspective, I need to regard the challenge of the organization as something interesting and engaging that I'm going to learn from and contribute to. I need to like the people with whom I will be working, and have a strong belief that they are capable and committed.

A coach can build the individual competencies of a top manager, but I believe that individual competency is leveraged enormously if it is put in the context of the top team and the building of organizational capability. If clients are not comfortable with that, I may still work with them, but more as a consultant providing my expertise. I don't consider my work coaching unless I am developing their individual and organizational capabilities.

———◆———

Fariborz Ghadar

STRATEGY IMPLEMENTATION: WHERE THE FUN BEGINS

 Fariborz Ghadar is the William A. Schreyer Chair of Global Management, Policies and Planning and Director, Center for Global Business Studies at the Pennsylvania State University Smeal College of Business Administration. He specializes in global corporate strategy and implementation, international finance and banking, and global economic assessment. He is the author of 11 books and numerous articles, including the *Harvard Business Review* article entitled "The Dubious Logic of Megamergers." His most recent research has been published as the first chapter in *Pushing the Digital Frontier, Insights into the Changing Landscape of E-Business*. He can be reached by e-mail via Penn State University at fghadar@psu.edu.

Some organizations can have a mediocre strategy, implement it well, and be successful. Others can have a wonderful strategy, implement it poorly, and waste everyone's time. As a coach, I work with senior leaders to identify a strategy that makes sense for their organization. Then, I help optimize the capability of the management team to implement it.

This is not without its interesting challenges. Most industries are experiencing a paradigm shift from long product life cycles to short product life cycles with significant ramifications for strategy implementation. Throw in the fact that the management team of the average global organization is almost always multicultural, multinational, and diverse in background and perspective; and you have a very new set of dynamics playing havoc with old ways of doing business. Strategy implementation is not as complicated as people think, but there are many different categories that need to be placed within a framework before the way forward becomes clear.

It helps to understand why those dynamics have changed. Many of the very smart, very capable leaders I work with think that the situation they're facing is unique. When they started in business, 20 years ago, everything was perfectly clear. Now that things have become complicated, frustrations and pressures are mounting. It's all too easy to blame the organization or the senior team. It's much more likely that the impact of a shortened product life cycle hasn't been factored into the strategy equation.

Organizations fall into four categories depending on where they are positioned in the traditional product life cycle. Common patterns of external and internal behavior exist for each group. *Group A* companies are those that have just been formed. Typically, they are high-tech companies that are considered leading edge, such as Cray Research in supercomputers or Genentech in the pharmaceutical industry. *Group B* companies are established, proven technology providers with a strong brand name, like IBM. *Group C* are customer-focused companies, like Toyota, which provide market-segmented products. *Group D* companies are low-cost providers that compete solely on price. They typically manufacture goods in cheap labor markets such as China. Years ago, Lucky Gold Star, which produced black and white televisions, exemplified a *Group D* company.

Naturally, CEOs are different in each category as well. *Group A* CEOs are visionary leaders, confident if not arrogant about their concepts and capability, caring only about the technology and the vision. *Group B* CEOs are highly polished, and talk and look as though they have received their MBA at Harvard or MIT. In *Group C*, the CEO is very market- and customer-focused and probably rose through the operational ranks. In *Group D,* the CEO is an efficient cost cutter.

In the old days, when product life cycles were long, these four categories of CEOs and strategies worked perfectly. But in most industries today, new products can be imitated within months. The company no longer has the time to go through the arrogant and visionary stage, the sensitive-to-the-customer stage, the price-conscious stage, or the efficient-cost-cutter stage. Instead, the leader in a time of short product life cycle needs to be all of these things at once.

This changes the leadership formula dramatically. The organization needs to innovate, manage the brand, listen to the customer, compete on price and become superefficient at the same time. Since no one person has all of these skill sets, the management team becomes very diverse. The team must be pulled together in new ways to deliver on the potential of the strategy.

Where to begin depends on where the organization is at in terms of its understanding of these new dynamics. Sometimes, the CEO has gone through all the transformations during his tenure and knows intuitively what has happened to the company. He just wants his team to come along with him. Sometimes, in what always proves to be a more complicated situation, the team has figured it, out but the light hasn't gone on for the CEO yet.

The strategy implementation coach needs to build credibility between the leader and the team, as well as between the team and the leader. Once that's established, the team is able to look at how other companies in other industries handled their transformation. From there, they can be guided to figure out their own best solutions.

At this point, strategy implementation becomes fun. Although we are engaged in developing a strategy for the future, we really don't know what that future will look like. How can we possibly know which direction the company should take? When I work with senior management, I challenge them to come up with two or three distinct future scenarios. It's amazing the level of creativity that emerges when people imagine and articulate what might happen to the world.

Picture an oil company. In one possible scenario, the Russians and Angolans decide to increase production and glut world oil markets. In another possible future, hydrogen fuel cell technology takes off and everyone begins driving hydrogen-powered cars. In a third, hydrogen fuel cells are a flop, and everyone in China buys a moped, and everyone in India purchases a Subaru. In each case, the implications for oil production, distribution, and marketing strategies are radically different. I encourage the management team to ask themselves where they would fit in each of those worlds. What would their strategy be if the future were to take that direction? All scenarios will not have the same level of probability. But what if one of the low probability futures were to actually occur? Without going through the exercise of imagining that possibility, an organization's strategy could be blown to pieces. If, on the other hand, it had prepared itself mentally for the otherwise unimaginable and even put metrics into place to track that development, it would be much more capable of shifting direction. To develop these ideas, we consider companies from other industries and other times that have experienced similar change and look closely at what they did in response. It's a game that everyone enjoys playing.

Throughout this process, managing the dynamics of cultural differences within the implementation team is a key challenge. After all, the chances are good that not everyone at the table is an engineer from Akron, Ohio, anymore. Some are in marketing, others design, finance, or operations. Some have start-up backgrounds; others are from consulting or manufacturing. Some are efficiency-oriented, others creative; some are revenue-focused, others cost-conscious. Culturally, they probably come from far and wide. The head of information technology, the guy you've always called Ken, may be called Kennichi when he e-mails his family in Yokohama or Krishna if he hails from Bangalore.

What I've found is that the diversity of the management team makes the company more likely to be successful externally, even though it makes the internal operations more difficult. The diverse group, though often in conflict, is able to see more possibilities and come up with a distinctly greater range of possible futures. Conversely, when the management team is consistent and similar, this makes the operation smoother internally while reducing the chances for external success. In other words, conflicts in point of view are not a bad thing—in fact, conflicts are one of the elements I measure from the first day.

Measurement is a key theme overall. Months or years down the line, as scenarios start coming true or, conversely, begin to diverge from what's been imagined, the organization's strategy needs to be revisited. The metrics are there to evaluate the strategy so that the team can judge progress periodically and stay motivated, united, and on track.

The process of engaging the management group as a team, making sense of their strategy issues, encouraging buy-in from those diverse perspectives, and figuring out the best implementation path can create a tremendous sense of energy. That wonderful happy feeling won't last forever, though. As soon as reality hits, optimism and focus can quickly be lost. To adequately prepare the organization for the future, the strategy implementation coach must stimulate senior managers with the possibilities for conducting new ways of doing business. I try to make it fun for everyone involved because it won't always be fun in the marketplace. If it's not an interesting journey, nobody will want to join.

Michael Hammer

COACHING FOR
OPERATIONAL INNOVATION

Dr. Michael Hammer is the author of four books, including the international best-seller *Reengineering the Corporation,* one of the most important business books of the
1990s. His latest book is *The Agenda: What Every Business Must Do to Dominate the Decade.* His articles have
appeared in periodicals from *Harvard Business Review* to
the *Economist,* and his work has been featured in every
major business publication. An engineer by training,
Dr. Hammer focuses on the operational nuts and bolts of
business; his work is relentlessly pragmatic and immediately relevant. Dr. Hammer was formerly a Professor of Computer Science at the Massachusetts Institute of Technology, and he is a founder and director of several high technology
companies. He was named by *Time Magazine* to its first list of "America's 25
Most Influential Individuals." He can be reached by telephone at (617) 354-5555
or by e-mail at Michael_hammer@hammerandco.com.

I don't see myself as a coach in the traditional sense of advisory leadership
development. What I'm trying to do is help leaders think about their business operations and business processes in a different way. The particular
point of view I bring has two major aspects: operational innovation and process management.

Operational innovation is largely terra incognita to executives. In order to
improve performance, most executives think about changing organizational
reporting lines, developing a new strategy, engaging in some kind of financial
transaction, doing a merger or acquisition, or launching a new marketing
campaign. They don't consider how customer service is delivered, orders are
filled, or products developed. Such issues are simply not on their radar
screen. If anything, this problem has gotten worse in recent years. The background that most executives have, the way business schools harvest their
MBAs, and the general cultural business milieu that we all operate in has become increasingly narrow. As a result, we're losing a lot of the perspective
that can inspire operational innovation.

The second aspect of my work relates to process. Process, in my terminology, means thinking about work cross-functionally on an end-to-end basis. I
want leaders to think outside the organizational chart and consider the organization's work holistically rather than narrowly. Instead of planning the
work of the sales department, or the work of the manufacturing unit, or the

work of the logistics division, I want the organization and its leaders to think about order fulfillment, which crosses all those boundaries and many others. In other words, I want leaders to look at their businesses in two new ways: first, that operational innovations can be a new and valuable source of strategic advantage; and second, that doing work differently does not require additional structural forms but rather an end-to-end orientation. Since most executives are not accustomed to these kinds of ideas, coaching in this area involves a fair amount of mental stretching.

There's nothing glamorous about the work I do. Deals are exciting. Hostile takeovers are dramatic. When an insurance company develops a new and profitable way of processing claims, however, or a manufacturer transforms its distribution process, it's not going to make headlines in the *Wall Street Journal*. Yet such operational innovation is the stuff of real strategic advantage.

I don't presume to offer advice on the particulars of a business situation. The executive knows his or her business much better than I do. He or she has talents that I don't, and it would be absurd to think that they need to hold my hand to do their job. My role is to help them get a new perspective on business that will help them create competitive advantage.

When I do this work, I am never doing it alone. I am not a guru who preaches from the mountaintop. Instead, I work collaboratively with managers inside the organization who already have this point of view and are trying to get their leaders to have it as well. As a rule, people who are not at the top of the organization often understand these ideas better than those who are higher up. They're closer to the problems. They haven't been acculturated away from it. They have to deal with the consequences of traditional ways of doing things.

Together, we make a multipronged effort to establish the operational and process innovation perspective in the minds of the leadership. My job is to articulate and communicate the ideas in ways that senior executives can absorb. There's a teaching element to that, and there's also a questioning element. I sit with them and listen. They have a lot of questions they need to ask as they grapple with the implications. What might this mean? How will it affect what we currently do? What is it, in fact, that we do now? The questions are all part of the struggle each person goes through in trying to internalize the conceptual shift. My job is to help them in that internal debate so that they can emerge with a new theory for how their organization can extract value from its operational and process strategy. If there's no struggle, there's no progress.

At the same time, my colleagues within the organization are collecting performance information that substantiates the concepts I am teaching to the senior leadership group. For example, they might collect data about the performance penalties incurred by the company's current organization and operations. In what constitutes a third prong of attack on the traditional viewpoint, I also encourage people at all levels to network with peers at other companies who've already embraced new ways of thinking. This helps everyone involved internalize the ideas while developing homegrown strategies.

When I think of what makes a good coach in this or any area, the word that jumps to mind is passion. Operational and process innovation is a mania for me. It's my mission because I think it is the single most critical thing that organizations need to do well. Leaders who are trying to get the rest of their organization to have a similar awakening need that kind of passion, also. I tell them, if you don't believe in this on a deep, personal level, how can you expect anyone else to get it?

Experience and expertise are obviously important. It's necessary to have helped make things happen in a variety of places in order to have relevant experiences to draw on. Just as critical is empathy. A coach must appreciate a leader's perspective to understand what is going on in their thinking, not just in terms of the business but in worldview. If a CEO is passionate about customers, for example, then that's the leverage point I can use to help them think passionately about the way operational innovations will provide better service.

At the same time, a coach needs to be respectful and humble. The leaders of the organizations I work with are truly impressive people. I know for a fact that I could not do their jobs. So I have a high regard for them and a sensible perspective on myself. I am valuable to them only to the extent that my point of view and experience might be helpful. This perspective enables me to work collaboratively with those leaders who are driving change within the organization. If I merely tell people what to do, none of us will get anywhere. I need to engage people so that the discoveries they make are their own. It's critical to the success of our efforts.

Most organizations are still operating with mind-sets that were forged at the beginning of the industrial revolution 250 years ago. As a result, they suffer from two severe problems. First, the operational strategies that were excellent for an emerging, high-growth economy are useless in a global customer-dominated economy. Inevitably, such an approach leads to performance that customers find unacceptable. Second, the mind-set of the traditional perspective on operational strategy creates organizations that a great many people find stultifying and unfulfilling. This might have been tenable when options were limited, but it simply doesn't fly in the face of the opportunities that exist today for employees and customers alike.

Operational innovation has two signal virtues. It transforms organizational performance to an astonishing degree, and it creates an environment for people working in the organization that is much more fulfilling and enriching. These are the reasons why I am passionate about operational innovation and why business leaders should be too.

Joel Barker

STRATEGIC EXPLORATION

Joel Barker is an independent scholar and futurist. He is known around the world as "the Paradigm Man" because of his videos on paradigms. He also was one of the first corporate educators, starting in 1982, to emphasize the importance of vision for all organizations. He is presently studying complex ecological systems for their lessons about innovation and collaboration. He has just finished a new book on twenty-first-century technologies. He can be reached by e-mail at Joel@JoelBarker.com.

Too many CEOs and top executives give little thought to an aspect of strategic thinking that exists between intuition and strategic planning. Sure of their personal judgment, they leap from intuition to planning without exploring the terrain of the new direction. In my work, I coach leaders to add a layer of thinking before they start their planning. I call it strategic exploration. Done properly, it will give them early information about potential long-term consequences. Strategic exploration occurs before the planning process begins and thus alerts the leaders and the organization to those dreaded unintended consequences. I believe this added capability to explore the future will be a key measure of great leadership in the twenty-first century.

A key part of strategic exploration is the understanding of paradigms within which an organization must compete. When a paradigm shift occurs, an organization that is dominating its industry can become a second-tier player almost overnight. Consider the way Motorola's strategy not to develop and release a digital cell phone in 1994 opened the door for Nokia. Motorola's situation today might be very different if it had explored how the long-term implications of not being first into the digital market would affect them. The Swiss watch industry made exactly the same mistake and chose to overlook quartz technology, allowing Seiko of Japan to become a world market leader. The decisions of an intelligent executive can look very stupid when the rules of the game are transformed. But as Edson de Castro, CEO of Data General, said in 1978, "Few corporations are able to participate in the next wave of change, because they are blinded by the business at hand."

Some executives, because of this close focus, develop tunnel vision. I want them to develop Funnel Vision. To that end, I teach them a schema I've called the Possibilities Cone®. (See Figure 8.1.)

The Cone is flared at its opening to allow a wide range of possibilities to be discovered and explored. Our paradigms determine how well we begin that capturing process. Once the idea enters the cone, it then flows through the intuitive judgment process, then through the strategic exploration process, then

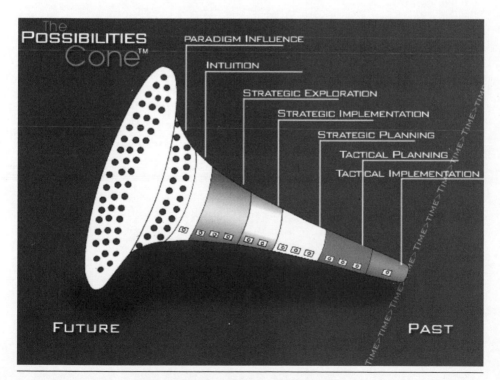

FIGURE 8.1   The Possibilities Cone

the strategic assessment process. All of this happens before strategic planning even begins.

Most executives leap directly from intuition to strategic planning and overlook the importance of strategic exploration. The analogy I use is of a wagon train heading westward. No wagon master would roll the wagons without first sending out scouts to explore the terrain that lies ahead. The wagon master has an intuition about what the future holds but needs details and specifics to educate that opinion. A good scouting team is diverse in background and experience. This diversity guarantees that they will see a broad spectrum of possibilities. Their job is to bring back information, almost always qualitative, that will illuminate the choices of the paths ahead. The wagon master assesses this information and, with the help of the scouts, picks a path. Once the pathway is decided, the wagon master meets with the members of the wagon train to share his vision of their collective future.

People think that the vision process is the last step in strategy planning, but I believe it needs to come at the end of the scouting process, when strategic exploration has taken place and many of the long-term consequences have been identified.

A deficiency in leadership today is its unwillingness to take the time to explore and consider the long-term positive and negative implications of a vision. When unexpected change occurs, organizations that have not planned for such possibilities retreat to the prevailing paradigm and willingly give up market share rather than deal with reality. It's the job of a manager to optimize the paradigm the organization currently occupies. But it's the job of the leader to lead between the paradigms. I tell leaders that 60 percent of their time should be focused on the future. No one will thank them for taking care of today, if they fail to provide for tomorrow.

PRACTITIONERS

Niko Canner

Niko Canner is a founder and Managing Partner of Katzenbach Partners LLC, a consulting firm with offices in New York and Houston. Niko was also a founder-member of the McKinsey Change Center and a cofounder of the Organization Practice at the Mitchell Madison Group. He has published articles on subjects ranging from the theory of financial asset allocation to the social context for knowledge management, and is working with Jon Katzenbach on a book regarding how leaders motivate performance by building pride. He can be reached by e-mail at niko.canner@katzenbach.com, via the Internet at www.katzenbach.com, or by phone at (212) 340-8282.

Strategy is the set of ideas that shape the way organizations make choices and take action. At its very best, strategy both expands the universe of possibilities that individuals and groups consider, and channels effort behind a small number of priorities. Great strategies answer the question "Why?" in the same moment as the question "What?" They help narrow and channel focus, while maintaining sufficient room for creativity about *how* to achieve an overarching goal.

Most of us think about strategy as a concept that applies primarily at the corporate, business unit and product levels. In fact, there is no level at which the concept of "the set of ideas that shape the way organizations make choices and take action" does not apply. Strategy is nested, dynamic, and ubiquitous.

The ubiquity of strategy presents a set of challenges that take us a long way from Boston Consulting Group's articulation of the growth-share matrix as a codification of the notion that some businesses are more worthy of investment than others. Three principles stand out:

1. All leaders are both consumers of strategy—as it is defined by customers and partners, as well as within their own organization—and producers of strategy.
2. Strategy is communication. The metaphor of "rolling out" needs to be replaced with the imperative to give people at all levels the tools to redefine the ideas that shape their choices and actions. Strategy must

create a language for people to solve problems laterally, as well as to facilitate decision making up and down the organization.

3. Strategy constitutes the most powerful lever for motivation—within and outside the organization. Strategy must provide meaning as well as guidance, and must be meaningful beyond the bounds of the enterprise. Strategy creates the foundation for brand.

In the broadest, most value-neutral sense of the word, strategy fulfills an ideological, as well as an informational purpose. Jack Welch and Sam Walton stand out as leaders who fulfilled both needs brilliantly. Many CEOs remain trapped in the equation of strategy with planning, and many leaders down the line fail to see themselves as strategists at all.

A strategic advisor can no longer be someone who primarily leads projects to assess market positioning or corporate portfolios. Both of these tasks continue to be important, but the capabilities to execute them have disseminated far more widely than in the golden age of the strategy consultant. The tasks of an advisor have evolved to include:

- Helping a leader understand the role that strategy must play at a given point in his or her organization's evolution
- Working with leadership teams to develop a discipline for working together to develop and articulate a strategy
- Determining the analytical basis for the small number of guiding ideas that drive the selection of a strategy
- Formulating strategy as a story that is compelling, memorable, and useful to internal and external audiences
- Finding ways to launch experiments that enable the learning necessary to refine the development of a strategy
- Developing a process by which the core ideas of a strategy can be shared, understood, and applied across an organization

My experience working as an advisor in this capacity suggests that neither the traditional strategy firm nor the solo practitioner model of coaching provides a good institutional context for this role. The leverage ratio at which strategy firms operate makes it very difficult for partners to focus on advisory work. Their minimum efficient scale in terms of monthly fee levels creates a bias for heavily resourced, analytically intensive efforts that typically must be pushed to closure faster than their client organizations can integrate these new ideas into their business.

Solo practitioner coaches face a different set of issues. Their model tends to emphasize serving as a sounding board for the senior leader and/or the supporting team. It is very difficult, however, for the solo practitioner to reach deep enough into the organization to experiment with how new ideas can re-shape the way day-to-day work gets done. They rely heavily on resources within the client organization, but these organizations often find it harder to focus on questioning and testing assumptions about themselves rather than outsiders. This difficulty arises as much from the challenge of creating time for that discipline as from the intellectual challenge of breaking frame.

My partners and I have been experimenting with an institutional form that we think will be more successful in advising clients who are engaged with questions of strategy in this newer and broader conception. We work best with clients who see the difference between "strategy" and "implemen-tation" as a false distinction, and who are willing to engage both their own organizations and external thinkers in developing and testing new ideas. Many of our clients are situated in companies that lead their industries. These clients are looking for new ways of conceiving how value can be cre-ated. They do not perceive strategy as a benchmarking exercise that will re-sult in an adaptation of practices that others in the industry have already proven. Our clients understand that strategy, organization, and people can-not be separated, and they look to us to help them consider how those three elements can evolve together.

To deliver this vision, we have had to do something new in the consulting industry:

- Focus at least as much on experiments that point the way to new strate-gic options as on studies that prove the case for a new strategy
- Maintain the levels of revenue per consultant necessary to attract and retain the very brightest people, while keeping project costs low enough that we can engage with clients over time frames much longer than a traditional strategy project
- Create an environment in which people who are "high/high" on intel-lectual and emotional intelligence feel valued for "critical doing" as well as "critical thinking"
- Develop communication approaches that work at both the most senior levels in an organization and at the front line

Although our efforts in this regard are currently distinctive, we expect, and even hope, that others will follow us in developing institutional forms that enable a new kind of advisory work around strategy. There is perhaps no more important question for an individual who seeks to be a world-class ad-visor on strategy than "What institutional context will enable me to provide the best help and counsel to clients?" As clients realize more and more that strategy *is* organization, *is* communication, and *is* brand, they will increasingly reach out to advisors whose own organizational context provides them the time, resources, and incentives to deliver the right mix of counsel, experimentation, and facilitation of organizational change.

⋙◆⋘

Julie Anixter

 Julie Anixter is Strategic Director of Lipson Alport & Glass (LAGA), a brand marketing and design consultancy, where she works with clients on brand strategy, new product and service development, and design innovation. She is also the Director of the alliance between LAGA and tompeterscompany! Consultant, coach, designer, speaker, and trend-spotter, Anixter specializes in developing successful business solutions at the intersection of client brands, business issues, and organizational needs. Prior to joining LAGA she was Managing Director of R&D for the tompeterscompany!, where she developed consulting solutions around Tom Peters' ideas. She has worked with a wide variety of clients. She can be reached by e-mail at janixter @laga.com, by phone at (513) 961-6225, or via the Internet at www.laga.com.

Most of the strategy coaching I do is in the domain of communications, brand, and innovation, and how those three disciplines can help an organization create competitive advantage and energy. Strategy, by definition, always requires thoughtful analysis and interpretation of the world. We all know it is an iterative process. The days of the lone executive preparing a five-year strategy are over. Strategy today is a fluid, complex, and collaborative process, more so than it historically has ever been.

From the start, I am not just coaching: I am collaborating with my clients. In my view, that is the essence of what makes me effective, and that's where the energy comes from. I always try to start exactly where the client is. Sometimes, they can articulate that, and sometimes they can't. I just try to understand them, and to communicate my understanding in such a way that it opens opportunities for trust and the freedom to explore what's missing. What is common to all the coaching I have done, and to the way I approach every new situation, could be summed up simply as "connecting to people's passion for their work." Passion, like so many great words, is overused. However, it is also instantly discernable in any conversation, meeting, or business. It is present in the leader, in the team and in the customers—or it is not. That distinction is what makes great organizations great.

Like a heat-seeking missile, I continuously look for passion and for what's missing. I observe the leader and the environment around the leader, and then feed back what I see, and make interpretations with the person I'm coaching that are designed to help elicit what they care about most. My goal is to find a way to help leaders tap the natural resource of passion, in themselves and others, and to allow that natural resource to provide the fuel and persistence needed to get almost anything important done.

When choosing to work with clients, I look for people who have real passion about what they are doing, and I look for chemistry. Another key prerequisite for any effective coaching relationship is trust and authenticity. Establishing a relationship and creating the necessary levels of trust and rapport takes a fair amount of chemistry, and enables you to become a "trusted advisor" as Maister says, or to paraphrase, a "trusted collaborator." In my experience, this coaching as collaboration means bringing your whole self to the table, engaging in deep listening, and not simply wearing one of the hats that we so often talk about to define professional roles. It also means rolling up your sleeves and working on getting inside the situation. Additionally, you have to be impeccable in keeping your promises. If a coach can care, listen, help clients read the world, and then collaborate with them on what is possible, that's a pretty good Petri dish in which to have a successful coaching engagement.

Conversely, or symmetrically, the client's *willingness* to learn, grow, explore, and collaborate on new approaches is, for me, the critical success factor for a good engagement. I also believe that people who want to work with a coach also want to be coached by people who can authentically deliver a sense of what's possible. There is no formula for this, but the truth is undeniable: if clients were not looking for new possibilities, they would not be working with a coach.

Success has many meanings, so I find that it is crucial to articulate the criteria for successful results in the client's language. I judge whether or not I've been successful by asking myself these questions:

- Are there results? Can we all see them?
- Is the client satisfied with those results?
- Have their work practices changed in positive ways?
- Is their business or brand more vibrant?
- Are their strategies producing more long-term sustainable advantage?

- Are they able to take advantage of change more easily?
- Are the people in the business using their full talents?
- Are they doing, to quote Tom Peters, "cool stuff"?
- Have they broken the code?
- Is there plenty of passion to go around—enough that good people want to work there?

Along the way, I want people to:

- *Read the world,* including the mess, the opportunities, the politics, or the fray, the beauty of the situation, the humor, the opportunities, and what it means for them.
- *Define the identity* they personally want to hold in the world and the identity their organization wants to have (and how the two are linked!). Identity is the heart of branding.
- *Decide on the highest leverage actions* it will take to get there in the most elegant fashion—what I mean by "breaking the code" (sorry, too many spy movies in my childhood and a worship of the Emma Peel character).
- *Pull in the talent* they have to help them take the actions and break the code as quickly as possible. I find there is a layer of subtle malaise and uncertainty hanging over many organizations like a cloud cover. We could use a corporate weather channel some days just to break through. Pulling a team of passionate people together to work a key project is one of the best antidotes to that malaise.

Bill Davidson

William H. Davidson founded MESA Research, a management consulting firm acquired by Deloitte & Touche in 1996. MESA's clients have included over half of the Fortune 100. He serves on the board of UTi Worldwide (UTIW), a fast-growing global logistics services provider, and on several private company boards. An active researcher and writer, he was acknowledged as the most widely cited academic in the field of international management during the 1985/1995 decade. His book *2020 Vision* (with Stan Davis) was selected as the Best Business Book of the year by *Fortune* in 1992. His latest book, *Breakthrough,* was published in the fall of 2003. Bill can be reached by e-mail at mesaresearch@aol.com or by phone at (310) 375-0020. MESA's web site is at www.mesaresearchgroup.com.

My group specializes in formulating and implementing *enterprise strategies.* Enterprise strategies are integrated master plans that require focused and coordinated implementation across an entire organization over an extended time period. Our efforts generally involve substantial changes in core strategies and performance management systems; and trigger efforts to create long-term IT architecture road maps, and new people strategies.

Typically, we work with a select set of senior executives to develop the enterprise imperative—the critical need for the organization to pull together behind a common strategy. It can be very difficult to establish an enterprise mind-set among an executive team. But we do not recommend proceeding with any strategic change program until the senior team is of one mind and one gut about the need for change. These executives are required to come to the strategy council wearing an enterprise hat: that is, with the best interest of the entire organization in the forefront of their minds. New goals, new strategies, and specific projects follow from that team commitment.

Much of our coaching effort occurs on the field of play. That is, we use the development and execution of the new strategy to reorient and fuse senior executives into a cohesive enterprise leadership team. Our framework, summarized as AIM, READY and FIRE, both shapes and supports those strategic change efforts. In the AIM phase, the senior team works together to assess current corporate identity, both in strategic and organizational terms. Considerable effort is devoted to real-time team building during this phase. The AIM phase culminates in the definition of a preferred future state, which serves as the beacon and destination for the development of core strategies and projects. In the READY phase, work includes assessment, alignment, communication, people strategies, and accountability exercises. The FIRE phase focuses on project launch, delivery of key strategy elements, and realization of strategic targets.

Our preferred clients are ready to embrace the enterprise strategy mindset, and they often possess a substantial base of existing strategy work. Their market is typically in transition with performance pressures intensifying. We also find, quite often, that our clients have operated with excessive decentralization and have taken initial steps to rebalance themselves with stronger corporate roles. Regardless of circumstance, the ideal client anticipates continuity in leadership and sees strategic change as essential.

We measure our success primarily in traditional terms: growth rates, market share, and financial metrics. However, we also take pride in observing senior teams discussing and deciding strategic issues efficiently and effectively. It is satisfying to witness such cohesive teamwork, especially when it is accompanied by accelerated corporate momentum and improved morale as clients consolidate newly won market positions.

⋙◆⋘

Judy Rosenblum

Judy Rosenblum is an expert in developing organizational capability through organizational learning tied to corporate strategy. Judy is currently Chief Operating Officer of Duke Corporate Education, a private for-profit corporation spun out by Duke University providing educational experiences that help companies link their investments in people and knowledge development directly to the execution of their business strategies. Prior to joining DukeCE, she was Chief Learning Officer of the Coca Cola Company and the Vice Chairman for Learning and Human Resources at Coopers and Lybrand. She can be reached via e-mail at Judy.Rosenblum@dukece.com.

Coaching skills training has been around a long time. What's new is the recognition that in order for coaching to add value in an organizaton, it must be aligned with both the culture and the business strategy. The purpose of coaching is improvement in performance and assurance that the firm will have successive generations of competent people who live the values of the organization. In order for coaching to really be part of the strategic agenda of the business, it needs to be aligned to the company's strategy and made relevant to both the coach and the coachee. My work focuses on creating that alignment organization-wide.

It's important to begin with a systemic analysis of why coaching is or is not working in an organization; otherwise, investments will fall into the same old cultural sinkholes. Using interviews, company survey data, benchmark data, and focus groups of successful coaches and those that feel they have been successfully coached, we construct the systems maps that describe what is happening in the environment that accelerates or inhibits a coaching culture.

Next, we use that analysis to design a coaching strategy for the company, based on the changes they are trying to implement. When the maps are completed, we discuss and adjust them with the client and then look at the kinds of interventions, both educational and otherwise, that will start the changes necessary to make coaching more successful. This can include coaching skill development but can also be focused on such things as communications, leadership symbolism, alignment around strategy, and examination of HR practices and tools.

The primary focus of DukeCE's work is the design of innovative educational interventions that create better coaches and coachees in the work environment. These interventions may live in company processes, in passage programs, in leadership development, and in job assignments. They are there to bring coaching to life in the business.

Effective coaching, in the context of an organizational change strategy, begins with the ability of the coach to translate that strategy into something meaningful to the person across the desk. Coaching has to have a starting point and a goal. By aligning it to the strategy, it becomes something that coachees can internalize to help them succeed in their careers and contribute to the company.

It's critical that the organization be willing to examine, from a systemic perspective, the question of: "What will it take to build a coaching environment in this company?" This requires looking at the inhibitors and enablers from the perspective of culture, mental models, norms, skills, communications, leadership, infrastructure, metrics, and symbolism. Equally important is the organization's willingness to face the complexity of the task rather than look for a silver bullet in the form of training. Skills may actually be an issue, but more often than not, the real inhibitors are found elsewhere.

In the training of coaches, it's important to engage outside resources that are willing to invest in knowing the company's business and culture. How else could they act productively as coach to those soon to be coaches? I find that it is very difficult to learn coaching from folks that have little understanding of what actually goes on formally and informally in the company. Understanding the business and culture makes outside resources credible as advisors to senior leadership who see coaching as a strategic tool. Educators must be trusted to knowledgeably bring that strategy and point of view into the classroom and be seen as coaches themselves. They need to create a challenging and engaging practice field for those new coaches, one that recognizes the complexities and cultural realities of their environment.

Measurement should be part of the coaching strategy. It's necessary to decide from the beginning what outcomes the organization is after and how it will know if it has achieved them. The organization might take particular inhibitors identified in the early analysis and look at whether they are still in place. It might want to see improvements in elements of the organization's people and pulse surveys measuring feelings and beliefs within the enterprise. Stories and qualitative evidence can also be very informative, as can an examination of particular elements of strategy execution. The important thing is to decide what success looks like up-front and to design to achieve it.

Part III

INTERNAL COACHING

CHAPTER 9

※◆◆※

Applying the Behavioral Coaching Model Organization-Wide

The following case study, "Expanding the Value of Coaching: From the Leader to the Team to the Company," provides a great example of how a behavioral coaching process can expand beyond an individual executive and ultimately have a positive influence on hundreds of people.

Expanding the Value of Coaching: From the Leader to the Team to the Company—Clarkson Products Case Study

Joe Smith is the President and Chief Executive Officer of Clarkson Products.[1] Clarkson Products is a key division of Clarkson Enterprises and employs over 40,000 people. Clarkson Enterprises is a Fortune 100 company that employs over 100,000 people and is a leader in its industry.

I had the opportunity to work with Joe as an executive coach for over a year. Although I am not sure how much Joe learned from me during this period, I learned a lot from him and from his team! I hope that the great work done by Joe and his team gives you a couple of ideas that you can use, either as a coach, or a person being coached.

This real life case study shows how an executive can expand a simple coaching assignment to benefit his team and the entire company. I hope it also reinforces my observation that the most important factor in executive coaching is *not* the coach. It is the executive being coached and his or her coworkers.

Getting Started

The project began when I met with Bruce Jones, the CEO of Clarkson, and Mary Washington, the EVP of Human Resources. Bruce was clearly a fan of Joe's. He let me know that Joe was a fantastic leader who had produced consistent results. He felt that Clarkson would benefit if Joe played a greater role in reaching out across the company and building relationships with his colleagues in other divisions. Mary agreed that Joe was a key resource for the company and that the entire company could benefit from his increased involvement. Clarkson, like many of my clients, is trying to increase synergy across divisions and build more teamwork *across* the company.

When I first met Joe, I was impressed with his enthusiasm and love for his job. He was clearly in a place he wanted to be. Joe was very proud of what Clarkson Products produced and proud of the people who worked with him. I have worked with over 60 major CEOs. I have met a lot of committed leaders. Joe is one of the most committed leaders I have ever met.

Joe liked the design of our coaching process. He developed a list of key stakeholders and called Bruce to validate his list. He decided to work with me.

Collecting Information

I conducted one-on-one confidential interviews with each of Joe's preselected stakeholders. Both colleagues and direct reports agreed that Joe was brilliant, dedicated, hard working, high in integrity, great at achieving results, well-organized, and an amazing leader of people.

Joe's peers felt that the company could benefit if he did a better job of reaching out and forming partnerships with them. Some believed that Joe and his team were so focused on achieving results for the Products division that they hadn't placed enough emphasis on building synergy and teamwork across the entire Clarkson business.

Joe's direct reports agreed that Joe, his team, and the company would benefit if the Products team did a better job of reaching out across the company. They also wanted Joe to focus on making sure that everyone felt included. Some mentioned that Joe was so focused on achieving his mission that he could (unintentionally) leave out people or ideas that were not on his radar screen.

All of the interview data was collected by topic, so that no individual could be identified. After reviewing the summary report of the interviews with Joe, he agreed that he wanted to work on "reaching out across the company and building partnerships with colleagues" as a personal goal. He also expanded the goal to include his entire team.

Joe also decided to work on "ensuring involvement and inclusion" with his direct reports. Joe checked in with Bruce and both agreed that these were worthwhile goals.

Involving Team Members

Our research on behavior change is clear. If leaders get feedback and follow-up, and involve their coworkers in the change process, they get better. If they don't follow-up and involve their coworkers, they usually are not seen as improving.

As part of the coaching process, Joe had one-on-one discussions with his colleagues and direct reports about what he had learned. He thanked them for their feedback, expressed gratitude for their involvement and positive comments, openly discussed what he wanted to change, and asked them for their input on how he could do a great job.

After the initial discussions with his direct reports, Joe made a minor modification in one of his goals. He decided that his direct reports wanted him to do a great job of "inclusion and validation." The Products Division was going through very turbulent times. Several of Joe's team members wanted to make sure that he was checking in with them and validating that they were headed in the right direction during these changing times.

Although I always recommend that my coaching clients follow up with their key stakeholders to get ongoing ideas for improvement, Joe came up with a much better idea. He got his entire team involved! Not only did Joe pick key colleagues to connect with on a regular basis, so did everyone on this team. This expanded the benefit, reaching out far beyond anything that Joe could do by himself. In fact Joe's team established a matrix with ongoing process checks to ensure that *everyone* was sticking with the plan. All members of Joe's team talked about whom they were contacting and what they were learning on a regular basis. They shared information with each other to help improve cross-functional teamwork, synergy, and cooperation.

In the area of ensuring inclusion and validation with direct reports, Joe developed an amazing discipline. He would consistently ask, "Are there any more ideas that we need to include?" and "Are there any more people that we need to include?" at the end of each major topic change or meeting. This gave everyone a chance to reflect and made sure that everyone had the opportunity to make a contribution.

Often in the meetings of high-level executive teams (like Joe's), there is an outer ring of people in attendance. These are people who may report to team members and may be providing information on key topics that are going to be discussed. Joe made sure that his team members were included in this outer ring. Equally important, he reached out to ensure that everyone from that outer ring present at various meetings did not feel like outsiders or interlopers. He did so by genuinely encouraging them to participate—and genuinely taking into account their resulting feedback.

Over the course of the year, I had follow-up discussions with Joe's direct reports. Not only did Joe pick an area for personal improvement, each one of his direct reports did as well. This way the process of change not only benefited Joe; it benefited everyone.

A couple of his direct reports showed great maturity by telling Joe, "When we started on this process, I was critical of *you* for not being inclusive. In the last few months, you have been doing everything that you can do to include people. You have asked me for my input on a regular basis. I have to admit something. You weren't the problem in the first place. Sometimes *I* just wasn't assertive enough to say what I was thinking. It was easier for me to blame you than to take responsibility myself."

A Year Later

At the end of the coaching assignment, I had the opportunity to interview each of Joe's 15 direct reports and his 10 colleagues from across the company. They were asked to rate his increased effectiveness on each item on a "–5" to "+5" scale (with "0" indicating "no change"). Not surprisingly, his improvement scores were outstanding. 40 percent of all numerical responses were a "+5" and over 85 percent were a "+3" or above. No individual had a negative score on any item. I have seen hundreds of reports like this. These scores were exceptionally positive.

In "reaching out across the company and building partnerships," both his direct reports and colleagues were extremely satisfied with his progress. They commented on his ongoing dedication to being a great team player. They noticed how he had gone out of his way in meetings, phone calls, and e-mails to be a good partner.

In "ensuring that his team does a great job of reaching out and building partnerships," his scores were equally positive. Both groups commented on the ongoing process that he put in place with his team. In fact, some of his direct reports commented that their colleagues across the company had also started becoming better team players. (It is much easier to be helpful and supportive to other people, if they are trying to be helpful and supportive to you!)

In "ensuring validation and inclusion," his direct report scores were not just positive; they were amazing! His 15 direct reports had over 100 positive comments and nothing negative to say. They almost all talked about the value of his asking for input on an ongoing basis and his including everyone who was involved in the decision.

Like many companies, Clarkson's business was dramatically impacted by September 11 and its aftermath. This was an extremely hard year for Joe, his team, and his company. Many of his team members noted how easy it would have been for Joe to lose it and not reach out to others during this tough time. He had every excuse not to put in the time. They were amazed at his ability to involve, inspire, and motivate people when times were so tough. Some of the written comments were more than positive; they were moving.

Learning Points for Coaching

- *The key variable in determining the success of coaching is not the coach; it is the people being coached and their coworkers.* Joe had greater challenges and problems than almost any of the people that I have coached. In spite of this, he achieved outstanding results in building relationships with his colleagues and being inclusive with his team. He didn't get better because I did anything special. In fact, I have put in much more time with people who have achieved much less. He reinforced an important lesson for me (as a coach)—only work with people who care!

  As a person who is being coached, never put the responsibility for your change on the coach. It is your life. Like a personal trainer, the coach can help you get in shape. You are the one that has to do the work.

  Not only was Joe a model of ongoing dedication and commitment, so was his team. Every team member had a positive, can do attitude toward improving teamwork across Clarkson. Joe's positive results were not just a reflection of his efforts; they were a reflection of this team's efforts.

- *True long-term change requires discipline over time and process management.* One of the great misassumptions in leadership development is "If they understand, they will do." If this were true, everyone who understood that they were supposed to go on a healthy diet and work out would be in shape. Every executive that I meet is smart. In terms of behavior, they all understand what they should do. Joe did it!

  Joe established an ongoing process and discipline and stuck with it. He managed a process. He made sure that follow-up discussions were scheduled. He had the discipline to ask, "Are there any people or ideas that we need to include?" over and over again.

- *By involving team members and key stakeholders, the value of the coaching process can be increased exponentially.* Not only did Joe get better, everyone around Joe got better! Joe's entire team was involved in the process. Everyone in his team reached out across the company to build partnerships and increase synergy. Everyone on Joe's team picked personal areas for improvement and focused on getting better. Many of the members of Joe's team began to implement the same process with their own teams. In some cases, people across the company began reaching out to Joe's team in a much more collaborative way.

❏ Have you reviewed the benefits and costs of using internal coaching?
❏ Are the resources available to train the internal coaches?
❏ Do the best candidates for coaches have the time to commit to a coaching relationship?
❏ Will the bosses of the coaches put the appropriate priority on the coaches' involvement in the initiative?
❏ How are you going to deal with the question of confidentiality?
❏ Do you have a plan to match the coaches with coachees?
❏ Are you going to designate coaches or allow coachees to have an option?
❏ Establish the ground rules for the relationship.
❏ Has the coachee agreed that the coaching engagement will be treated as an opportunity or is the coachee reluctant? The more reluctant the coachee, the more an external coach may be more helpful.
❏ Establish and agree on the steps in the process.
❏ How is the coach going to get the information to correctly assess the development needs of the coachee?
❏ Is the coachee's boss fully supportive of the initiative?
❏ Is coaching being used as a substitute for dealing with a performance problem?
❏ Have you agreed on how frequently you will communicate with each other?
❏ How will the coach know when the end of the coaching relationship is reached?
❏ What will success look like?

FIGURE 9.1 Coaching Checklist: Internal Coaching

Joe was given a simple challenge to change his own behavior. Through his effort at personal improvement, Joe ended up benefiting hundreds of people across Clarkson.

- Internal HR coaches can use this process if:
  —*They have the time to do it.* In many cases coaching is an add on for HR professionals and they are just not given the time to do it right.
  —*They are seen as coaches, not judges.* Clients may not open up to HR professionals if they are later going to use what is being shared as part of a performance appraisal.
  —*Their internal clients give them credibility.* In some cases internal people can say exactly the same thing as external coaches but not be listened to.
- GE Capital did some wonderful research using this behavioral coaching model with internal HR coaches.[2] Their results were just as positive (if not more so) than the same research that we have done with external coaches.
- Figure 9.1 on page 230 provides a simple but effective tool that you can use when designing and implementing an internal coaching process.

CHAPTER 10

The Leader as Coach

David Kepler and Frank T. Morgan

David Kepler is a Corporate Vice President and the Chief Information Officer of The Dow Chemical Company. Dow is a global diversified chemical company with sales of more than $33 billion. Since joining the company in 1975, he has held numerous leadership positions in the United States, Canada, and Pacific regions of Dow. He is a member of the U.S. Chamber of Commerce Board of Directors, the American Chemical Society, and the American Institute of Chemical Engineers. Dave graduated from the University of California at Berkeley with a degree in chemical engineering.

Frank T. Morgan is Global Director of Executive Development and Leadership at The Dow Chemical Company. Prior to Dow, Frank was Professor of Management and Director of Executive Education at the University of North Carolina at Chapel Hill and the Darden Graduate School at the University of Virginia. He was also Senior Group Vice President for an American firm and ran companies in Latin America and Europe.

The opportunity to be a leader and coach occurs for everyone throughout his or her life. Many times, people miss the opportunity. In this essay, we will discuss why the leader-coach role is so critical in today's organization. To begin, Dave Kepler shares how a simple family experience in his life provided the foundation for his philosophy on leadership and coaching.

Who Should Build the Car?

Several years ago, my young son and I enjoyed an experience in the Indian Guides. It was time for the annual Pine Wood Derby. Each father and son

233

team was sent home with a small block of wood, two steel rods and a set of four plastic wheels. After careful planning, cutting, shaping, sanding, painting, and assembly, the teams returned to the next meeting with a racecar.

The objective was to create a car that rolled down a sloped track faster than all the other cars made from identical kits. The only variables were the shape and size of the car, and the careful placement of the axles and wheels. A winning car must minimize friction and resistance, and maximize effect of the car's only power source—gravity.

As the coach of our two-person team, I made sure my son understood the assignment and the challenges we would face in building our racecar. I outlined our strategy and lined up the resources (tools) we needed. As the coach, I had two options: I could dictate how the car would be built and do the work myself, or I could provide an appropriate level of input and coaching while my son did the work. Fortunately, I chose the latter option.

In my mind I pictured a sleek, Indy-style racecar. My son, however, pictured a "racing van." So we built a van. In retrospect, it was more like a blue brick on wheels, but it was my son's creation, and he was proud of it and felt a great sense of accomplishment. It even rolled reasonably straight. So off to the races we went.

As soon as we entered the race, two things became clear. First, our van was in trouble racing against all the sleek Indy-style race cars. Second, many of the other fathers took a much more hands-on approach to building their cars. Several of the pine wood models looked like concept cars from Detroit, with smooth, aerodynamic shapes and glistening lacquered finishes.

The laws of physics were all too predictable. While our van had the other cars beat in cargo space, it lacked considerably in speed and finished near the end of the pack. Our first Pine Wood Derby experience was a failure.

Or was it? My son had the satisfaction of approaching a *challenging assignment* (a block of wood, two steel rods and four plastic wheels) and emerging with a racing van. He had a *structured learning experience* of using woodworking tools for cutting and sanding, and techniques for painting. He also experienced first-hand how to evaluate *performance and results* to determine the best approach to future challenges. And these valuable lessons were capped off with a pleasant surprise.

After all the speedy winners received their trophies, my son's van was chosen as winner of the design class. Thankfully, the judges recognized the creative design capability of a seven-year-old over the advanced engineering prowess of the parents. We still have that van on display, after all these years, as a symbol of the lessons learned. I sometimes wonder what lessons were learned by the sons on other teams whose fathers stepped beyond their coaching role and built the cars themselves.

The Leader as Coach

A leader's primary function is to set the strategy and direction for the organization, and align the resources necessary to be successful. Of course, results and success are very important for any organization. If an organization is to have a future, the leader must produce results and develop the organization's assets—the most important of which is the performance capability of its people.

Great leaders (and great organizations) view continued people development as a high priority. Great organizations focus not just on results, but also on sustainable success through people development. Recent research indicates that people-centric firms have significantly higher financial returns when compared with less people-oriented companies in the same industry.[1]

As outlined in Figure 10.1, effective leaders contribute to a people-centric culture and thus influence employee satisfaction. Satisfied employees tend to stay with an organization longer, and to work harder and more effectively. The end result is better operational performance, higher levels of customer satisfaction, and, ultimately, business success.

How do organizations develop people? That's the role of the training department, right? Not really—training departments *train,* leaders *develop.* One model of individual development (Figure 10.2 on page 236) shows that structured learning experiences (e.g., organized training and education efforts) are but one aspect of development. In fact, for most people, structured

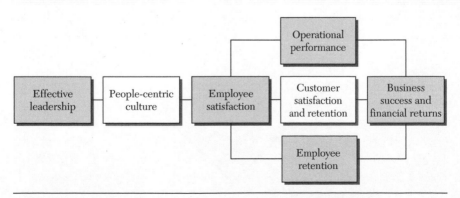

FIGURE 10.1   The People Development Value Chain

learning represents only 10 to 20 percent of their development experiences. The vast majority (80 to 90 percent) of professional growth comes from on the job experiences through completing challenging job assignments, being accountable for measurable performance results, and receiving coaching and mentoring from leadership.

As a coach, the leader is the touchstone for all the aspects of professional development. The leader not only makes job assignments, he or she also sets the direction for structured learning experiences and performance measurements, gives feedback, and provides the individual mentoring that is often the critical ingredient in developing an individual.

The role of a coach in business and in sports is very similar. For example, a sports coach determines the overall strategy for the team; aligns the resources (chooses the players); assists with key decisions in the game; and works with individual players to develop their personal skills, attitude, and approach.

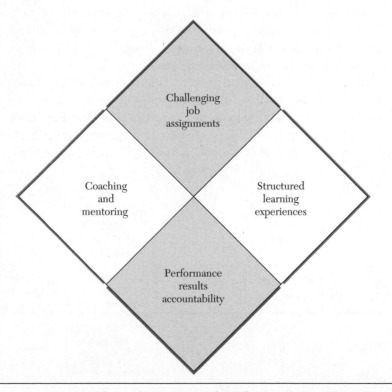

FIGURE 10.2   The Sources of Professional Growth

Likewise, the business coach determines the overall strategy; aligns the resources (in this case, both people and finances); assists with key decisions; and works with individuals to develop their personal skills, attitude and approach.

One additional challenge for business coaches, however, is that their role is not as clearly defined. Trailing by one point in the NBA finals with two seconds left on the clock, Pistons coach Larry Brown will likely design the in-bounds play and decide who takes the final shot. But he will *never* come off the bench and take the final shot himself.

In other words, a business leader is more of a player-coach. Business coaches must provide the strategy, align the resources, and provide individual development. But business coaches have the option to jump into the game. In business, the leader-coach *can* choose to take the final shot.

Most business leaders are promoted through the ranks. They are first recognized as effective doers. They are promoted to be managers and closely direct the work of others. Then, some evolve into a leadership position in which they must direct and influence business outcomes without being as intimately involved. Unfortunately, many leaders have a hard time evolving their role along with their responsibilities.

In business, a leader-coach faces a daily decision process to balance:

- Results versus Development
- Motivation versus Critical Assessment
- Being an Evaluator versus a Being a Developer
- Risks versus Learning Opportunities
- Delegation versus Direction versus Doing

These decisions have significant consequences. For example, a business coach who jumps in to take control of a given situation might have a positive impact on short-term results—while negatively impacting team development and long-term success.

Returning to the Pine Wood Derby metaphor, if Dave had dictated that his son build an Indy-style racecar, and taken a more hands-on approach to its construction, they certainly would have built a faster, more competitive car. But Dave's son would have lost out on some of the personal accomplishment from completing the assignment himself.

Dave's son would have lost out by not learning how to use woodworking tools. And he might have missed the design award won by his unique van. The long-term success of the team (Dave and his son) would definitely have suffered if Dave had focused on short-term objectives and built the car himself.

Leaders are doers, working alongside the individuals they lead. The player-coach in business must exercise judgment to determine the trade-offs between long-term, short-term, and immediate results versus development opportunities. Leaders need to have the judgment to know how and when to bring their skills and knowledge to task to support the individuals working with them and the organization they all serve.

Effective Coaching: Challenging Assignments

Individuals need challenging assignments to continue growing and developing. As a coach, how do you determine when and how to delegate an assignment? How do you balance the need to deliver business success with the need to provide employees with flexibility and the opportunity to learn through experience? Certainly, a risk-reward tradeoff enters into every decision.

There was little risk involved in encouraging Dave's son to design and build his own Pine Wood Derby car. Suppose the task had been purchasing his first real car as a 16-year old? With the stakes being his personal safety and significant financial consequences, Dave would have taken a much stronger role as a coach.

When approaching challenging assignments in an organization, the leader-coach must be able to evaluate the potential positive and negative impacts of the assignment. A coach must judge the abilities of their individual team members, and decide who is best suited and ready for a particular assignment. And, finally, a coach must decide how much of his or her personal involvement is required. Allowing employees greater freedom on the smaller tasks can better develop their decision-making skills and self-confidence to handle the bigger assignments that will arise.

The more a given assignment is beyond an employee's past experiences, training, and skills, the more a leader will need to be involved in coaching and support. When an assignment requires changes, resources, or commitment of others beyond the individual responsible, the coach may need to be more engaged. Certainly, the attitude and approach of the individual will dictate how much the coach is involved. Some people inherently have a higher tolerance for frustration, ambiguity, and problem solving, and thus need less coaching.

A common failure by coaches is not recognizing the differences in individual needs and thus approaching all situations in the same way. Inevitably, this mistake leaves some people undersupported and frustrated, and can lead to failure. At the same time, overcoaching individuals who don't need it leaves them discouraged, unchallenged, and underdeveloped. The ability to recognize and provide the *appropriate* amount of coaching is a hallmark of an effective leader.

Finally, although delegation is key, not all leaders have developed habits that foster success. In each situation, the leader should consider:

- Is the assignment understood?
- Can you measure the results?
- Does the individual understand and accept his or her role in implementing the assignment?
- Is there a deadline?
- Have key issues been evaluated and addressed?
- Are all necessary resources available?
- Do I, as a leader-coach, understand and accept my role in supporting the individual implementing the assignment?

Effective Coaching: Structured Learning

As addressed earlier in this chapter, the majority of individual development occurs through on-the-job experiences, but structured learning is an important piece of the puzzle as well.

Most people have access to structured learning opportunities through the organization they work for, or through private and public training and education organizations. Learning opportunities may be focused on specific skill sets required in a current job, on expanding existing skills into a broader role for the individual, or even on developing new skills to prepare for a job or career change.

What role should a leader-coach play in structured learning? The most obvious role is for the leader to strongly support and encourage continued learning. A leader who focuses on his or her own professional growth and encourages growth in others will foster a team that values learning and development. Coaches often help decide who on their team should participate in structured learning programs, what learning is required, and at what stage of their career they should participate.

Perhaps a subtler, but more important role for the coach, is helping the individual properly apply their structured learning experience to the real-world situations they will face. The closer the structural learning is to the assignment, the higher the employee's knowledge and skill retention. "Training on the job" and "on the job training" are both important, and they are most effective when used together.

As his son's Pine Wood Derby coach, Dave encouraged him to learn how to build the car, helped determine which skills were required (e.g., using a saw to shape the car or painting the finished piece), and took the time to teach him these skills. But more important, Dave explained to him the impact these skills had on the finished car. And since that time, Dave has helped him expand, develop, and apply these same basic skills to other, more advanced projects.

Ultimately, each individual employee must take responsibility for his or her own professional development. But leaders have a responsibility to support employee development, provide ongoing feedback and coaching, and ensure that employees develop some plan for their own growth.

Although many organizations have a formal employee development planning process, an effective leader-coach can support their team members by:

- Encouraging self-evaluation to determine the career aspirations of each individual. It helps to understand your destination before you begin the journey.
- Providing feedback on their specific strengths and weaknesses, particularly any gaps that may exist in skill sets required for them to follow their preferred path.
- Defining and documenting a plan to fill the gaps or develop the skills they will need to succeed. Coaches can play a critical role in helping employees uncover the best learning opportunities and helping apply them to the needs of both their individual career and the success of the business.
- Making sure the plan is implemented and evaluated, and that it is developed and expanded in the future.

Effective Coaching: Performance and Results

Ultimately, the development of employees is dictated by how they evaluate their own performance, and how it is evaluated by the organization. Employees who monitor and adjust their activities, and capitalize on learning opportunities to address performance successes and failures, will have the best long-term growth.

Here again, the leader-coach plays a critical role. A coach's feedback should be timely, specific, and as positive as possible. Input should focus on competencies (how the job was done) and on performance toward goals (what was accomplished). By providing ongoing input, and dealing quickly and directly with any issues that may arise, the coach develops a stronger relationship with the employee and prevents minor incidents from becoming significant problems. Ideally, both will view their relationship as a partnership to develop the employee's career and professional growth.

Returning one last time to the Pine Wood Derby story, the results might seem obvious on the surface. Digging deeper, it's the relationship and partnership that emerged as the greatest success.

Naturally, Dave's son was thrilled to have won his first trophy. Perhaps more important, however, was the satisfaction he got from seeing Dave's pride in his accomplishment. This combination of recognition by his peers and the joy his coach took in his success gave him confidence to undertake other challenges in the future.

When a leader-coach provides a team member with feedback and evaluation, heor she fosters a strong relationship of growth and development. Feedback works best when it is specific, directed at behavior, and not criticizing the person. For example, instead of saying "that was a good meeting," this feedback can be more effective if directed toward the behavior that helped produce the favorable result: "You did a great job preparing the agenda, and that made for a productive meeting." Giving sincere, specific feedback like this not only helps individuals develop, it helps cultivate relationships. And, strong coaching relationships between a number of leaders and team members throughout an organization foster a people-centric culture that, in turn, breeds sustainable success.

Conclusion: Learning for Leaders

The fundamentals of leadership and coaching, in sports, business, and life have remained largely unchanged. But how the rules are applied has changed dramatically.

For example, in business, we have evolved from the command and control pyramid structures of decades ago to flatter organizations made up of empowered teams. Today, business coaches must be flexible, use good judgment, and strive for a solid partnership with their team members, based on common goals for the individual and for the business.

Business cycles are shorter, and the amplitudes greater, so leaders themselves must be lifelong learners, constantly evaluating how their own roles evolve as the world and their organization change.

More than ever, it's critical for business leaders to lead by example. Can you expect your team members to place high value on their own growth and development if you ignore your own? Will your team members be willing to take reasonable chances and try new opportunities if you criticize their every "failure?" Will team members learn to make their own decisions if you dictate their every move?

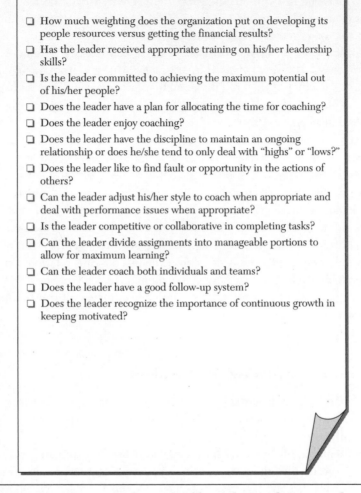

- ❏ How much weighting does the organization put on developing its people resources versus getting the financial results?
- ❏ Has the leader received appropriate training on his/her leadership skills?
- ❏ Is the leader committed to achieving the maximum potential out of his/her people?
- ❏ Does the leader have a plan for allocating the time for coaching?
- ❏ Does the leader enjoy coaching?
- ❏ Does the leader have the discipline to maintain an ongoing relationship or does he/she tend to only deal with "highs" or "lows?"
- ❏ Does the leader like to find fault or opportunity in the actions of others?
- ❏ Can the leader adjust his/her style to coach when appropriate and deal with performance issues when appropriate?
- ❏ Is the leader competitive or collaborative in completing tasks?
- ❏ Can the leader divide assignments into manageable portions to allow for maximum learning?
- ❏ Can the leader coach both individuals and teams?
- ❏ Does the leader have a good follow-up system?
- ❏ Does the leader recognize the importance of continuous growth in keeping motivated?

FIGURE 10.3   Coaching Checklist: The Leader as Coach

On the other hand, if you provide your team with *challenging job assignments,* support their *structured learning opportunities* and recognize their accomplishments toward specific *performance results,* you'll find your coaching job gets easier and the success of your organization more sustainable well into the future. Figure 10.3 provides a valuable tool for leaders acting as coaches.

And remember, sometimes it's okay for your team to build a racing van.

THE COACHING ALMANAC

CHAPTER 11

⪻⪼

Is Coaching Worth the Money? Assessing the ROI of Executive Coaching

Any person looking at the value of executive coaching must bear in mind that its practices are changing alongside broader business practices. Since the recession of 2001, much conventional business wisdom has become open for reexamination. The cult of the strong, forceful leader, for instance, has been replaced by a more humble model. At such a turning point, we need to examine not only how coaching has worked in the past but where it is headed in the future. This does not give us a reason to avoid exploring coaching best practices and ROI, but it does provide a caution that we are unlikely to reach any final answers in the near term. As Fredrick Reicheld recently commented, the careful study of business is a relatively new thing. We write this book at the beginning of the study of executive effectiveness—not at the end. The coaches represented in this book are pioneers. It is only in the decades ahead that we will come to a full understanding of the ground that they cover. Some would see this as daunting. We see it as exciting.

What Is the Business Impact of Executive Coaching?

We know that executive coaching is increasingly popular. On its own, this fact would tend to argue for its value—companies don't have a habit of throwing away money and those that do rarely live to throw it away for long. Still, there are nagging concerns about just how much coaching adds back to the bottom line. To borrow an argument from the Nobel Prize-winning economist Robert Solow, there is a fundamental difference in the return on investment in, say, a new factory and a new recreation room.[1] Both, technically, may contribute to increased productivity. One does so rather more directly.

Which is coaching? Is it more like investing in the new factory—investment that makes a direct and measurable impact on financial performance? Or is it more like buying the new rec room—helping the bottom line because happy employees tend to be productive employees? The answer has everything to do with how coaching is done. The available evidence suggests that many companies are investing heavily in coaching hoping to get the first kind of return (the factory) and actually getting the second (the new rec room). In this section, we will examine some of the research done over the last few years that helps to clarify how companies can get the most economic impact from their investment in coaching.

First, we need to look at what research has been done and separate the wheat from the chaff. Ten minutes on the Internet will prove that there is no shortage of what calls itself research on coaching. To be charitable, most of this material is not useful. Anecdotal stories of individuals who found greater effectiveness through their relationship with a coach, or elaborate case studies of coaching effectiveness told from the standpoint of the coach don't advance our understanding of the root effectiveness of coaching as a practice. What we need are careful quantitative studies of actual coaching engagements. We want to ensure that we are measuring the effectiveness of coaching and not of some other learning experience that might be going on while coaching is underway. We need a better sense of the periods in an executive's life when coaching is most beneficial. And we want to determine the relationship between what might be called customer satisfaction, and actual performance improvement.

How do we determine that it is coaching that is leading to performance improvement, and not some other activity, experience, or pressure? Particularly in situations where coaching is encouraged on an executive either by his or her superiors or by some broader part of the organization, we need to make sure that it is the coaching that is helping the executive improve, and not just his or her awareness of the expectation of change. Put on the spot, most executives are intelligent enough to temporarily change their performance in desired ways. What is less certain is that this forced change leads to permanent behavioral change. One of the claims made by effective coaches is that the coachee is learning new *habits*—that is, that the points of discussion and the lessons learned will be lasting. Good research allows us to zero in on the impact of coaching—and coaching alone—an important question for determining the return on investment.

Second, good research will reveal quite a bit about the timing of effective coaching. In coaching, as in life, timing is everything. Three questions are important in this regard. What is the best time to expose an executive to coaching? Are there windows in an executive's career when the organization would be earning better ROI than at others? Finally, are there unique periods when coaching is unlikely to be productive? These questions can only be answered by carefully studying how coaching works in large numbers of cases across a variety of companies.

Related to this is the question of performance improvement lag. Briefly stated, lag has to do with the amount of time that passes between the coaching event and the performance improvement. Adult education tends to have quite a bit of lag built into it. After learning something, adults tend to digest it—to make it their own and put it into practice in their own environments. The actual performance impact of a useful developmental experience, then, will likely start off low, gradually climb and then diminish as the executive wrings the lasting benefit from that experience. Well-conducted research on coaching will give a better sense for what these lags might be and how we can design our coaching interventions to impact our organizations as much as possible.

Finally, good research will allow us to differentiate between improved effectiveness as an outcome of coaching and mere customer satisfaction. Think, for a moment, about our above example of the recreation room. If asked, employees may say that their satisfaction is enhanced by a new recreation room. They may even report that they are more productive as a result of increased relaxation, happiness, or other related factors. In the end, however, it is not their own conclusions that are definitive, but actual hard data showing an increase in productivity. Stated bluntly, people can be wrong about how much more effective they are becoming. If people were able to accurately assess and remedy their own performance, there would be less need for executive coaching. In other words, determining whether or not executives are happy with their coach is not the same thing as carefully measuring the improvement each executive achieves as a result of coaching. Executive satisfaction will tend to measure, among other things, how well the coach and executive get along. At best, questioning the coachee will obtain his or her self-evaluation of increased effectiveness. We shouldn't lose sight of the fact that this runs the risk of significant bias. Good quality research will keep this fact in mind.

What's Out There Now: Early Research on the Value of Coaching

What would quality research look like, and does it exist now? To answer the first question, we should make a list of the qualities that the best research would have. Once we have such a list, it will be much easier to evaluate what's out there.

First, we are looking for efforts to measure the exact impact of coaching in a relatively large sample. The larger the sample, the more confident we can be that we are measuring actual effectiveness, as opposed to something that might be happening for local reasons. We also become more confident that best practices work from company to company.

Second, we'd love to find research where participants are selected randomly. This is important because it will help us avoid something called selection bias. Selection bias occurs when individuals are selected for possessing some initial quality or attribute; inevitably, subsequent measurement efforts pick up this quality or attribute. An example might be selecting a company's high potentials, for coaching and then comparing them after coaching with employees not on the high potential list. Understandably, you'll never be sure whether you are measuring the effect of the coaching or the fact that they were already high potentials. Selection biases can be very subtle but can have dramatic effects. The most well-known statistical example concerns a headline from the 1948 presidential race. On Election Day, the *Chicago Tribune* famously printed the mistaken headline "Dewey Defeats Truman," despite the fact that Truman had actually won the race. What happened? The *Tribune* relied on a poll in which participants were drawn from Department of Motor Vehicle records. In 1948, however, people who owned cars were a bit wealthier than the average American. The poll sampled these slightly wealthier individuals, who voted for Dewey slightly more than the actual rates in the population. Because the sample had selection bias, the results were useless— and quite embarrassing for the *Chicago Tribune*.

There are many contexts where true random sampling is difficult or impossible to achieve. In a coaching setting, randomness is unlikely to make sense. You give coaching to people who need it and avoid it for people who do not. Although it is true that the expense of coaching as a practice makes random sampling less feasible, we should look to cases where researchers have done what they can to avoid selection bias. At a minimum, what we would hope for is some comparison between a group of managers subject to executive coaching and those who weren't. We'd want these two groups (those selected for coaching and those not) to be as similar as possible in terms of rank and context. We'd then want to define what we mean by coaching as clearly as possible—making it easier to figure out what exactly was working if we find any effect. Is there research out there that meets these demanding standards? Some.

We chose to look at one study that is representative of good early research on the subject. It appeared in the journal *Personnel Psychology* in the spring of 2003. In this study, the authors looked at the effectiveness of 360-degree feedback when participants met with a coach versus the effectiveness of the 360-degree feedback alone.[2] The authors found that individuals who met with a coach to discuss their feedback and their action plan were more likely to set specific goals and achieve them in the year ahead. What is good about this research is its specificity. At the end of reading it, we know what has and what has not been demonstrated, and thus, what does and does not work. Other research that would fit this bill includes such work as:

- Gerald Olivero, Denise K. Bane and Richard E. Kopelman, "Executive Coaching as a Transfer of Training Tool: Effects on Productivity in a Public Agency" that appeared in *Public Personnel Management*, vol. 26, no. 4 (1997), pp. 461–469.

  Summary: Describes the advantages of one-on-one executive coaching in positively influencing transfer of training. Examines the effects of executive coaching in a local government agency. Thirty-one managers took a management development program, followed by eight weeks of one-on-one executive coaching. The study finds that training increased managerial productivity by 22.4 percent, while coaching increased productivity by 88 percent.

- Andrea D. Ellinger, "Antecedents and Consequences of Coaching Behavior," *Performance Improvement Quarterly*, vol. 12, no. 4 (1999), pp. 45–70.

  Summary: Discusses the use of coaching to facilitate the development of learning organizations. Presents the results of a study to determine the outcomes of coaching interventions. Finds that managers' commitment to coaching can impact employee, manager, and organizational performance.

- Carol Patton, "Rating the Returns," *Human Resource Executive*, vol. 15, no. 5 (April 2001), pp. 40–43.

  Summary: Outlines a nine-step ROI process that determines the value of executive coaching. Claims that this process must be applied consistently through the organization. Includes a list of measurement tools and important ROI measurements.

What we see when we look at this research is a fairly compelling case for the cost effectiveness of executive coaching. We would add that this effectiveness can be enhanced if a number of careful steps are followed. First, the coaching should be as specific as possible in terms of its goals. This doesn't rule out what we would call opportunism—cases where we find something worth working on in the course of our engagement—but it does help to have a specific set of goals agreed to early on in the engagement. Second, there should be some sort of agreement about what will count as meeting those goals. If the executive has a problem motivating team members, an agreement should be reached prior to the engagement about how a change in this skill will be measured. This system of measurement need not always be quantitative. Some of the best coaches rely far more on interview-based feedback. What is important is that this agreement be reached before the engagement begins. Otherwise, there will be the temptation to define success based on where you end up rather than on where you wanted to go. Third, getting to know your coach as well as you can before an engagement is a good idea. Ask questions. Talk about results. Evaluate the decision to hire a coach as carefully as the decision to buy a piece of major equipment. Do you know the brand? Do you need the features, and do they fit in with other aspects of your business?

The sheer diversity of coaching research tells us where we are in the developmental phase of the industry. Like the automobile industry in the early twentieth century, we are in a situation where the need for the product has become clear, but where the exact form that product will take is still very much under development. What is important in this development phase is reliability of the product and reputability of the person or company providing the service. In the next 20 years, we will see a consolidation of the coaching field around accepted best practices and a further refinement of the research studying coaching. For now, the best advice for those who would seek coaching is to know your practitioners; evaluate his or her reputations; and have detailed conversations about expectations before the engagement begins.

Conclusions and Recommendations

What becomes clear when we look carefully at the existing research is that asking the question "Is coaching worth the money?" is like asking the question "Is training worth the money?" The question itself is too broad. Unless you know quite a bit about the proposed intervention—what are its specific goals? who will do the training? how will the success of the training be measured?—you will not know enough to answer the ROI question. Coaching *can be* worth the money, but the consumer must purchase wisely. The two best reasons that coaching *can be* worth the money have to do with (1) the disproportionate influence exerted by executives and (2) the increased effectiveness of one-on-one training.

The Disproportionate Influence of the Executive

Many studies of coaching ROI assume what we are calling the disproportionate influence exerted by executives. The argument goes something like this:

John Smith, executive, controls the fate of a company that generates $5 billion annually. A 1 percent improvement of his effectiveness, it is suggested, will translate into a $50 million dollar savings for the company. Even if the rate of return is less (or even far less) than the estimated $50 million, the savings would still be substantial—and worth it for the organization. Small increases in executive effectiveness are able to have large effects on organizational performance. This makes executive coaching appealing because a little effort can have a large impact. Although it's probably a good idea to be cautious about the wilder claims made on the basis of this assumption (it's not uncommon to see a 100 to 1 return on investment claimed for coaching), there is certainly something to this rationale.

Two suggestions are important here for getting the most bang for the buck. First, coaching should have a discernable effect on business-critical skills. If the executive is regarded as too abrasive, for example, the net result of the coaching should be a reduction in the perception of abrasiveness on the part of the people with whom the executive works. If the issue is an unwillingness to engage in conflict, colleagues, superiors, and subordinates should regard the executive as better able to engage in effective conflict at the end of the coaching engagement. If all of this sounds very obvious, it is. Nonetheless, most coaching engagements are not structured so clearly. Accordingly, even though the executive has an enormous amount of influence, the coaching engagement often becomes too watered down to have concrete business impact, and thus any appreciable ROI. As many of the coaches in this volume will tell you, one key way to enhance return on investment is specific and prearranged goals and a way of measuring whether or not those goals have been accomplished. This can take the form of a written action plan with specific follow-up, or it can take the form of an agreement between the coach and the executive to find some way of measuring progress.

Second, coaches and executives alike should be aware of what could be called nonlinear skills or attributes. A nonlinear skill or attribute is one where one of two things is true: either a small change will have a dramatic effect on the effectiveness of the executive, or a large change will have a negligible effect on the effectiveness of the executive. The first case is called an amplifier, where a small amount of improvement facilitated by the coach has a large effect on performance. The second is called a damper where a coach can work and work and not make much of a mark on the effectiveness of the executive.

Coaches and executives should be on the lookout for these amplifiers. A good example of this is some engagements we have seen that have centered on effective conflict management. Because conflict is, in most cases, somewhat rare, and because most people have a negative emotional response to conflict, small improvements regarding conflict management skills tend to result in large changes in perceptions of effectiveness. Indeed, too much change and the perception of the executive's effectiveness can go down—we start running into concerns about assertiveness. Amplifiers help to achieve good ROI because they are cases where a little bit of work by the coach and the executive result in quite a bit of perceived improvement.

Dampers, on the other hand, are pitfalls to be avoided. These are skills or attributes in which large amounts of work can be invested, and actual change is achieved, but there is little perception of increased effectiveness. A good example of this might be work we have seen in increasing the organization skills of an executive. Even relatively large shifts in an executive's ability to be organized are often not noticed by his or her peers or superiors. This is true for a number of reasons. First, it is assumed that executives are going to be organized to at least a certain level. Below this level, even improved performance is unlikely to earn much credit. Second, the skill is often seen as cost-effectively delegated. If a coaching engagement will cost more than other solutions that are more likely to lead to effectiveness, such as delegating more authority to an office manager, then coaching won't make a great deal of sense. Self-esteem probably works like a damper as well—it takes quite a bit of increased self-esteem to make a noticeable impact on others. This has led many of our authors to be wary of deeper psychological issues. They are more likely to require large amounts of work for what may well be only small improvements. This is not an argument against an executive working through these issues. It is an argument that says that a coach might not be the person who can help most effectively.

The Effectiveness of One-on-One Training

Second, much of the research seems to assume that executive coaching works as a form of one-on-one training. The claim goes something like this: since we know that training in a group setting works, and since executives tend to be too busy to participate in group training, one-on-one training (which we'll call coaching), will work as well. This makes sense. Just as a one-on-one session with a teacher is likely to get certain concepts and practices across, so too the one-on-one relationship established as part of the coaching process is an effective way to impart new practices and ideas.

A couple of guidelines are important here. First, we have to be careful to include enough people in the coaching process to get the advantages of both the classroom and the one-on-one session. Many who have experience in group educational settings can tell you that some of the most valuable lessons come not from the teacher, but from the other students in the class. This unexpected benefit often comes from the quiet members of the class—the one's you'd least expect to provide a frame-changing comment. Coaching can be similar. We need to make sure to include enough input to allow for surprises, both for ourselves as coaches and for the executive. This is a good argument for the inclusion of interviews in at least some component of the coaching process.

❏ As an organization, are you committed to coaching as a process rather than just an event?

❏ Is the coachee's immediate supervisor committed to the coaching process?

❏ What are the types of changes that you hope will result?

❏ Have you established internal measurements to identify when you have achieved success?

❏ Do you have benchmarks on those measures to identify the baseline?

❏ Do you have a control group identified?

❏ Are you using the right period of time to properly achieve the results you are looking for (at least 18 to 24 months)?

❏ Have you considered indirect measures such as employee satisfaction or turnover?

❏ Are you measuring the coach on the results that the coach achieves or the time that the coach spends?

❏ Have you ensured that one of the measurements is perceived improvement, as viewed by those who work with the coachee on a frequent basis?

❏ Based on everything that you know about the coachee, is there a reasonable probability that the coachee will change?

FIGURE 11.1 Coaching Checklist: Enhancing ROI

Second, we need to be a bit careful about the fundamental differences between training and coaching. Training assumes a lesson in place and ready to go. It assumes that there will be a more or less effective reception of this lesson and an application after the fact. Coaching often works differently. The coach works to facilitate progress in a number of areas, but it is the experience of the executive that serves as the foundation for any lessons learned. The coach needs to walk a thin line between too little and too much structure—between adding value and turning the coaching discussion into a monologue. Good coaches have great skill at walking this delicate line.

Conclusion

A brief look at the quality research available on the ROI of coaching gives us grounds to be optimistic. Measuring impact remains an underexplored issue; and yet there are solid reasons that coaching can make a significant impact on the bottom line of our organizations. Despite the significant cost associated with executive coaching, such costs can be carefully and wisely managed to the benefit of all concerned. Coaching is a good way to improve individual executive effectiveness. When planned and executed well, it will likely lead to more effective organizations.

Figure 11.1 on page 253 provides a useful coaching tool for enhancing ROI.

CHAPTER 12

Interpretative Data:
*What's Shaping the
Coaching Marketplace*

In launching a survey through Linkage, our goal was to obtain important information on coaching trends. We wanted to report on what's completely new in the field, not merely on changes in techniques, tools, and methods. We also wanted to learn more about focus; for example, where are organizations investing in coaching? We segmented our questions into internal coaches (employees providing coaching) and external coaches (outside consultants supplying coaching services to organizations). We asked about evaluation, measurement, and assessment, hoping to determine how analysis was taking place.

We also applied qualitative methods in our survey. Every day, Linkage discusses coaching trends with internal/external coaches all over the world. These data are included in our summarization.

We believe that over time, as this data is collected on an annual basis, it will provide valuable information to those inside companies who are making decisions based on benchmarks; and also be of great service to external coaches who study the market in order to better meet organizations' needs.

This chapter is meant to summarize important data that we collected from the *Linkage Best Practices in Coaching Survey*. The survey was sent to thousands of organizations around the world, representing industries of all sizes, including those in government services, nonprofits, and associates. Over 235 surveys were completed, assuring us a stratified random sample that represented organizations with fewer than 100 employees up to those with more than 20,000 employees. For the most part, the largest representative groups included those employee-based company respondents with 1,000 to 5,000 employees and those with more than 20,000 employees. The latter group accounted for approximately 37 percent of the total number of survey respondents.

About the Sample Group

There were 19 countries represented in the survey data. The United States, Canada, and Mexico accounted for 74 percent of the survey respondents, Europe was the second largest respondee group, followed by Asia, representing a little less than 5 percent.

We surveyed organizations from virtually all sectors, representing a wide range of industries, as well as government organizations and nonprofits.

The following is a list of those industries that comprise more than 1 percent of the sample:

- Academic/Educational
- Aerospace/Defense
- Arts/Entertainment/Recreation
- Automotive
- Banking/Finance
- Communications/Information Technology
- Retail
- Constructing
- Mining/Oil/Gas
- Manufacturing
- Government Agencies/Public Administration/Nonprofit
- Health care/Pharmaceutical
- Engineering
- Transportation
- Agriculture

The Data

Our analysis of the quantitative data follows. After each question, interpretive comments and perspective are added:

1. In which of the following areas does your organization currently use coaching?

    Respondents indicated that they most frequently use coaching for developing leaders when they are facing specific instances of career/life transition, making organizational change, or determining strategy.

Analysis and Discussion: Our conclusions from this survey question and our qualitative data are that organizations use coaching most frequently for developing leaders. Our other leadership surveys also indicate that leadership development is a primary focus of organizations' development efforts. Surprisingly, organizational development and change scored higher than our expectations.

2. Where do you see your organization's most significant coaching needs for this year?
   Here are the top five in rank order:
   1. Leadership coaching for behavioral change
   2. Career transition/succession coaching
   3. Performance and development
   4. Communications and interpersonal skills
   5. Lower-tier employee coaching

Analysis and Discussion: No surprise here, as the top five ranking came in as expected.

3. How does your organization currently use coaching?
   The top six ranked uses for coaching within organizations are as follows:
   1. Enhancing current performance
   2. Correcting performance issues
   3. Team building (tied)
   3. Change management (tied)
   5. Succession management
   6. Ensuring the success of new executives

Analysis and Discussion: It was most interesting to note that enhancing current performance was noted by 78.3 percent of survey respondents, whereas correcting performance was at 71.3 percent; team building and change management 45 percent, succession management 37 percent, and ensuring success of the new executive 32 percent. Respondents strongly indicate that the issues confronting those who manage coaching within organizations are strongly weighted toward enhancing and correcting performance. We believe there is a big missed opportunity for ensuring the success of the new executive, which scored only 32.3 percent. We also believe that, as organizations begin to see the benefits of coaching for new executives, this type of coaching will increase significantly in the years to come.

4. Why do you choose coaching over other methods?
   The responses in rank order:
   1. Customized application
   2. Flexibility/timeliness
   3. Outside perspective/objectivity
   4. Personal privacy
   5. Subject expertise
   6. Expense
   7. Minimizing company liability

Analysis and Discussion: It is not surprising that survey respondents rated expense low, since coaching is more costly than other methods. There is an obvious and increasing clarity expressed by our analysts that coaching is a preferred developmental method because an organization can customize a specific intervention with explicitly designed behavioral objectives.

5. How do you characterize the effectiveness of past coaching interventions at your organization?
   Seventy-five percent of survey respondents rate the effectiveness of coaching as a 3 or better on a scale of 1 to 5, with 5 being very effective and 1 not effective. Only 15 percent of respondents rate coaching as a 1 or a 2.

Analysis and Discussion: Unfortunately, 15.8 percent rate past coaching interventions not at all effective or hardly at all effective. The good news is that the majority consider it to be somewhat effective or very effective. We interpret this data to indicate that overall there is high degree of satisfaction with past coaching interventions with room for improvement.

6. How many years has your organization been using internal coaches?
   Of the total group, 9 percent indicated that they had been using internal coaching for less than 2 years; fewer than 2 percent for less than 1 year, while 55 percent of respondents have been using coaching for between 3 and 20 years.

Analysis and Discussion: It's clear that internal coaches have been in place for many years in most organizations. In fact, the majority of organizations in our survey indicate that coaching has been institutionalized in their organization. We also interpret from our data that a certain percentage—perhaps as high 33 percent—have not institutionalized an internal coaching process.

7. How many years has your organization been using external coaches?

   The majority of respondents report they have been using external coaches for less than 10 years. It is interesting to note that approximately 12 percent have institutionalized external coaches during the last 2 years.

Analysis and Discussion: We believe that external coaching is growing at a stable rate. At the same time, more than 40 percent of the organizations in the survey have not institutionalized an external coaching program.

---

8. Has your organization's use of coaching increased for external coaches?

   In those organizations that use external coaches, 57 percent suggest that they're using coaches at an increasing rate. Moreover, we estimate that the organizations using external coaches will increase 27 percent per year on a going forward basis.

9. Has your organization's use of coaching decreased for external coaches?

   Respondents indicated that use is decreasing in less than 10 percent of those who are currently using internal coaching.

10. Has your organization's use of coaching increased for internal coaches?

    Internal coaching is growing at about the same rate as external coaching or decreasing at about the same rate as external coachings.

11. What percentage of your organization's coaching needs is met internally versus externally?

    Of those surveyed, approximately 75 percent go outside only 28 percent of the time to meet their coaching needs, while 22 percent go outside slightly more than 50 percent of the time, and 13 percent go outside less than 25 percent of the time.

Analysis and Discussion: This data suggests that many organizations are attempting to answer most of their coaching needs through internal coaching. This is understandable given the nature and volume of coaching that has increased over the last 5 to 10 years. Companies may also be investing in building skills for coaches to handle the growing needs for trained coaches.

---

12. Which management levels in your organization currently receive coaching?

    Lower leadership—53 percent
    Middle leadership—31 percent
    Senior leadership—52 percent
    Executive leadership—64 percent

Analysis and Discussion: It was clear in this data that the major investments are being expanded. Executive and senior leaders receive coaching twice as much as middle leadership. It is very interesting to note, however, that lower level leaders (i.e., entry level) receive coaching 53.6 percent of the time. One could look at this data and infer that middle management gets the least amount of coaching. One would have to wonder whether this is a big opportunity for organizations or whether middle levels of leadership simply do not have the front-burner issues.

13. What is the average duration in months of a coaching intervention?
    Lower leadership—6.6 months
    Middle leadership—7.3 months
    Senior leadership—12.5 months
    Executive leadership—14 months

Analysis and Discussion: This indicates that there is a correlation between length of coaching assignment and leadership level in the organization supplying data. The more senior the leader, the longer the coaching relationship. This may suggest that higher-level coaching is more intense and is conducted over a longer period of time. Since there is a relationship between expenses and duration, there may be an obvious conclusion that higher-level coaching is perceived to be of higher value to organizations.

14. What are your greatest concerns in selecting, hiring, and using a coach?
    Validating coaching expertise—60 percent
    Determining coaching needs—31 percent
    Assessing fit—25 percent
    Ensuring return on time and expense for coaching engagement—55 percent
    Determining appropriate length of coaching time—34 percent
    Gathering information about coaching—24 percent

Analysis and Discussion: It is clear from the respondent data that there is significant concern in measuring impact and assessing fit. There is only moderate to low concern on how to gather information on coachees. The second most pressing concern among respondents is ensuring return on time and expenses. Getting the right expertise is the greatest concern.

15. How important are the following considerations in selecting a coach?
    Cost—57 percent

Area of expertise—68 percent
Coaching experience—78 percent
Gender—20 percent
Level of business experience—63 percent
Industry—34 percent
Direct referral—40 percent
Reputation—65 percent
Whether the coach and the coachee get along—71 percent

Analysis and Discussion: Coaching experience and area of expertise, along with reputation, combined with the ability of the coachee and the coach to get along, are the most important aspects in selecting a coach. Business expertise and gender are the least important.

16. How do you evaluate/measure the success or impact of the coaching intervention?
Pre and post self-assessment—54 percent
Pre and post multirater assessment—44 percent
Accomplishing agreed-to changes and objectives—78 percent
Satisfaction of coachee—69 percent

Analysis and Discussion: The two most important measurements are accomplishing agreed-to changes and objectives, and the satisfaction of coachees, while pre- and postself-assessment is not as important. There seems to be overwhelming agreement that coaching has to produce results (i.e., change in behavior that is observable).

17. How effective is internal/external coaching?
Forty-four percent rate internal coaching very effective or most effective, while only 13.6 percent rate their internal coaching as not effective. Twenty-nine percent rate external coaching as a very effective or most effective while only 10.7 percent rate their external coaches as not effective.

Analysis and Discussion: There was only a slight difference between how organizations rate their external and internal coaching. Although there is a slight increase in assessment of the external coaching, overall, in both internal and external coaching, the ratings are significantly higher than anticipated.

18. Please indicate which of the following statements apply to your organization.

Do you have an internal coaching and mentoring system in place?—
74 percent
Do you apply certification standards to internal coaches?—11 percent
Do you provide training for internal coaches and mentors?—
65 percent

Analysis and Discussion: Surprisingly, even though the vast majority (74 percent) of respondents do, in fact, have an internal coaching and mentoring system in place, only 11 percent apply certification standards and measures with respect to those coaches. We expect that the use of such standards and measures to increase over time. Indeed, some of the underlying training is already in place, as nearly two-thirds of respondents currently provide training for internal coaches and mentors. We believe that this is higher than in the past as derived from the qualitative data.

19. What leading-edge coaching models, tools, techniques, methods, and approaches does your organization use?
    Action learning—48.1 percent
    Appreciative inquiry—32 percent
    Behavior modeling—35 percent
    360-degree feedback—62 percent
    Quick feedback survey—27 percent
    Peer interview—40 percent
    Supervisor interview—48 percent
    Shadowing—29 percent

Analysis and Discussion: Clearly, 360-degree feedback has really caught on in the last 10 years. It is becoming customary in approximately two-thirds of the cases where internal and external coaching is provided by an organization. Surprisingly, action learning is being used (i.e., tailoring on-the-job learning for the coachee) in almost 50 percent of the coaching situations. Advanced concepts such as shadowing, although significant, are used in less than 30 percent of the internal and external coaching situations.

20. How frequently are your coaching needs delivered through the following means?
    Face to face—greater 75 percent
    Phone—greater than 50 percent
    Teleconference—less than 20 percent
    E-mail—approximately 50 percent

Videoconferencing—less than 10 percent
Group—greater than 20 percent

Analysis and Discussion: There are some surprising results here. For instance, e-mail, at 50 percent, is far above the expectations of our analysts. These data suggest that technology is becoming part and parcel of the coaching experience for both internal and external coaches. In fact, e-mail and phone rated approximately the same—a big surprise.

21. How do you contract/structure a coaching intervention?
    Specific timeframe—greater than 70 percent
    One-time event—less than 30 percent
    Ongoing event—greater than 60 percent of the time

Analysis and Discussion: Respondents rated one-time event coaching lowest. In fact, 58 percent of respondents noted "never or almost never" for coaching as a one-time event.

22. On what basis do you purchase coaching expertise (in rank order)?
    1. Daily rate
    2. Fixed rate for assignment
    3. Contingency basis
    4. Per individual intervention

Analysis and Discussion: It's clear that daily rate is the most important consideration in how respondents purchase coaching expertise from the qualitative discussions with organizations, the higher the level of coaches the more inclination to daily rate arrangements.

23. Do you expect your coaching investment to increase this year (check all that apply)?
    Entry-level leadership—17 percent
    Middle-level-leadership—30 percent
    Senior-level leadership—25 percent
    Executive-level leadership—35 percent

Analysis and Discussion: What's interesting about this is that whereas current spending on various levels of management and leadership clearly is skewed toward senior and executive leadership, these data suggest that this might change. Respondents suggest middle-level leadership spending will increase at a significantly higher rate than entry-level leadership, and even more than at senior-level leadership.

This may indicate that there is a growing recognition of the need to develop middle managers and leaders.

Summary

In addition to our survey data, we have collected many comments from organizations and individuals using internal/external coaches from interviews over the past year. Here are some of our overall conclusions:

- Investments in all areas of leadership coaching appear to be on the increase, with approximately 33 percent of the respondents indicating increases in budgets going-forward for all categories.
- There is surprising evidence from respondents that investment in mid-level managers and leaders will increase disproportionally to the current spending in that category.
- There appears to be strong evidence that coaching through electronic mediums, including telephone and e-mail, is increasing, with e-mail and telephone indicated by respondents to be greater than 60 percent. Nevertheless, face-to-face interviewing still ranks as the most prevalent form of coaching.
- Respondents rated cost as an important aspect in the selection process of outside coaches. However, the most important aspects of coach selection are coaching experience, level of business experience, and area of expertise. It is suspected that once a decision is made to expend funds on coaching, cost becomes less important.
- There is no question that 360-degree feedback in the coaching process plays the biggest role in setting up the relationship, as well as in assessing the success of the coaching intervention.
- It is significant that among respondents there is a high degree of satisfaction for both internal coaching and external coaching with a slight statistical advantage to external coaching. This is good news for those practitioners of coaching.
- It is interesting to note that there is a strong indication that there are new leading-edge coaching methods and models being used by coaches inside of organizations and by outside coaches (e.g., action learning, appreciative inquiry techniques, and behavior modeling). However, tried and true peer interviews and supervisory interviews are still significant techniques used by respondents.
- There seems to be evidence that there is a trend toward open-ended coaching assignments, as well as coaching assignments in specific time frames.

- Overall, the greatest concern in selecting, hiring, and using internal/external coaches is aligning the right coach with the coachee.
- Responses in our survey and our interviews indicate there is a growing trend toward external use of coaches for all levels of managers and leaders.
- There is no question in the minds of our analysts that currently, executive leadership and senior leadership levels within the organization are receiving more coaching, for longer periods of time, with greater levels of expenditures.
- There appears to be a significant increase in coaching entry-level managers and leaders, which indicates the high payoff of such efforts.
- Overall, there is no question that organizations primarily use coaching to enhance current performance and correct performance issues. The growing evidence from respondents is that team building and managing change, as well as succession management and ensuring the success of the new leader are also important. Overall, coaching is most frequently used for leadership development, followed by change management, strategy, and then career development.

We received many contributions both in written form within the questionnaire and verbally through interviewing coaches during this process. We have included here a number of comments that were especially noteworthy. As you will see, many of these come from the heart and speak to many of the larger issues that were supported in the data.

Here is the case of Barbara Beath of Ernst & Young, who expresses how 360-degree feedback as a coaching tool improved scores year over year:

After utilizing 360-degree feedback for a division's executives, 100% of execs in the bottom 15% of results received one-on-one coaching to help make behavior changes and improve their scores. 100% of the bottom 15% in scores (12 out of 12 executives) improved their scores the next year and only one of those 12 execs were in the bottom 15% of scores in the second year.

You will note in the data, 360-degree feedback is, without a question, a critical part of today's coaching interventions, and we predict it will be so in the future.

It was encouraging to hear so many touching stories of internal coaches who are truly making a difference, as in Sylvia Brown's experience at Boeing:

I was an internal coach for a member of the Boeing Executive Development Program. The coachee was high-potential and intelligent but frequently was stonewalled by her peer team on projects. Coaching enabled her to see her actions and gave her an opportunity to practice some changes in her be-havior, resulting in good working relationships with her team and with the executives to whom she was assigned.

Some offered caution like Eric deNijs at Capital One, who helps us to be-ware of the concern that too many people are cashing in on the recent popu-larity of coaching. Exemplary internal coaches like Eric who are dedicating their lives to the profession of coaching are truly making a difference:

My biggest concern for coaching today is growing the coaching value proposition. It seems that many people are trying to cash in on the recent popularity of coaching. However, this is a profession complete with lan-guage, technology, values, and risks. If we want to protect and enhance the future of coaching we need to do a better job of educating the consumer about the standards of coaching excellence.

The rewards are great. As Bruce A. McGuiness of the Department of De-fense helps us to see, "it is the unselfish coach that succeeds." Bruce also notes that tools, like books and materials, can help a person along the way in addition to the exemplary coaching provided by the coach.

Prasanta Kumar Padhy shared this wonderful quote: "explore something out of nothing." This is what he is doing at Berhampur University in India.

Then there is the issue of integrating coaching results/solutions and cre-ating a whole system. As Mary Anne Rasmussen at Allianz AG advises, there needs to be "a stronger organizational commitment to the coaching effort."

Clearly, the data and the comments from those who contributed indi-cate that it does take an organization to coach a person. Coaches who have learned how to employ the resources of the organization, the commu-nity, internal/external coaches and mentors, and team efforts provide the best results.

Some of our respondents expressed concern, as did David Proctor of the United Way of Rhode Island, who talks about how sometimes organizations will put a "hammer on someone" through coaching. He uses a great metaphor in saying, "much more helpful imagery is seeing the client and the coach as fellow pilgrims on a journey with the coach bringing some of the resources such as a wilderness guide brings while leading a group."

Kenneth Yap at Meta HR & Communication explains it well when he says, "Coaching is to be a guide by the side, not merely a sage on the stage."

Patti Waterbury says it well, too, when she says, "When you understand your old maps, you can decide whether to let them define your future."

Lucille Peeters-Adriaens' quote is a great place to complete and summarize: "Creating a coaching culture is only possible with full commitment of the executive team and both bottom-up and top-down initiatives."

We look forward to conducting a similar survey in the future so that we can compare this survey's results and help define how coaching is changing. Our objective is to anticipate trends and provide direct and clear analysis from the data that we receive. If you would like to participate in such future surveys, please e-mail pharkins@linkageinc.com, and we will put you on the list of future survey respondents. We wish to thank the many hundreds who participated in the quantitative and qualitative responses that made the current survey successful. And here are a few final thoughts from some of those participants.

The higher one gets on the echelon climb, the lonelier is the journey. A coaching hand is a welcomed rope to ease the challenge for secured footing.

—Sharifah Maria Alfah, MIHRM

One of the most critical competencies is for today's organizational leaders to value the people relationships to accomplish the task. Many managers are so task-focused, they are blinded to the greatest tool at their disposal: the people. My suggestion to any manager seeking to become a great leader is to cultivate the people relationships with those you lead. If you do this, you will not have to do the tasks; your people will be glad to take on those responsibilities.

—Tony Preston, Lake Community Action Agency

The value of executive coaching is revealed when trust develops between the coach and the coachee, allowing the executive a place for honest, direct feedback that doesn't compromise the integrity of his or her position. When it's "lonely at the top," a coach becomes a safe ear for thoughtful analysis without risking professional reputation or the confidence of the staff.

—Susan O'Leary, Chanticleer Foundation

Coaching is an Art and a Science. However, in my work I find that it's more about the art. Each relationship requires the ability to adapt to individual needs and learning styles, as well as grasping the motivation underlying the perceived need to change.

—Jerome J. Behne Sr., The Behne Group

NOTES

Chapter 4: Coaching Leaders/Behavioral Coaching

1. In fact, five of the coaches have been coaches or mentors for me: Frances Hesselbein, Paul Hersey, Richard Leider, David Allen, and Niko Canner.
2. See Marshall Goldsmith, "Try Feedforward Instead of Feedback," *Leader to Leader* (Summer 2002), pp. 11–14.
3. This has been updated from Marshall Goldsmith, "Coaching for Behavioral Change," in *Coaching for Leadership,* eds. Marshall Goldsmith, Laurence Lyons, and Alyssa Freas (San Francisco: Jossey-Bass/Pfeiffer, 2000).
4. See James M. Kouzes and Barry Z. Posner, *The Leadership Challenge* (San Francisco: Jossey-Bass, 2003), for a comprehensive discussion of the Five Practices of Exemplary Leadership™, the research behind them, and real-life stories of leaders who serve as exemplary leadership role models.
5. See James M. Kouzes and Barry Z. Posner, *The Leadership Practices Inventory* (San Francisco: Jossey-Bass/Pfeiffer, 2003), for more detail.

Chapter 6: Coaching for Leadership Development

1. David Whyte, *Crossing the Unknown Seas: Work as a Pilgrimage of Identity* (New York: Riverhead Books, 2001), pp. 240–241.
2. Rosamund Zander and Benjamin Zander, *The Art of Possibility* (Cambridge: Harvard Business School Press, 2000).
3. Parker J. Palmer, *The Active Life: A Spirituality of Work, Creativity, and Caring* (New York: Harper & Row, 1990).
4. For an excellent example, see the work of Rob Nickerson (www.robnickerson.ca), who originally worked with Toronto's famous improv group, The Second City, and now works around the world providing interactive, improv-based workshops, seminars, and keynotes to a wide range of industries and audiences.
5. David Whyte, *The Heart Aroused* (New York: Currency Doubleday, 1994), p. 287.
6. See note 2, p. 24.

Chapter 9: Applying the Behavioral Coaching Model Organization-Wide

1. All names of people and companies are fictitious.
2. Linda Sharkey, "Leveraging HR: How to Develop Leaders in Real Time," in *Human Resources in the 21st Century*, eds. Marc Effron, Robert Gandossy, and Marshall Goldsmith (Hoboken, NJ: Wiley, 2003).

Chapter 10: The Leader as Coach

1. See, for example, Watson Wyatt, "Human Capital Index: Human Capital as a Lead Indicator of Shareholder Value," available from www.watsonwyatt.com /research/resrender.asp?id=W-488&page=1.

Chapter 11: Is Coaching Worth the Money? Assessing the ROI of Executive Coaching

1. Robert M. Solow, "Mysteries of Growth," *New York Review of Books* (July 3, 2003), p. 49.
2. James W. Smither, Manuel London, Raymond Flautt, Yvette Vargas, and Ivy Kucine, "Can Working with an Executive Coach Improve Multisource Feedback Ratings over Time? A Quasi-Experimental Field Study," *Personnel Psychology*, vol. 56, no. 1 (2003), pp. 23–44.

INDEX